CUTTING THE LION'S TAIL

MOHAMED H. HEIKAL

CUTTING THE LION'S TAIL

SUEZ

Through Egyptian Eyes

ANDRE DEUTSCH

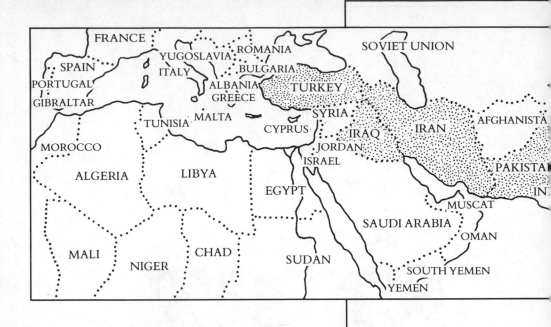

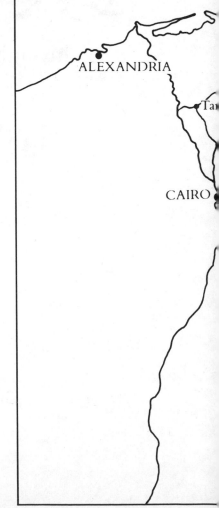

First published 1986 by
André Deutsch Limited
105-106 Great Russell Street London WC1B 3LJ

British Library Cataloguing in Publication Data

Heikal, Mohamed
    Cutting the lion's tail : Suez through
    Egyptian eyes.
    1. Egypt——History——Intervention, 1956
    I. Title
    956'.044   DT107.83
    ISBN 0–233–97967–0

Phototypeset by Falcon Graphic Art Ltd
Wallington, Surrey
Printed in Great Britain by
Ebenezer Baylis and Son Ltd, Worcester

LEBANON

SYRIA

Lake Tiberias

Mediterranean Sea

● AMMAN

TEL-
AVIV ●

● JERUSALEM

Gaza

Dead Sea

Port Said

El Arish

Rafah

ISRAEL

Lake Bardawil

Abu Aweigla ●

El Quseima ●

JORDAN

Ismailia

Abu
Suweir

*Great
Bitter
Lake*

● Bir Rod Salim

Suez Canal

Suez

⊐⊏ *Mitla Pass*

Ras el Naqb ●

E   G   Y   P   T

Eilat ● Aqaba

Sinai Peninsula

Gulf of Suez

Gulf of Aqaba

SAUDI ARABIA

Red Sea

Sharm
el Sheikh

Epigraph

'The British lion has tried to roar, but everyone can see that it has got no teeth, and now the Egyptians are going to cut its tail off.'

Nikita Khrushchev, in conversation with the Egyptian ambassador, at a party in the Romanian embassy in Moscow during the Suez crisis.

CONTENTS

LIST OF ILLUSTRATIONS

1. Sir Anthony Eden and Colonel Gamal Abdel Nasser, in conversation with the British ambassador, Sir Ralph Stevenson, in Cairo, February 1955. (© Topham)

2. Eden and John Foster Dulles, the US Secretary of State. (© The Press Association)
Eden and Christian Pineau, the French Foreign Minister. (© The Press Association)

3. Krishna Menon, the Indian Minister without Portfolio. (© The Press Association)
Robert Menzies, the Australian Prime Minister. (© The Press Association)

4. Two Egyptian views of the developing crisis. (© Rose-El-Youssef)

5. Nehru, depicted in cartoon form as the sole dove at a meeting of otherwise irate Commonwealth leaders. (© Rose-El-Youssef)
An Egyptian cartoon providing a remarkably accurate forecast of the eventual outcome of the Suez conflict. (© Rose-El-Youssef)

6. A striking convergence of views from the two sides of the Anglo-Egyptian divide. Both the British cartoonist Vicky and his Egyptian counterpart see Eden ensnared by the wiles of the French. (Vicky cartoon © *The New Statesman*, print reproduced courtesy of the British Library; Egyptian cartoon © Rose-El-Youssef)

7. In Britain, as the cloth caps and bowler hats in this Giles cartoon suggest, reaction to the Suez crisis was split along party lines. (© *The Sunday Express*; print reproduced courtesy of the British Library)
The Trafalgar Square demonstration of Sunday, 4 November 1956, called to protest against Anglo-French action. (© BBC Hulton Picture Library)

8. Nasser leaving the Al-Azhar mosque on 2 November 1956 after delivering his address to the Egyptian people.

9. The havoc wrought by British air raids.
After the British attack on Port Said the Egyptians sank block ships in the canal, closing it to traffic for six months.

10. America, depicted here as the clear victor of the whole episode. (© *The New Statesman*; print reproduced courtesy of the British Library)
Britain and France, forced into the position of supplicants. (© The Estate of David Low; print reproduced courtesy of the British Library)

11. Israel appearing unabashed before the court of world opinion. (© Rose-El-Youssef)

12. Dr Fawzi, the Egyptian Foreign Minister, in conversation with Dag Hammarskjöld, the UN Secretary General.
A British cartoon featuring Eden, Macmillan and Butler and highlighting the motives that determined American policy. (© *The Daily Express*; print reproduced courtesy of the British Library)

PREFACE

SUEZ IS ONE of the place-names, like Munich or Yalta, which contain within themselves the still smouldering passions which were aroused when they first forced their way into the headlines. Suez was a war, but if wars are to be categorized by the number of their casualties, a small one. During the few days of actual fighting, at the end of October and the beginning of November 1956, the Egyptians suffered much the highest casualties, 921 killed, while the Israelis, according to their own figures, lost 200, the British 22, and the French only 10. But Suez was much more than a war. The fighting came as the climax to months of diplomatic, political, and military manoeuvring; and these manoeuvres were, in their turn, the inevitable outcome of the positions taken up in the Middle East by outside powers and by the countries of the region themselves. Each link in the chain has to be examined if Suez is to be properly understood.

No event in our time has been more fought over in print than Suez. For nearly thirty years the flow of books and articles on the subject has shown no sign of slackening. Many of the main actors in the drama — Eden, Selwyn Lloyd, Eisenhower, Ben-Gurion, Dayan, Pineau, Nutting, Burns — have written books recording and justifying the part they played in it. The soldiers and sailors have made their contribution. Why, it may be asked, should I at this late date join the throng?

My answer would be that almost everything has been written from the Western point of view. Though often highly critical of the military operation and of the events leading up to it, these books and articles have looked at Suez from the vantage point of London, Paris, Washington, or New York, and have been based on the material available in those cities at the time or subsequently. The Cairo end of the story has necessarily not been so well documented. This does not mean that many authors have not tried, often most successfully, to explain the Egyptian attitude during the dispute. Several of them consulted me before they wrote and were good enough to express in print their thanks for such assistance as I was able to give them. It is now my turn, having profited from what they wrote, to express my thanks to them in public and my hope that by retelling from the Cairo end the story of what was probably the most acute international crisis since the end of the Second World War, I may have been able to make a contribution which will supplement theirs.

I was very closely involved in the unfolding of the Suez affair, both as a newspaper editor and as a friend of President Nasser who saw him or spoke to him on the telephone every day. I made a point of keeping every document which came my way and which I thought might turn out to be of lasting significance, and made many notes about events and conversations. 'What on earth are you going to do with all those bits of paper?' Nasser used to ask, half jokingly. 'They'll come in useful,' I told him. 'One day you and I are going to have to sit down and write an account of all this.' 'Not me,' he said. 'You'll have to do it on your own. Anyone in a job like mine burns the candle at both ends. I almost certainly won't be there when the time comes to do the writing.'

In this prophecy Nasser was proved right, and there can be no substitute for the account that would have emerged if he had lived and had the leisure to reminisce. All I can do is attempt to recapture the spirit of the time as we experienced it. I have tried to fill in the background, drawing on evidence not always publicly available; mainly of course from Cairo but also, where relevant, from London and Washington.

In retrospect, a clash of arms between the British, who had left Egypt so reluctantly after an occupation lasting seventy years, and the forces of Arab nationalism, which Nasser came to personify, can be seen to have been inevitable. I have tried to show how it came about.

I hope that this will correct the impression some writers have liked to give that Suez was essentially a private duel between Nasser and Eden. It was never that. It has to be seen in a global and not a personal setting. But because on the Egyptian side all the decisions were Nasser's, because the strategy was of his making and the risks were ones he had to weigh and accept, this is a book which owes everything to him, and which I therefore dedicate to his memory.

PROLOGUE

✠ ✠

WHY NOT A HUNDRED PER CENT?

JOHN FOSTER DULLES, the American Secretary of State, received the Egyptian ambassador in his office at 6 p.m. Washington time on Thursday, 19 July 1956. He told him that the American government did not feel able to ask Congress for a long-term commitment to finance the proposed High Dam at Aswan. His government was, therefore, withdrawing its previous offer to join forces with the British government and the World Bank to undertake this project. He spoke for the President, 'and I am sure,' he added, 'that I am expressing the feelings of Congress and the country.' Dulles presented the ambassador with an aide-mémoire on the subject which had already, together with news of the government's decision, been given to the American press.

Nasser heard of the American action over the radio in the plane which was carrying him and Nehru back from the island of Brioni in Yugoslavia, where they had been conferring with the third of the 'big three' leaders of the Third World, President Tito. But it was only when the plane landed in Cairo, at 2 a.m. local time on Friday, 20 July, that he was given the full text of the American aide-mémoire. He realized immediately that this was something much more than a financial blow which threatened Egypt's entire development programme. That blow he had already anticipated. But the studied offensiveness of the language made it clear that Dulles' action was also a deliberate snub, a political challenge to Egypt's dignity as well as to her aspirations. It was a challenge to which he would have to find an effective response or get out.

Nasser asked some of his closest associates to make suggestions about what they thought should be done, and we all spent Friday in that endeavour. In my case, it was, ironically enough, something that the British Foreign Secretary, Selwyn Lloyd, had said when he was in Cairo earlier in the year which gave me what I thought might be a lead. He had spoken about the importance of the Suez Canal, not simply for navigation but as what he called 'a part of the whole oil complex'. Discussing Lloyd's visit after his departure, Nasser had taken up the point. He contrasted the miniscule return that Egypt derived from the canal and the huge profits of the Suez Canal Company with the situation in the oil-producing countries, where agreements had been negotiated with the oil companies that gave the governments a full fifty per cent of the profits. Was there not, he asked, a lesson which could be drawn by Egypt?

So when I telephoned him at 9 o'clock on Saturday morning I said: 'I've been thinking about that which we discussed, and I think I've got an idea. You remember when Selwyn Lloyd was talking about the oil complex and the fifty-fifty agreements?' Nasser was normally willing to talk freely over the telephone, but on this one occasion the enormous security implications of what he had in mind took over. 'That's enough,' he interrupted me. 'Come round and see me.'

When I arrived, a strange scene confronted me. Nasser was in a small room on the left of the entrance to the modest suburban house that was his home in Heliopolis, in which was nothing but a desk, a chair, and a telephone. It had been arranged that during the summer months a new study for the president was to be built onto the house, and the workmen had already taken over. Nasser had rented a house in Alexandria for the summer, and his family had been installed there while he was in Yugoslavia. Meanwhile he was camping out.

Nasser was dressed in grey slacks and a short-sleeved shirt. 'I think our minds must have been working on the same lines,' he said to me. 'But why fifty-fifty? Why not a hundred per cent?'

I was taken aback, momentarily, by the audacity of the idea: 'It's too much,' I said. 'Why is it too much?' asked Nasser.

To that, I realized, there was no answer.

AFTERMATH OF WAR

At 6 a.m. on 1 September 1939, German planes dropped the first bombs on Warsaw. World War Two had begun. At 9.15 on the morning of 6 August 1945, an American plane dropped an atomic bomb on Hiroshima. World War Two came to an end. To a devastated Europe was now added a devastated Japan. Between these two extremes, at the great cross-roads of the world, lay a region which by comparison seemed, on a superficial view, relatively unscathed — the Middle East. That view was illusory.

For much of the six years between the summer of 1939 and the summer of 1945 the Middle East had been one of the principal theatres of war. Soldiers, sailors, and airmen of many nationalities — British, German, French, American, Italian, Polish, Indian, Greek, African, both white and black — had fought and died there. More than four million troops had passed through Egypt, spending shorter or longer times there. Presidents and prime ministers had flitted through the area, conferring, quarrelling, bargaining. Royalty had moved there into exile; revolutionaries plotted there. To suppose that all these dramas had somehow been divorced from those who were the permanent inhabitants of the region was to suppose the impossible.

There was, in fact, not a single inhabitant of the Middle East who had not been directly affected by the war. Shortages and inflation had disrupted the economic pattern of every community. New jobs had been demanded, new skills taught, old conventions and usages pushed aside. Everybody, even in the smallest villages and in the nomad tents, had been subjected to a growing barrage of propaganda through the novel medium of the radio.

Whatever fate had in store for the Arabs of the Middle East, one thing was quite certain: 1945 would mark a turning point in their lives – the second within a generation.

For an earlier convulsion in world history, the Great War of

1914–18, had already seen the destruction of the system which had provided the Middle East with a semblance of order for the previous four centuries – the Ottoman Empire.

The Arabs had accepted the Ottoman Turks as a military race which would protect the *Dar el-Islam*[1] at a time of crisis, in the fifteenth and sixteenth centuries, when it seemed threatened by encirclement or even extinction. But, though the Ottoman emperors adopted the caliphate for themselves, they never really understood the spirit of the civilization they were supposed to champion. By 1914 they had exchanged the universality of Islam for a narrow Turkish nationalism. When that was defeated in war, the caliphate collapsed with it.

In 1918 the Arab world was up for grabs, and there was never much doubt as to who would be the principal grabbers. Britain was already installed in Egypt, the Sudan, Aden, and Cyprus, while France considered it had historical claims over the Levant. So although the full partition plan envisaged in the Sykes-Picot Treaty of 1916 proved too unwieldy to implement, something along the same lines eventually emerged. A new formula, the mandate, was invented by the colonial powers, Britain securing the mandates for Iraq and Palestine (with Transjordan), and France the mandates for Syria and Lebanon. Italy maintained its control over Libya, and France over the rest of North Africa.

But in spite of new boundaries and new labels, there was an air of improvisation and impermanence about the post-1918 settlement. The empires of Britain and France were long past their youth and middle age. They could use and collaborate with the same classes which had profited from the Ottoman connexion — the landowners, merchants, and tribal leaders — but they were at a loss when it came to dealing with the exponents of new ideas for which they themselves had been to a large extent responsible — the ideas of liberalism, secularism, social progress, and national self-expression. Faced with these they could only react and improvise, alternating uneasily between conciliation and suppression, always searching for a formula which would leave themselves with the reality of power and their increasingly restless critics with a comforting illusion of it. And in the background were two restless giants, America and Russia, one in self-imposed isolation, the other ostracised, but both capable of throwing a devastating new ingredient into the equation, should they choose to do so.

* * *

To the victor belong the spoils, and when at last in 1945 victory came to Britain nowhere would the spoils be more welcome or, surely, more deserved, than in the Middle East where, militarily and politically, its role had all along been predominant. And as the guns fell silent it was excusable for an observer in London to draw the reassuring conclusion that peace was indeed about to bring its just rewards.

It was easy to identify many familiar landmarks in the Middle East. Friendly monarchs held sway in Iraq, Transjordan, and Saudi Arabia; the Egyptian king might be tiresome but it had been shown that he could be kept under control; a British High Commissioner and Governor General ruled in Palestine and the Sudan; Libya was under British military occupation; Aden and Cyprus were British colonies and apparently quiescent. Almost everywhere the politicians were men with whom the British had worked closely and over a long period. Indeed, in one important respect the situation looked even more propitious than it had when the war started. France, always, in this part of the world at least, much more a rival than an ally, had been virtually eliminated. Its hold on the Levant had been broken. De Gaulle might have succeeded, by sheer force of personality, in securing for France a seat among the mighty in Europe and at the United Nations, but it would have to be a France shorn of most of its empire. In Syria and Lebanon during the last four years it had been Englishmen like Spears and Wilson who were the arbiters, not Frenchmen like Catroux and Dentz.[2]

How far, in fact, were the British really controlling events, or to what extent were they simply being hurried along by ineluctable forces? Had it really been the British who rescued the Levant states from a French military reconquest, or had it possibly been the Syrians and the Lebanese themselves? Could the British really take credit (or, in the eyes of the Zionists and French, the blame) for the creation of the Arab League?[3] Sir Anthony Eden, the British Foreign Secretary, was widely credited with having given the 'go-ahead' for the development when, in November 1941, speaking at the annual Mansion House dinner, he had referred to the 'long tradition of friendship' between Britain and the Arabs. 'Many Arab thinkers,' he went on, 'desire for the Arab peoples a greater degree of unity than they now enjoy. In reaching out towards this unity they hope for our support . . . His Majesty's Government for their part will give their support to any scheme that commands general approval.'

But it is one thing to recognize a political trend, as Eden, thanks to the advice of men on the spot, was able to do, and it is quite a different matter to harness it. Those who believed that the Arabs would express their gratitude for the fair words with which the idea of Arab unity had been sped on its way by placing their united strengths at the service of Britain's postwar policies were to be disappointed. The Arabs were not to be willingly consigned to a subordinate position. Nor, for that matter, as soon became apparent, was Britain's closest wartime ally, the United States.

---

[1]'The Abode of Islam', that part of the world under Moslem rule as opposed to *Dar el-Harb* (the Abode of War) which was not.

[2]General Sir Edward Spears was head of the British mission to Syria and Lebanon following the invasion in July 1941 of those two countries, then under Vichy and so, indirectly, under German control, by a combined British and Free French army under General Sir Henry Maitland Wilson. General Henri Dentz was High Commissioner in Syria and Lebanon when war broke out and remained loyal to the Vichy government after the fall of France, being replaced after July 1941 by General Georges Catroux, de Gaulle's representative in the Middle East.

[3]A conference attended by representatives of seven Arab states — Egypt, Iraq, Lebanon, Syria, Transjordan, Saudi Arabia, and Yemen, with an observer from Palestine — met in Alexandria in September 1944. This led to the formation of the League of Arab States, the pact of which was signed in Cairo on 22 March 1945. The purpose of the league was defined as being 'the common good of all Arab countries, the improvement of their status, the security of their future, the realization of their aspirations and hopes'. The pact laid down in twenty articles areas for future cooperation, and as other Arab countries subsequently achieved independence they adhered to the pact.

THE STRAINED
ALLIANCE

AMERICAN TROOPS in uniform began to be seen in the Middle East a few months after America entered the war on 11 December 1941, but, to begin with, American efforts in the area were concentrated on the delivery, through Iran, of arms and equipment for the hard-pressed Russian ally. Their initial impact on Egypt was slight. On 25 June 1943 Sir Miles Lampson, the British ambassador in Cairo, recently created Baron Killearn of Killearn, sent a personal letter to his friend Anthony Eden, the Foreign Secretary:

> Dear Anthony,
>   I think the enclosed may interest you?
>   As I think you know, the Americans haven't gone down very well with the local populace here for one reason or another, so I was diverted the other day when my people brought me these two 'exhibits'. One is a sweet which the American troops are handing out to all the *wallads*[1] they meet in the street; the other is a small mirror which apparently is being sent by the American propaganda people to local women's clubs, etc.
>   Pretty primitive, don't you think? It's all looked upon as rather a good joke by the locals.
>
>   Yours ever
>   Miles W K

Eden minuted the letter 'Thank. Diverted. But not tempted to eat the sweet.'

An attitude of patronizing jocularity came naturally to the representative in Cairo of His Britannic Majesty. Ever since a British army under Sir Garnet Wolseley had defeated the Egyptian army at the battle of Tel el-Kebir on 13 September 1882, Egypt had in effect, if not in name, been as much a part of the British Empire as India or Canada. There might be a khedive (later a king) in the royal palace, deputies, and senators might make up a parliament, elections might be held and cabinets formed, but the final word belonged to the man who lived and worked in the large white building on the east bank of the Nile in Cairo, whether he called himself simply the British Consul-General or the British High Commissioner. For in each government department there were British advisers who controlled policy and the purse-strings, and, more important, in Cairo the barracks housed a British battalion and in the harbour at Alexandria British warships rode at anchor.

In 1936, under the shadow of Mussolini's invasion of Abyssinia and the ever-growing threat of war, the British and Egyptian governments had signed a Treaty of Alliance by which some concessions were made to Egyptian national sentiment, though the essentials of power were retained. The most important of its provisions stated that:

> In view of the fact that the Suez Canal is a universal means of communication and an important link in Empire communications, British troops are to be stationed in the vicinity of the canal, in a specific zone, to ensure, with Egyptian cooperation, the defence of the canal. The presence of these troops does not, however, constitute an occupation, and will in no way prejudice the sovereign rights of Egypt.

Not more than 10,000 British troops and 400 RAF pilots were to be stationed in the zone in peacetime, but in time of war Egypt was to allow its ally the use of all the ports, aerodromes, and communications it might require. Britain would also sponsor Egypt's membership of the League of Nations, this being intended to demonstrate that the country was now well and truly independent. The treaty was signed on behalf of Britain by Anthony Eden, then enjoying his first spell of office as Foreign Secretary, a fact to which he was to draw attention when, twenty years later, he occupied the same post but had a new and very different lot of Egyptians to deal with. He hoped this would persuade them of the sympathetic understanding which he brought to their problems.[2]

One clause in the 1936 Treaty stipulated that Britain's representative in Cairo should cease to be called a high commissioner and should become simply an ambassador – though always having precedence over all other diplomats. Not that this change in style made any difference to the attitude of the current holder of the post.

Killearn looked like the popular idea of a proconsul, a role which he thoroughly enjoyed playing. Well over six feet tall and massively built, often to be seen dressed like the Viceroy of India in grey frock coat and grey topper, he was well equipped to overawe physically as well as diplomatically most of the Egyptians with whom he came into contact. The most notorious incident in his long term of office (1934–46) was when, on 4 February 1942, he drove in the company of General Stone, the GOC Land Forces in the Middle East, backed by a squadron of tanks, to Abdin Palace where he presented King Farouk with an ultimatum — either appoint the prime minister of Britain's choice or abdicate. 'I must confess,' he cabled to Eden that same evening, 'I have never enjoyed myself so much in all my life.'

If Killearn found it difficult to share authority with an Egyptian king or Egyptian politicians, he was going to find it even more difficult to share with these American newcomers. He understood the country; they did not. There were thousands of Britons who had worked in Egypt, knew its people and their language, whereas, except for a handful of missionaries and university teachers, the Americans were strangers there. American moral and economic backing for what Britain was trying to do in Egypt would be as welcome as its military strength on the battlefield, but they could hardly expect to be treated at once as equal partners. Yet soon there were indications that that was the line along which American minds were working. And eighteen months after Killearn's letter to Eden a much more significant figure than the sweet- and mirror-bearing soldiers appeared on the scene.

On his return from the Yalta Conference, where, with Churchill and Stalin, he had been settling the fate of the postwar world, President Roosevelt had asked to meet three key figures in the Middle East — King Abdel Aziz ibn Saud of Saudi Arabia, King Farouk of Egypt, and Emperor Haile Selassie of Ethiopia.

The choice was an astute one and reflected Roosevelt's determination that, in the Middle East as elsewhere, America should take up the reins of world power. Saudi Arabia represented the United States' existing foothold in the area. For the British government, having been assured by Shell that no oil was to be found in the kingdom, had made no serious efforts to add it to its sphere of influence, and the vast oil reserves which had subsequently been discovered were now being exploited by a consortium of American companies. Farouk spoke, in theory at least, for populous and potentially the most powerful of the emerging Arab nations. And Ethiopia, together with the British at their base in Aden, controlled the strategically vital straits between the Red Sea and the Indian Ocean.

At noon on 13 February 1945, Roosevelt received Farouk on board USS *Quincy*, anchored in the Great Bitter Lake. To an unresponsive monarch, more interested in complaining about the iniquities of Killearn, he suggested that it might be a good idea to break up the large landed estates in his country and hand them over for cultivation by the *fellahin*. At noon the following day he received the King of Saudi Arabia. They considered the question of homeless Jews in Europe, the King insisting on the impossibility of cooperation between Arabs and Jews, in Palestine or anywhere else, and the President promising that he would do nothing to assist the Jews against the Arabs and that he would make no move hostile to the Arab people.

The two leaders then went on to discuss the British and the French. 'We like the English,' said the President, 'but we also know the English and how they insist on doing good themselves. You and I want freedom and prosperity for our people and their neighbours after the war. The English also work and sacrifice to bring freedom and prosperity to the world, but on the condition that it be brought by them and marked "made in Britain".' Ibn Saud smiled, and nodded assent.

Later the King said that he had never heard the English so accurately described. 'The contrast between the President and Mr Churchill is very great,' he told the American Minister in Jeddah. 'Mr Churchill speaks deviously, evades understanding, changes the subject to avoid commitment, forcing me repeatedly to bring him back to the point. The President seeks understanding in conversation; his effort is to make two minds meet; to dispel darkness and shed light on the issue.' On his return Roosevelt told Congress that he had 'learned more about the whole problem, the Moslem problem, the Jewish problem, by talking with Ibn Saud for five minutes than I could have learned in the exchange of two or three dozen letters.' An era of postwar harmony between America and the Arabs seemed to be about to open. Two months later Roosevelt was dead.

*   *   *

In November his successor, Harry Truman, called the heads of American missions in the Middle East to Washington. He told them that a 'more active policy' was to be conducted in the area, and that the American government would 'look with sympathy upon the efforts of certain countries in the Near East to extricate themselves from commitments which they were forced to make before the beginning of the Second World War to various great powers, giving these powers special positions and privileges which detract from the full independence of these countries.' It was all too obvious which 'great power' Truman had particularly in mind.

It soon emerged, however, as the wartime Grand Alliance disintegrated and the Cold War began, that there was one issue concerning the Middle East on which Britain and America could agree wholeheartedly, at least in principle. Both governments were convinced that the area was threatened by Soviet aggression, and both were determined that it must be defended. In Europe the lines of demarcation between East and West were already hardening into the Iron Curtain and it was clear that the Soviets could advance further only at the risk of provoking a new war. In the Far East, despite the devastating blow of the 'loss' of China, the threat of further communist aggression seemed remote until the outbreak of the Korean War in the summer of 1950. But the Middle East was eminently vulnerable. It was now known to contain by far the biggest reserves of the commodity on which the existence of Western industrialized nations depended — oil — and this made it a prize of incalculable value. Nobody could forget that when Stalin was Hitler's ally he had shown his desire to obtain access to the Persian Gulf, or that after the war he had tried to secure for Russia the trusteeship (a new form of mandate) over the former Italian colony of Tripoli.

But how was the Middle East to be defended? To the British it seemed clear enough. In the course of the war there had been built up in Egypt what was by now the biggest military base in the world, straddled over an area 120 miles long and 30 miles wide on the west bank of the Suez Canal. Its headquarters, appropriately sited at Tel el-Kebir, alone covered an area of 35,000 acres in a perimeter fence 17.5 miles long. This huge complex was manned by British troops but serviced by Egyptian labour. To protect the Middle East this base, or a large part of it, would have to be preserved; and to ensure that, two things were necessary: the

Egyptians must be persuaded that it was in their interests that the base should be there, and the Americans must help in persuading the Egyptians and in keeping the base going.

To begin with, the Americans showed themselves reasonably willing to learn and to cooperate. This is illustrated by the curious incident of Admiral Conolly's arrival in Egypt. In June 1949 the American Naval Commander-in-Chief in the eastern Atlantic and Mediterranean was due to 'direct and coordinate Anglo-American emergency planning for the Middle East'. He had had one meeting with his British opposite number in Malta, and the next was due to take place at Fayid, in the canal zone. The admiral wanted to anchor his ship in the Bitter Lakes, close to Fayid, but it was pointed out that this would be a violation of Article 7 of the Suez Canal Convention. Whitehall commented:

> It is true that in the past British warships have frequently stopped in the canal and even now this occasionally occurs. On the other hand, the warships of no other power do so and our practice has arisen because of our peculiar relationship to Egypt and the Suez Canal. We do not ask Egyptian authorities for permission to make these visits but merely notify them of our intention. We are aware that our action is, strictly speaking, illegal but as the admiralty attach importance to certain visits of our warships a decision was taken some time ago to continue the practice at least until a protest is made against it.
>
> If Admiral Conolly were to have asked permission to stop in the Bitter Lakes, the Egyptian authorities would have had no legal right to grant this permission and if they were, nevertheless, to do so, they would be implying that they no longer recognized the validity of the Suez Canal Convention, to certain provisions of which we attach vital importance. If, on the other hand, Admiral Conolly were merely to notify the Egyptian government authorities of his intention, his action would very likely draw their attention to our own practice and lead them to question it. It was therefore suggested that it might be better for Admiral Conolly and any members of his staff to disembark at Alexandria and proceed by other means to Fayid.

This is what appears to have been done. The Americans were not always to be so biddable in canal matters.

All those on the spot were soon to realize that the Americans were bringing to their dealings with Egypt the same enthusiasm with which they had waged war — the belief that all problems, political as well as economic, were capable of solution if only they were tackled with sufficient energy and resources. They began by looking around for local elements with whom they could work, and considered first King Farouk, but quickly abandoned him. Nor did they get far with the old land-based middle class which was used to dealing with the British and found these newcomers too impetuous and unpredictable for its liking. So they turned hopefully to the younger generation, the thirty- and forty-year-olds, many of them educated in the States, progressive, technically qualified, accessible.

To symbolize this new approach the Americans appointed a new ambassador. They had won one of their first skirmishes with the British and got their legation in Cairo upgraded to an embassy, and in September 1949 a very high-powered figure appeared on the scene. This was Jefferson Caffery, a wealthy Southern aristocrat, who had for the previous five years been ambassador in Paris. He approached this 'special appointment' as it was called with some reluctance, but once arrived he set about his duties with confidence. A man who had successfully dealt with de Gaulle could surely manage King Farouk and the Egyptian politicians — and the British.

There were to be many complaints about Caffery from the British side over the years. One, from the minister at the British embassy in Washington in November 1951, is typical: 'I was apprehensive as to the reception which Caffery might have given to the King's Chef de Cabinet who approached him. If he had shown any kind of sympathy this would be the beginning of the historical pattern which we know so well, where the Americans intended to give us their support but the Oriental received the impression that he could stick in his wedge.' A lot of wedges were to be successfully stuck in.

In the course of the difficult negotiations with successive Egyptian governments which followed, the British came to feel that they enjoyed considerably less support from their American allies than they were entitled to expect. The Americans were no less convinced than the British of the need to defend the Middle East, but they showed an infuriating eagerness to distance themselves publicly from their ally. They were desperately anxious not to appear to be supporting the 'special positions and privileges' which Truman had spoken about. In other words, Britain was a colonial power, while they were not, and it was not America's job to pull Britain's colonialist chestnuts out of the fire.

The position was summed up in language which displayed some impatience by the then Foreign Secretary, Herbert Morrison. In a despatch to the American Secretary of State, Dean Acheson, written at a moment of particular tension in Anglo-Egyptian affairs (15 August 1951), he said: 'As you know, the question of Anglo-Egyptian relations has been looming large in our minds here recently, and I am disturbed at indications which I have seen that there is some divergence of view between you and us as to what our attitude should be.'

After reminding Acheson that Britain was in Egypt as the result of 'a freely negotiated treaty', Morrison went on:

> We cannot hope to defend the Middle East with the forces now at our disposal, or likely to be at our disposal in the foreseeable future, without the existence of a main base in Egypt. That base must be already there in time of peace, if we are to have a chance of holding the Middle East on the outbreak of war; and it must be there not merely as a dump, but as a live, going concern. What the Egyptians cannot do, and of this we are convinced by our many years of dealing with them, is to maintain the base itself as a live organization.

After making the not very realistic analogy between the American bomber bases in Britain and the British bases in Egypt — 'we do not see why the Egyptians should object to our presence for similar reasons in their country' — Morrison went on: 'I should just like to repeat that we do not regard ourselves as being in Egypt simply for the maintenance of our own interests, or those of the Egyptians for that matter, but because we feel that we must bear this responsibility on behalf of all freedom-loving nations. No question of imperialism exists.'

The military used blunter language. A telegram from the Chiefs of Staff to Air-Chief-Marshal Sir William Elliot in Washington, sent at the same time, complained that it was the Americans themselves who had suggested a joint approach to the Egyptian government.

> Now we are told, when the prospects of a showdown against Egypt are real and imminent, that the basic reason for the crisis in our

relations with Egypt is our 'rigid' attitude and that the only possibility of averting collision is for us to take an 'initiative' . . . The only 'initiative' that we can imagine as being in the mind of the State Department is a capitulation to Egyptian demands and the total evacuation of Egypt . . . Their policy in the event of an Anglo-Egyptian clash is now apparently to 'dissociate themselves from us in every way' — in other words to let us down flat and in effect take the Egyptian side. What influence they imagine they will retain in Egypt or the other Arab states if they sabotage our whole position in the Middle East we are not clear. It is an illusion to imagine that the influence of the dollar or of supply of arms can hope to be effective with people who respect only strength, if they have been treated to the public spectacle of one of the only two Western peoples who really count in Western military strength supporting the Egyptians in making the military position of the other in the Middle East impossible.

Very similar language, expressing a very similar sense of grievance, was to be heard five years later.

---

[1] *Walad* is the Arabic for 'boy'.

[2] To commemorate the 1936 Treaty, Egypt issued a series of stamps, on one of which Eden's head appeared — ironically, the only Englishman ever to be thus honoured.

✥ 3 ✥

DEALING WITH THE
ANCIEN REGIME

As THE END of the war came in sight the Allies laid down that only those countries which were in a state of war with Germany and Japan on 1 March 1945 would be invited to the conference at San Francisco at which the Charter for the United Nations was to be drawn up. It was obviously important for Egypt to be represented there, and the Prime Minister, Ahmed Maher, went on 24 February to Parliament to announce Egypt's declaration of war, but while moving between the Chamber of Deputies and the Senate he was assassinated.

A new Prime Minister, Nokrashi Pasha, was installed. The war ended, and all parties and peoples looked for the justice from their British ally which they felt was their due — in other words, for a revision of the 1936 Treaty which should accord Egypt independence in fact as well as in name. In December Nokrashi presented the British government with a note which made two principal demands: the evacuation of all British troops and the effective union of Egypt and the Sudan with Farouk as king of both countries.[1] The British government took five weeks to answer, and when it did, though it accepted the idea of negotiations, it maintained that the war had proved the effectiveness of the treaty, which was therefore still valid.

For the next five years there was to be an almost continuous dialogue between the two governments, aimed at putting their relations on a new footing, but since they started from wholly different premises it is hardly surprising that no agreement emerged. The British insisted that they must retain a military base in Egypt. Ernest Bevin, Foreign Secretary in the Labour government which came to power in the summer of 1945, put it succinctly as early as March 1946: 'Our major base must continue to be located in Egypt; we must continue to maintain forces in Egypt; and if the defence of the Middle East on a regional basis is to become a reality the main headquarters must be located in the canal zone.'

For their part, the Egyptians were insistent that they were quite capable of looking after the defence of Egypt and the Suez Canal themselves, provided they were given the arms with which to do this. They suggested that a start might be made by Britain sending the arms which had been due to be delivered to Egypt when war intervened, and by returning the arms, mainly anti-aircraft equipment and armoured vehicles, which had been 'borrowed' from the Egyptian army when the British army in the western desert ran short.

Feeling in Egypt on all these issues ran extremely high, but it was no longer necessary for the dialogue to be only a two-way one. In January 1947 the Egyptian government announced that it would be taking its case to the United Nations. When eventually the case came before the Security Council, in August, Nokrashi argued that the 1936 Treaty was incompatible with the UN Charter, to which both Britain and Egypt were signatories. 'The condition of stability and well-being necessary for peaceful and friendly relations,' he said, 'can be brought about in this part of the world only by the complete withdrawal of British forces from Egyptian territory and the termination of the separatist British administration of the Sudan.' He warned that 'as long as the occupation continues popular resentment cannot be stilled. Its flare-ups cannot be prevented. Such a situation can easily get out of hand.' No agreement was reached, and Egypt's case was 'left on the agenda'.

But by now another case had come before the United Nations in which both Britain and Egypt had a vital interest. In February 1947 the British government finally acknowledged that the promises it had so rashly made in the First World War to Arabs and Jews were irreconcilable and turned responsibility for the resulting mess over to the UN. When this new organization proved equally unable to solve an insoluble problem the British government announced that, whatever happened, it was going to quit Palestine in the following May.

The likely consequences of the British decision were all too obvious. The guerrilla warfare between the Palestinian population and the Jewish settlers which had driven the British to take this desperate action would explode into open civil war. In such a war the Palestinians would inevitably be the losers – unless their Arab neighbours could provide them with effective support. Moreover, if the Arab governments did not rise to the challenge, then not only would the Palestinians be driven from their lands but an alien state would come into being at the very crossroads of the Arab world.

What action should — or could — the Egyptian government take? Like all Arab countries Egypt took a passionate interest in the fate of Arab Palestine, a country with which it shared not only a strategically vital frontier but also a common identity and commitments. The question of Palestine had figured prominently in the debates which led up to the formation of the Arab League, and continued to preoccupy its Council. But in April, during a secret session of Parliament, Nokrashi explained the dilemma facing him. 'Of course,' he said, 'Egypt felt strong solidarity with the Palestinians; but, in view of Egypt's quarrel with Britain, intervention would be difficult.' Britain controlled the supply of arms, and British troops lay across the lines through which Egyptian forces would have to advance. If Egypt fought in Palestine and failed to achieve its objects the British would claim that their case had been proved — that Egypt was not capable of filling the defence vacuum that would be caused by a British withdrawal. Egypt risked, he said, 'losing both its army and its argument'. Yet a month later, just a week before the last British soldier was due to leave Palestine, his attitude had completely changed. 'Yes,' he said, 'Egypt must intervene.' Egypt could not be seen to betray Arab solidarity.

What had brought about the change? There is some evidence that the British encouraged Egyptian intervention. A foreign adventure, they no doubt argued, would divert public attention from the quarrel with Britain, and war would make the Egyptian army more dependent than ever on its British ally for arms.[2] In this calculation they could count on the support of King Farouk, who was conscious of his growing unpopularity. The country was suffering from postwar economic depression, and a military triumph was exactly what the monarch, now a British honorary colonel as well as an Egyptian field marshal, needed.

There is also evidence that the British were prepared to arm Egypt in a most unusual way — by conniving at theft. The army command in the canal zone reported that in the five months following the outbreak of fighting in Palestine sufficient arms 'to equip a fair-sized force' had been stolen from the base. These included eight 500-lb bombs and sixty-eight 20-lb fragmentation bombs, nearly two thousand shells of various calibre, half of them

3.7-inch heavy anti-aircraft shells, thousands of mortar bombs, nearly half a million rounds of .303 ammunition, twelve 3-ton and seven 15-cwt trucks, as well as 'various quantities of miscellaneous explosives, mattresses, motor vehicles, spares, thousands of yards of cable and various other types of war material'. 'Nothing will convince me,' the Foreign Office minuted, 'that 500-lb bombs can be stolen without the connivance of those guarding them.'

So desperate, in fact, did Egypt's need for arms become as a consequence of the war in Palestine that missions were sent to try to purchase arms in France, Belgium, Switzerland, and Czecho-slovakia (which country was, with Russian encouragement, busily supplying arms to Israel), but these met with little success. When, after the first UN-organized truce in the fighting, the Israelis made a breakthrough at el-Arish in Sinai, the Minister of War, General Haidar Pasha, begged the British ambassador for planes, tanks, and guns, saying he was even prepared to accept these with British crews under Egyptian markings, if that was the only solution. But these were not forthcoming. When Air Marshal Sir Sholto Douglas saw King Farouk[3] in January 1949 the King complained strongly about the official arms embargo on the combatants: 'Could you not let some of the stuff slip through?' he asked. Egyptians were being killed trying to remove the stuff from the dumps, and the King 'appeared to think this was a bad show on our part'.

The Palestine war ended in the disaster for Egypt which Nok-rashi had originally feared. The Egyptian forces fought bravely, but they were handicapped by a shortage of arms and equipment and betrayed by corrupt contractors and politicians. The young men of the regular army, and many others such as the volunteers led by Colonel Ahmed Abdel Aziz, who so distinguished themselves in battle, were welcomed home as heroes. But they remained bitter about their experiences. As one officer who had himself fought with distinction, Gamal Abdel Nasser, would later put it, they returned from the war 'convinced that the real enemy was in Cairo'.

In this period of ferment various more radical political elements began to surface, of which the Moslem Brotherhood was un-doubtedly the largest. Founded in 1928 by a schoolteacher, Hassan el-Banna, it could claim at the height of its popularity a hundred thousand militant adherents. Many of them fought well in Pales-tine, but Nokrashi, who held the Brotherhood responsible for outbreaks of violence in Cairo directed against Jews and foreigners, dissolved it in November 1948. Shortly afterwards a member of the Brotherhood shot him dead in his office. The communists were always much smaller in numbers, probably never more than a few thousand, led largely by intellectuals and suffering from the usual ideological squabbles. The Misr el-Fattat group claimed to be socialist and had a fascist background. But all dissidents reflected the sense of disillusion which pervaded the country in the aftermath of the war, and, as a result of the failure to achieve any results either through direct negotiations with Britain or through the UN, a bitterness which was directed at the palace and the old parties alike.

It is difficult to overemphasize the significance which every aspect of the 1948 war was to have for a subsequent history of the Middle East in general and for Egypt in particular. Two examples must suffice.

The conditions under which Egyptian troops entered the war were absurd and humiliating. Nasser used to speak of the outrage he felt when, as staff officer in the Sixth Infantry Battalion, having entrained at Abbasiyeh Barracks in Cairo, his and all other units had to be checked through the Ferdan Bridge over the canal by the British military, a British officer with a torch making a thorough inspection of the carriage in which he was travelling and of the baggage he and his brother officers had with them. They also had to wait until the signal was given by an official of the Suez Canal Company that it was permitted for the bridge to be open to rail traffic. Here was the Egyptian army on its way to fight a new enemy, but obliged to pass on sufferance through the lines of its old enemy. It was a bitter paradox that was not to be forgotten. Nor was the situation which he met when he reached Rafah and found that the Egyptian army was required to facilitate the passage of the British First Division, retreating from Palestine to take up a new position in the canal zone.

Then there was the extraordinary story of Umm Rashash, the most southern point of Palestine, where a narrow strip of land gives access to the Red Sea. When, in May 1948, the Jordanian army (the Arab Legion) was moving into Palestine, a detachment occupied this strategic position. What happened subsequently was recounted by Tewfiq Abul Huda Pasha, Prime Minister of Jordan, when he was addressing the meeting in Cairo of Arab heads of government in January 1955:

> The number two at the British embassy in Amman came to see me and explained that it was in the interests of neither Jordan nor the empire that the Jews should be allowed to reach Umm Rashash. He suggested that a British battalion should go to Aqaba to prevent the Jews from reaching the Gulf of Aqaba, but as Britain's treaty with Transjordan only allowed them to use the RAF, I would have to give permission for land forces to be deployed. I agreed to this. But after some time we received information that the Jewish advance had reached the Gulf. I asked the commander of the British forces now installed there why he had not stopped them. He said that his orders were that he was only to intervene in the case of an actual act of aggression against Transjordan. So I saw the embassy official again and asked him what was going on, but I could see that he was playing tricks with me. Then another embassy official came to me, bringing a message from Mr Bevin, who said that he had genuinely wished to prevent the Jews from occupying Umm Rashash, but the American government had put pressure on them to adopt a new policy.[4]

Whatever the true story may have been, there can be no doubt that the British moved out and the Israelis moved in, and Umm Rashash became the Israeli port of Eilat and so Israel's opening to the Red Sea and the Indian Ocean. The line of imperial communications between the canal zone and Habbaniya in Iraq, which the British had appeared to set so much store by, was cut, as was the land link between the Arab countries of Africa and Asia. A potentially fatal blow had been struck at hopes for a practical union of Arab states.

In January 1950 elections were held which resulted in the return to power of the Wafd Party, the only political party which could, in the period between the wars, claim mass support in the country. Once again Nahas Pasha became Prime Minister, but soon a strong whiff of corruption enveloped the government. The King, who was more corrupt than anyone else, tried to outmanoeuvre his government, but the main concern of everyone in the country by now was what had become known as the 'national cause' — that is,

the complete evacuation of British troops. Sensing the way the
mood of the country was going, on 8 October Nahas took the
dramatic step of unilaterally denouncing the 1936 Treaty and
proclaiming Farouk King of the Sudan as well as of Egypt. This
was of course a direct challenge to Britain. In the canal zone, where
the British forces were now concentrated, the situation steadily
deteriorated. Guerrilla groups, with the unofficial backing of the
Egyptian army, carried out attacks against British troops and
installations, until a state of virtual undeclared war prevailed, and
continued throughout the following year.

On 23 October 1951, Middle East headquarters sent an appreciation of the situation to London, in which they declared their
conviction that there was no hope of any agreement with the Wafd.
'We must bring about a complete collapse of the Wafd government,' their telegram went on,

> by making the Egyptian people realize that their government has
> failed them and that the situation is hurting them much more than it
> hurts us. Probably the only foundation on which an alternative
> government can be erected and a satisfactory agreement concluded is
> represented by the King and his armed forces. Therefore we must be
> careful to avoid conflict with these elements. When the time comes
> we must be ready to go into the Delta with our troops in order to
> place them firmly in the saddle.

Four days later the Middle East Commanders-in-Chief suggested
to the Chiefs of Staff in Whitehall ways of countering the Egyptian
government's policy of obstruction. Possible sanctions were discussed, including the cutting off of oil supplies.

> We can apply a stranglehold on the Egyptian economy and deprive
> the population of Cairo and the Delta of power on which sewage
> disposal amongst other things depends, of kerosene for cooking. . .
> Our attitude to all questions which really affect the security of
> British families should be quite ruthless. . . We should intensify our
> campaign to undermine the faith of the Egyptian people in their
> present government and to convince them that the present game is
> not worth the candle.

What was described as the 'mass desertion' of the 70,000 Egyptians employed in the canal zone, either directly by the army or

through contractors, came next, and the general officer commanding was authorized 'to expel anybody, official or unofficial, who impedes him from maintaining the security of the canal zone'. This could begin with 'the small fry', but might well have to be extended to include senior police and government officials as well as governors and subgovernors. The army was also authorized to expel leaders of the Moslem Brotherhood, but only if it was certain that they were terrorists or if they were caught in the act.

There was much discussion of Operation Rodeo, which envisaged the military reoccupation of Cairo and Alexandria. It was pointed out that 'the occasion for intervention in Alexandria would be the loss of British lives' (as in 1882). 'If serious trouble arose in Alexandria a riotous mob would not distinguish between Englishmen and other Europeans. In these circumstances it would appear reasonable that the Americans should provide a contingent to accompany our naval force.' British troops might have to be sent to Egypt from Libya, and if they were it might be helpful if the Americans sent a warship to Tripoli. But when the new ambassador, Sir Ralph Stevenson, spoke about 'intervention if the worst comes to the worst', Churchill, who was now Prime Minister again, telegraphed: 'Does he mean the forcible occupation of Cairo? The Cabinet must be consulted before any movements are made to "intervene" outside the canal zone.'

Among those civilians in the canal zone for whom the British army was asked to arrange protection were officials of the Suez Canal Company. Since Egypt's nationalization of the company was the spark which touched off the Suez crisis, some explanation of its position needs to be given.

The original concession for constructing the canal was granted by the Khedive Said to the Frenchman, Ferdinand de Lesseps, in 1855. It was to run for ninety-nine years from the opening of the canal, which took place on 17 November 1869. The work was financed by the company formed by de Lesseps, the Campagnie Universelle du Canal Maritime de Suez, with a capital of two million francs, made up of 400 thousand shares of 500 francs each. The company was an Egyptian one, but de Lesseps also registered it (unnecessarily) in Paris, adding the word *universelle*, which had the double effect of complicating the legal status of the company and enabling it to engage in activities other than those connected with the canal. In November 1875 the British government bought almost half the issued capital, the 176,602 shares belonging to Ismail, Said's successor as khedive, for £4 million.

After the British occupation of Egypt the company recognized the fact that Britain had now, in effect, replaced Egypt as custodian of the canal by opening an office in London and by increasing the number of British directors from three to ten. Negotiations for a new international status for the canal resulted in the signature at Constantinople on 29 October 1888 of a convention, the first article of which read: 'The Suez Maritime Canal shall always be free and open, in time of war as in time of peace, to every vessel of commerce or of war, without distinction of flag. The canal shall never be subjected to the exercise of the right of blockade.' The convention was ratified by the governments of Britain, France, Germany, Austria–Hungary, Italy, Russia, Spain, Turkey, and the Netherlands.

The company naturally paid particular attention to the interests of Britain, as the largest user of the canal, by giving preferential rates for British shipping. The British Admiralty was always represented on the board of directors, and during the 1914 war supervision of the canal was virtually taken over by the Royal Navy. The same happened in World War Two, when the British armed forces made use of the company's facilities, eventually receiving a bill, when the war was over, for £254 million (which was in fact never paid). Many British officers found the social opportunities offered by the company's dependants, especially in Ismailia, the occasion for delightful relaxation.

When in 1940, during World War Two, France fell, the company was one of France's assets which de Gaulle hoped to be able to lay his hands on. In this he was not successful; but somehow, after the fall of France, the company managed to transfer some of its assets to Algiers and became, in fact, one of de Gaulle's principal financial backers, contributing no less than £12 million to Free France in nine instalments. From Algiers it was also in contact with elements of the mainland Resistance, including the important Jewish elements there. Many of those in Egypt who worked for the company, as lawyers, agents, and so forth, were Jewish, though this was not felt to be of any particular significance until the creation of Israel in 1948.

In Egypt the company behaved as a state within a state. It considered itself immune from Egyptian law and in the canal towns behaved as if it, and not the Egyptian government, were the real authority. Port Said and its communications were treated as if they were company property. (The company had, of course, its own direct cipher link with Paris.) Politicians and newspapers had always been heavily subsidized by the company, and no doors, from the highest, were closed to it. One director was permanently resident in Cairo, and his house in Garden City was so imposing that later it became the official residence of the Prime Minister. The annual visit to Egypt by the company's Chairman, François Charles-Roux, was almost a royal progress. He was received in audience by the King in Cairo, and thereafter he would stay at the company's headquarters in Ismailia, where de Lesseps' room was kept as a shrine, exactly as he had left it. Charles-Roux was always referred to as 'Monsieur l'Ambassadeur'. The Director General of the company, Jacques Georges-Picot, was the son of that Georges-Picot who had signed, with Sir Mark Sykes, the secret 1916 Sykes-Picot Agreement by which Britain and France carved up the Middle East between them.

After the conclusion of the Anglo-Egyptian Treaty of 1936, two Egyptian directors were for the first time included on the company's board, a further five being added in 1949 (all replacing an equivalent number of French directors, who, however, maintained an overall majority). How representative these directors — they were nominated by the company — were of Egyptian opinion can be judged by naming some of them: Mahmoud Fakhri Pasha, son-in-law of King Fuad, who lived in Paris; Sherif Sabri Pasha, a cousin of King Farouk and brother of Queen Nazli; Wasif Butros Ghali Pasha, son of that Butros Ghali who, when Prime Minister, had been assassinated in 1910 in protest against his proposal to extend the company's concession by forty years; Ahmed Abboud Pasha, reputedly the wealthiest man in Egypt and certainly one of the most corrupt; Ali Shamsi Pasha, Chairman of the National Bank after it had been 'Egyptianized', and Karim Thabit, King Farouk's Lebanese confidant and press counsellor. The official representative of the government on the board was Elias Andraos Pasha, who was responsible for the conduct of King Farouk's personal affairs. The Egyptian directors played no significant part in the company's business, being relegated to unimportant committees. They were, in any case, no match for the other directors, who included top British and French businessmen and politicians.

On the principle, expressed by Charles-Roux, that the company had 'a responsibility to the community of nations', he and Georges-Picot were to be seen in attendance at all the major postwar international conferences. Their main concern was, naturally enough, the course of Anglo-Egyptian negotiations, and there were strong suspicions that they gave more than moral encouragement to the 'Suez Group' in the House of Commons which opposed any idea of British withdrawal. The company's fears in this connexion were well expressed in a letter written on 21 May 1946 to the Foreign Office by Lord Hankey, the former Cabinet Secretary and Secretary to the Committee of Imperial Defence, at that time one of the government-nominated directors of the company:

> The directors present [at the Comité de Direction], as might be expected, do not like the withdrawal [of British troops] — I do not suppose anyone does — but such observations as I heard were made in no carping spirit. They had not forgotten the French misfortunes in Syria which helped them to understand our predicament. It must be remembered that for sixty out of its seventy-eight years of existence, the company has relied for protection in its essential work of keeping the canal open on the British naval and military forces. Twice in the present century its security had been menaced by external attack. . . In both wars the company went 'all out' to support the military effort, and the value of their assistance was acknowledged in cordial terms by the respective commanders-in-chief. On each occasion it was the British forces that saved the canal and the company were very grateful.
>
> They have shown their gratitude by doing everything in their power during the wars and between the wars, up to and including the present year 1946, to provide amenities for the British forces of all ranks and have spared neither time or money. They remember that their official and social relations with all three arms of the services have been particularly close and they are proud of the fact.
>
> I gathered that my colleagues are not much impressed by the argument that the Egyptians will cooperate more closely owing to our opening gesture of withdrawal. The company, as a matter of fact, found that the Egyptians have not responded well to its own gesture of goodwill and are not much influenced by gratitude.

Lord Hankey went on to show that the company, like the Defence

Departments in Whitehall, was already considering the alternative bases that might be available for the defence of the canal in the event of a withdrawal from the canal zone itself.

> Some anxiety was expressed about the Arab League in which Egypt has taken the lead, especially in connection with the Palestine position. Would not an acute situation in Palestine, it was asked, exercise greater influence in Egypt than the 1936 Treaty itself, and militate against their carrying out their obligation to the canal? Would the British government always be able to maintain sufficient forces in Palestine, and would they be sufficiently free to come to the aid of Egypt in an emergency? Was there any reasonable prospect of British forces being available in Libya? Those were among the questions touched on in these quite informal references to the subject.

Six years later such contingencies no longer seemed remote and the 'Israeli option', as it became known, loomed larger in British military thinking.

The climax to the escalating violence in the canal zone came on 25 January 1952. The British army authorities were convinced that the auxiliary police were largely responsible for arming and aiding the guerrilla groups, and on that day a British armoured force surrounded the headquarters of the auxiliary police in Ismailia, giving them an ultimatum of one hour in which to surrender their arms. They refused. The building was stormed, leaving forty-three dead and many wounded. The next day ('Black Saturday') Cairo erupted. Many buildings associated with the British, including the famous Shepheard's Hotel, were destroyed by fire and lives were lost. The mob then turned its attention to cinemas, bars, and nightclubs; none of those in the centre of the city escaped the incendiaries.

Farouk dismissed the Wafd government and appointed first his old associate, Ali Maher, and then, in March, a lawyer of proved integrity, Neguib el-Hilali, whose programme was first to clear up the internal mess and then to move on to securing the final evacuation of the British. He was given no chance to do either. Three months later, as a result of one of Farouk's most cynically corrupt deals, he was dismissed.[5]

A month after 'Black Saturday' the British ambassador, Sir Ralph Stevenson, sat down to consider the implications of the current situation and the possibility, as he saw it, 'of a rapid decline of Egypt to financial bankruptcy, administrative chaos and possible civil war'.

> Hitherto [he wrote], our policy towards Egypt has derived principally from our defence planning for the Eastern Mediterranean and Middle East, which itself has rested on the assumption that Egypt would remain a moderately stable and reasonably friendly state. On this basis, our policy has been directed to reaching a defence agreement whereby Egypt would be the hub of our defensive system in this part of the world, and simultaneously to giving Egypt every support which it is within our power to give. Recent events, however, have made me doubt whether either of the assumptions above — moderate stability or reasonable friendliness — are valid today or likely to apply in the future. . .
>
> I feel it necessary to warn you also that, in my view, we are no longer justified in counting in any foreseeable circumstances on Egyptian agreement to a British reoccupation of the Delta, and the use of it as a base, in time of war. . . In my view the present state of Egyptian opinion is such that we would have to count on strong resistance to an attempt to obtain by force the facilities we required in the Delta, and with a continuing commitment in troops to 'keep Egypt down' on a scale which, I imagine, might well prove unacceptable in a major war, particularly at the outset. Egypt is now so full of unrest and riddled with agents and organisations of a nationalist or revolutionary (and in both cases anti-British) character that even after succeeding, by force of arms and against the resistance of the Egyptian regular forces, we should be faced with a very active and troublesome fifth column of enemy sympathisers.

The ambassador went on to consider possible strategic alternatives:

> (a) that the defence system of the Middle East should be centred in the area to the north-east of Egypt in which Israel and the Levant states would play important parts and the former would have a key position; this would suggest the gradual transfer of some of our combatant land forces to a site where they could cooperate with the Israeli army and develop a 'backdoor' for lines of communication (as at Akaba); (b) that some further guarantee of Western control of the Suez Canal should be created, either by the internationalisation of the zone or otherwise, to take the place of the nineteenth-century concept which was workable solely on account of our own dominant position in Egypt itself.

'Our own dominant position in Egypt', Israel, the Suez Canal, internationalization. The menu for Suez was being prepared.

---

[1] The question of the Sudan, the so-called 'unity of the Nile Valley', played a vital part in these postwar negotiations. It was, understandably, an issue dear to the heart of King Farouk and one which none of his ministers could ignore. But after the 1952 Revolution, when the monarchy disappeared, the way was cleared for the Sudan to become independent of Egypt as well as of Britain.

[2] On 20 May 1948, a few days after the start of the war, the British ambassador in Cairo, Sir Ronald Campbell, reported on a talk he had had that morning with Nokrashi: 'He gave me a list of the Egyptian government's [arms] needs and asked me to take the matter up urgently with HMG. He said the matter was pressing and he hoped as much as possible would be supplied from the Middle East, as he believed was possible. . . . The Prime Minister based his request on the conviction that any Zionist state would have strong if not total Communist complexion, and he hoped HMG would therefore regard Egypt and other Arab states as pioneers in claim against spearhead of Communists in the Middle East and be ready to cooperate on that basis.'

[3] Farouk was not above applying the policy of divide and rule to the British. Though he detested Killearn and his successors in the embassy, he had a liking for the company of senior officers in the British armed forces. When he saw Field Marshal Slim, the Chief of Imperial General Staff, in 1949, he suggested to him, without consulting his own government, the possibility of a new military alliance between their two countries.

All members of the royal family were told by Farouk to follow his example and cultivate the company of British officers. So successful was this policy of Anglo-Egyptian fraternization that one army commander, with literary leanings, fell in love with the wife of a prominent politician and sent her every day a poem and a rose. Of another commander it was said that he conducted the desert campaign from the bedroom of a glamorous socialite.

[4] Truman, against the advice of most of his officials, gave all-out support to the Jews, prompting the bitter reflection by Bevin that the American attitude appeared to be 'Let there be an Israel, and to hell with the consequences.' So, for very different reasons, did the Soviet Union. See 'The Soviet Role in the Emergence of Israel' by Oles M. Smolansky in *The End of the Palestine Mandate*, edited by Wm. Roger Louis and Robert W. Stookey, London 1986. 'Moscow's primary objective was to force Great Britain to abandon Palestine. That goal was most likely to be served by supporting Jewish aspirations for a state in Palestine. . . . In retrospect it would appear that Stalin's handling of the Palestine problem was one of his most successful political ventures.'

[5] Abboud Pasha, one of the richest men in Egypt, owed £E11 million in back taxes on his sugar empire. Hilali demanded payment. Abboud went to Farouk, and a gift of £E1 million secured the downfall of the government. Abboud was regarded as a man close to the British embassy, which thereby became branded as an accessory to his intrigue.

❧ 4 ❧

THE COMING AND
THE GOING

IN THE EARLY HOURS of Wednesday, 23 July 1952, a small number
of young officers belonging to the Egyptian army and air force
seized army headquarters, the radio and communications centre,
and a few other key buildings in Cairo. A proclamation read over
the radio stated that the army was to be purged of traitors and
incompetents 'and put in the hands of men in whose ability,
integrity and patriotism you can have complete confidence'. Assurances were given concerning the safety of both foreign lives and
property.

Discontent in the armed forces had been smouldering for a long
time. At the beginning of 1946 there had been massive demonstrations by students and workers in Cairo, Alexandria, and other
towns, involving loss of life. Then had come the defeats and
humiliations of the Palestine war. Two prime ministers had been
assassinated, as had been Hassan el-Banna, the Supreme Guide of
the Moslem Brotherhood, the latter by members of the special
police. All this continuing unrest and frustration increased the
contempt felt in the armed forces for their nominal head, King
Farouk. At some time in 1949 a founding committee, calling
themselves the Free Officers, of which Nasser was the guiding
spirit, came into existence. Shortly before the events of 23 July
General Mohamed Neguib, who had won a reputation for bravery
and leadership in the Palestine war and whose election in January
1952 as President of the Army Officers Club had been seen as a
direct challenge to the King and his clique, was brought in by the
Free Officers as a figurehead whose presence would inspire confidence at home and abroad. It was in his name that the first
proclamation was issued. Three days later King Farouk and his
family sailed away into permanent exile.

*   *   *

The army took over in Egypt because there, as in all Third-World countries where there is no really recognizable class structure like that in most developed countries, it was the only body which was able effectively to initiate change. Inevitably in such countries the feelings in the street seep into the barracks, and by now the street was clamorous for change. As Nasser wrote in *The Philosophy of the Revolution*: 'Was it incumbent upon us — the Army — to undertake what we carried out on July 23? The answer to this question was definitely in the affirmative. It was inevitable. There was no escaping it.'

When the revolution took place the British ambassador, Sir Ralph Stevenson, was at home on leave, as was the general commanding British troops in Egypt. All the foreign embassies were taken by surprise, none more so than the British embassy, which was supposed to be better informed than the others. Though everyone had been expecting something to happen, those responsible for the coup were not the sort of people foreign diplomats or their informants knew personally. The initial British reaction was therefore restrained. Had the King commanded the smallest degree of confidence they might have backed him, but he did not. Nor was there any real excuse for forcible intervention. The claim by the Free Officers to be the guarantors of public order and the security of foreign property was quickly justified by events. Moreover, Britain already had enough trouble on its plate with Mossadeq in Iran, and the amiable pipe-smoking General Neguib, then regarded by all as the revolution's leader, was in no way comparable to the tearful figure in pyjamas who had engineered the seizure of Britain's largest Middle East investment the year before.

Not that the idea of forcible intervention was abandoned easily. On 28 July, five days after the coup, Michael Cresswell, the British Chargé d'Affaires, suggested in a telegram to London that the failure 'to give outward evidence of our readiness to act' might have encouraged Neguib 'under pressure from the younger officers' to change his plans, and instead of simply taking over the army, which he seemed to think had been the original idea, to go ahead and take over the whole country. 'If King Farouk and Maraghi [his last Minister of the Interior] were right,' his telegram continued, 'and many of these officers are really gangsters, we can still stop them by a clear show of determination and by an immediate show of force at the appropriate moment.' This hankering for instant action when the 'appropriate moment' for it — if there ever had been one — was clearly past, was yet another foreshadowing of the Suez mentality.

Stevenson had hurried back to Cairo as soon as news of the revolution reached him. His first aim was to try to find out as much as possible about the new men with whom he was going to have to deal and their intentions, but this took time. To begin with he found himself talking to a familiar figure, Ali Maher, the Free Officers' first choice as Prime Minister, who had been Prime Minister at the outbreak of war in 1939 and, again, immediately after 'Black Saturday' earlier in the year. The two men had a long talk in the embassy on 4 August. They discussed the state of internal security, on which Ali Maher spoke reassuringly, and the state of negotiations for a new Anglo-Egyptian agreement. When Stevenson reported to London on this talk he reverted to the thoughts about the defence of the area which he had outlined in his earlier telegram of 25 February.

With the Conservatives now back in office under Churchill, there had been discussions in both London and Cairo during the first half of 1952 about the possibility of developing Gaza, which was under Egyptian administration as a result of the Palestine war, into a 'back-door' base. On 17 December 1951 Selwyn Lloyd, the Minister of State in the Foreign Office, had met the Israeli Foreign Minister, Moshe Sharett, who had asked him if there was any truth in reports that Britain was considering Gaza as a base. If there was, he said, Israel would be glad to cooperate. Two weeks later the Chiefs of Staff agreed that a move to Gaza was practicable, subject to Britain's being granted security of tenure. But, they said, a large part of the refugee population of the Gaza Strip would have to be shifted elsewhere, and this would be expensive.

Now Stevenson's telegram continued:

> Assuming, as I think we may, that any removal of our striking force to the Gaza area would have to be preceded by an Anglo-Egyptian settlement, and by the adherence of the Arab states as a whole to the Middle East command, I do not think we should have too much difficulty in securing Israel's agreement as we might have had twelve months ago. Undoubtedly the Israelis would try to drive as hard a bargain as they could, and might well attempt to make conditions about the settlement of the Arabs and the equal status of the Arabs in the Middle East command. But we do not think that in the last resort they would press these conditions to breaking point.

The Egyptian Revolution had clearly encouraged a fresh look at the 'Israeli option'.

Apart from getting rid of the King and his corrupt associates, the Free Officers had few plans. The deliberations of the body now running the country, the Revolutionary Command Council (RCC), in these early days show its members casting around for some sort of programme. They knew they had to operate in three fields: they had to do something about the country's social and economic problems; they had to tackle the problem of the army; and they then had to pursue more purposefully than those they had supplanted the goal of complete independence. But there had been little or no preliminary debate or decisions on any of these topics.

After a while Nasser, who from the outset dominated the discussions, came to the conclusion that the greatest obstacle to progress on the home front was the paralysing bureaucracy. To get round this he created two new bodies — a High Council for Production headed by Hussein Fahmi, who had been Minister of Finance before the revolution, an able but traditional administrator, and a High Council for Services, headed by Fuad Galal, a sociologist who was also Minister of Social Affairs. Regarding the army, there was some talk of setting up a special school for selected officers, but, to their credit, it was rejected by Nasser and Neguib on the grounds that it would create a new military caste divorced from the people. Instead security was to be maintained by keeping some of the original Free Officers inside the armed forces.

That left independence. Nasser, thinking back to the Palestine débâcle, decided that this and the army were the two matters which he must keep in his own hands. The revolution would stand or fall by its success in dealing with them. It had to produce a truly independent Egypt, and an army strong enough to defend that independence. So he had to prepare for an approach to the British.

First contacts were not encouraging. When the Foreign Minister, Mahmoud Fawzi, met Stevenson and asked him about the state of negotiations, he was presented with a paper which informed him that, while the British government was anxious to go as far as it could to meet Egyptian aspirations, it had to insist on the validity of the 1936 Treaty. Certain requests for cooperative action by the

Egyptian government in the canal zone, which had been made to previous governments, were repeated.

Then, in October, Nasser made his opening move. He gave an interview to Margaret Higgins of the *New York Times*, in which he stated categorically that there must be a complete evacuation of Egypt by all British forces within six months. Stevenson protested. That sort of talk, he said, could only exacerbate things and risk provoking fresh explosions like those in the canal zone and Cairo earlier that year and the year before. However, in another interview in April 1953 with the correspondent of the *Observer*, Nasser said he might be willing to let civilian technicians keep the base prepared for use in time of war, provided this was not allowed to become a disguised occupation. Negotiations were restarted in Cairo the same month, Nasser leading the Egyptian team.

But now it was not just Egypt that was involved. 'The whole of Egypt will welcome this news,' the first revolutionary broadcast on 23 July declared. That was a reasonable prediction, but what nobody had been prepared for was the tidal wave of enthusiasm which swept the country and spilled over into the whole Arab world. Egypt had always been the country to which Arabs everywhere looked for a lead; now that lead had been given. Every move in Cairo found an echo in Damascus, Baghdad and all other Arab capitals. Thus, the day after the Margaret Higgins interview, which had, of course, been broadcast over Cairo radio, four Iraqi parties issued a joint statement demanding land reform and the cancellation of the Anglo-Iraqi Treaty. Events after 23 July brought to Cairo many Arab leaders anxious to find out what the makers of this revolution were really up to; the visitors including such diverse characters as the Syrian dictator, Colonel Adib Shishekli, and King Idris of Libya.

Like everybody else the Americans were both fascinated and puzzled by what had happened. They felt instinctively that these young and energetic soldiers were a decided improvement on their predecessors, and therefore people with whom it might be possible to do business, but they knew as little about them as did the British.[1] Nasser and his colleagues looked at the Americans with continuing hope. They had had no previous direct contact with them, but America had emerged from the war the most powerful nation in the world, and one that seemed to be unburdened by any imperial past. The first tentative steps towards getting further acquainted were made in Washington and Cairo.

Two important visitors from Washington arrived in Cairo before the end of the year. In October Kermit Roosevelt[2] paid his first visit since the revolution — it was to be the first of many. He was in charge of CIA operations in the Middle East, and at that time deeply involved in Operation Ajax which was to secure the overthrow of Mossadeq and the triumph of the Shah. But all this was unknown at the time to the new revolutionaries who accepted without any suspicion the credentials under which he travelled, his passport describing him as 'Special Counsellor to the President of the United States of America'. Washington may have felt that Caffery was going to find it difficult to get on easy terms with the Free Officers and would need reinforcing. Roosevelt brought a double message: America was prepared to support the new regime, and the question of aid was already under discussion. Consideration was even being given to the idea of transferring funds left over from the Marshall Plan for Europe to countries of the Middle East. Roosevelt's first meeting with Nasser and Neguib was arranged by Caffery, but thereafter he was always to act independently of the embassy. Roosevelt cast another fly over Neguib; would he be interested in paying a visit to the United States? An invitation had been extended to King Farouk by President Roosevelt and renewed by Truman, but never taken up. Now it could be transferred to the General. Neguib was much taken by the idea of standing in for Farouk, but the opportunity to do so never arose.

The next official American visitor was William Foster, Truman's Assistant Secretary of Defence, who arrived in November. Caffery gave a dinner in the embassy which was attended by Neguib, Nasser, and other members of the RCC. Nasser said he had seen the memorandum in which the prerevolutionary Hilali government had given the American ambassador a list of the arms it required, but he and his colleagues wanted more than these minor items. Foster appeared very cooperative. He said his government was willing to help and asked to be told exactly what the new regime wanted. Nasser had a list prepared and it was sent to Foster when he got back to Washington. Doors seemed to be opening, and it was thought essential to strike while the iron was hot. The American-educated Ahmed Hussein became the new ambassador in Washington, and Ali Sabri, Director of the President's Office, was sent to follow up the request for arms. Meanwhile, Eisenhower had won the presidential election and in January was installed in the White House.

The new administration did not, however, seem in any hurry to follow up the promises, or half-promises, that had been made by their predecessors. It had been assumed that Ali Sabri's mission was to finalize the sale of the arms required by Egypt, but it soon became plain that he was expected to observe and assess but not to buy. He was shown round a great many military bases, but when the question of buying came up he was always put off — there were the Christmas and New Year holidays; there was the inauguration. Finally Nasser told him to get a firm answer — were the Americans prepared to sell or not? But the answer he got was very unfirm. There were still difficulties, he was told; more discussion was needed. The most that the administration could offer was to speed up delivery of some of the arms arranged for by the Hilali government. But even this concession was subsequently revoked. Ali Sabri was informed that Eisenhower had received an emotional telephone call from Churchill — 'My dear friend, surely you are not going to start your term in the White House by supplying arms to Egypt which may well be turned against the former comrades who fought under your command in the great battle for the liberation of Europe.'

Though the welcome extended at this time to Egyptians in Washington was very warm, it could also, as I found for myself, be short on comprehension. I was in the States in November to cover the electoral campaign for my newspaper, and had been asked by Nasser to make my own assessment for him of the political scene. One of the many doors opened for me was that of General Olmstead, who was in charge of the Pentagon's military aid to foreign countries. After we had been talking for some time he pressed a knob and a huge map of the world descended on the wall behind him. It was covered with buttons and flags, in Western and Southern Europe and in the Far East, each representing an American garrison or base. But the Middle East was largely bare.

'Don't you think we could do with some buttons and flags in your part of the world?' said the General. 'But General,' I protested, 'we are talking about people, about their hopes and aspirations.' He seemed surprised.

General Olmstead mentioned to me an alternative plan which was well thought of in Pentagon circles at the time. Why not an Islamic pact? Because of its religious connotation this would provide a natural bulwark against communism. The list of potential candidates looked impressive — Turkey was militarily the strongest country in the area, Pakistan the most populous, Saudi Arabia the custodian of the Islamic Holy Places, and Egypt could supply the cultural focus. It might also be hoped that the existence of such an alliance would have an unsettling effect on the large Moslem populations in the Soviet Union and China and have a chastening effect in India. This idea, which was not endorsed by the State Department, also showed a certain lack of comprehension of the area.

But if progress on the arms front seemed to be slow, there had been more encouraging developments in other directions. These had followed the reappearance in Cairo of Kermit Roosevelt. Although his passport still described him as Special Counsellor to the President (by now Eisenhower), it soon became known that he had particularly close relations with Allen Dulles, head of the CIA, who was in continual confidential contact with his brother John Foster Dulles, the Secretary of State, who in his turn had the complete trust of the President in all foreign policy matters. So there could be no question of Kermit Roosevelt's impeccable qualifications as a negotiator. The news he brought with him this time was that the new administration had decided to give top priority to the Middle East, and this was confirmed by a personal letter to Neguib from Eisenhower, sent off only two weeks after its inauguration.

In this letter, which had obviously been drafted with great care,[3] the President spoke as one soldier to another about the way in which the Middle East could best be defended: 'I have personal views on this subject which I believe would commend themselves to you.' He expressed the understanding of 'the American government and people' for 'the natural aspirations of Egypt for full sovereignty over its own territory', since 'similar aspirations have

their deep roots in the traditions of America', and expressed
confidence that an agreement could be reached with Britain, which
only wanted to avoid a military vacuum in the area, and to be
reassured that 'the immensely costly base facilities can be readily
available in time of crisis'. He concluded with discreet flattery about
'the great strides made by Egypt in solving her internal and external
problems under your leadership', claiming that these had 'won the
admiration and respect of the American people'. It looked as
though Eisenhower, while keeping all his options open, was
offering the new regime the active friendship of the richest and
most powerful nation in the world.

The President's letter received a most searching analysis in Cairo.
It seemed to hold out the prospect of benefits which it would be
folly to refuse, but it was not clear exactly what the Americans were
aiming at. It was felt that the last sentence in the letter, proposing
that Egypt might become a 'keystone in any structure which may
be built for the defence of the Middle East', revealed American
thinking as being closer to the British than to the Egyptians.

As a start Ahmed Hussein was sent off to his new post in
Washington taking with him, as a personal gift for the President, an
ancient Egyptian statue of an ibis from the Cairo Museum. This
brought another extremely cordial letter to Neguib from the White
House:

> May I express my heartfelt thanks for the beautiful work of art
> which you were gracious enough to send me. . . . I appreciate
> particularly the wonderful workmanship and perfect state of pre-
> servation of this beautiful ibis, described to me as representing
> Thoth, the God of wisdom and science in ancient Egypt. I shall keep
> this as a valued reminder of your kindness and of the firm bonds of
> friendship which unite our two countries.

Finally a reply to the President's original letter was drafted:

> Dear Friend,
>   I have read with genuine pleasure and utmost care the letter you
> sent me with Ambassador Caffery. Your thought with regard to the
> questions pending between Egypt and the United States can only be
> of immense interest to all concerned. [Nasser altered 'all concerned'
> to 'me', and added in the margin of the draft: 'Does this not give
> them an established right to interfere?'] Nothing could have made

me happier than did your assurance that your government and the
people of the United States appreciate the natural aspirations of
Egypt for full sovereignty over its territory, and your reference to
the fact that similar aspirations have their deep roots in the traditions
of America. The people of Egypt profoundly admire and cherish
these traditions, and they consider your country as the standard-
bearer of freedom and of progress. We cannot subscribe to the
British claim that the withdrawal of the armed forces of the United
Kingdom from Egypt would create a military vacuum. The real
vacuum results from the continuance of present conditions against
the determined will of our people. Indeed, any gap could be more
than filled by earning the friendship and cooperation of the people
and by helping them morally, economically, and politically to build
up their country so as to make it a sterling and reliable bulwark
In its insistence on the withdrawal of British forces from its territory
Egypt is fully aware of its responsibilities in relation to its own
defence and the defence of world peace and security against aggression in accordance with the letter and the spirit of the Charter of the
United Nations.

So far, so good. The conclusion to be drawn was that the
Americans now saw the Middle East as a fluid and therefore a
dangerous area. Britain, so long the dominant force there, they saw
floundering, so that it was the turn of America, however tentatively
and tactfully at first, to replace it.

The pace of diplomatic exchanges was maintained. In line with the
decision to give top priority to the Middle East, the first journey
abroad by the new Secretary of State, John Foster Dulles, was to be
to Egypt, and a letter from the President, dated 8 May 1953,
heralded his arrival, in the company of Harold Stassen, 'to establish
those personal bonds of friendship which contribute so much to
understanding between nations'.

By the time Dulles set out, American policy towards the Middle
East had been formulated in two papers, prepared soon after the
Republican administration took over. The first of these, NSC No.
5428, postulated:

a) that we should move continuously towards the depth of the
Middle East with the aim of reaching a settlement of the Arab-Israeli

conflict as a necessary introduction for a stable Middle East; b) to move continuously and energetically to build the northern tier in the Middle East and have it connected through security arrangements with the heart of the Middle East (Arab world).

The second paper, NSC No. 5401, declared: 'United States policy is to keep the sources of oil in the Middle East in American hands and defend them at all costs, and deny them to the Soviet Union, even if this led to a confrontation or to the destruction of these resources by the Americans themselves.'

In Washington the so-called Alpha Group was set up in the State Department, headed by Francis Russell, with the task of initiating practical steps towards achieving the first policy aim — a settlement of the Arab-Israeli conflict. It was this body which, among other things, originated the Johnston Plan.[4]

Dulles arrived in Cairo on 11 May. He brought with him a leather case containing a brace of pistols. It was a present for Neguib, the careful symbolism of which was explained by Kermit Roosevelt. They were appropriate not simply as coming from one soldier to another but as reflecting Egypt's concern over the supply of arms. 'Don't worry,' was the message. 'You may be disappointed at the lack of results so far, but there are better times ahead.'

But Dulles made a bad start when he announced at the airport that he came to Cairo in an effort to enhance the security of the free world. When he read this statement Nasser said, 'Mr Dulles has made a great mistake.' He attended a dinner that evening in Caffery's house, and Dulles had somehow heard that Nasser was unhappy about his airport remarks, so he asked what was the objection. 'Mr Secretary,' said Nasser, 'it is a problem about the use of words. "The Free World" have become ugly words in Egypt.' Dulles asked why. 'Because,' said Nasser, 'the British have occupied Egypt for seventy years. At first the excuse was the need to protect the empire — imperial communications — but in two world wars Britain has claimed to be in Egypt on behalf of the security of the "Free World". So when you used these words they came as an unpleasant echo of the past.'

Dulles turned to Caffery and said: 'We must issue a corrective statement. I never meant it in that sense.' And this was done. A

e

ad

State Department spokesman issued a statement: 'The Secretary used the expression "free world", and still uses it, in a sense and context which have nothing to do with the way in which those meanings were used in the days of colonialism.'

The two men met for talks the next day in Nasser's office. In the memorandum which Nasser wrote following their discussions he recorded that Dulles began by bringing up the question of the defence of the Middle East against aggression.

> I told him about the Arab Mutual Security Pact, and he said that this was directed solely against Israel. I said that it could become the basis for the defence of the Arab world against any form of aggression. 'But you are threatened by the Russians,' said Dulles. I said I couldn't see the Soviets attacking the heartlands of the Middle East except in the event of a global war. I said I was ready to agree that the communists could represent an internal threat, but this was largely due to their ability to exploit the long-standing grievances which we have against the West and the injustices of Egyptian society. The best way of combatting communism would be to carry out a reforming programme and keep our distance from the West. I must insist on telling you [Nasser said emphatically], that I cannot see Egypt participating in any defensive pact except the Arab Mutual Security Pact. I agree that this is weak, but that is because the Arab countries lack the arms they need, and because their forces are inadequately trained. I must admit that not all their leaders see things as I do, but I think that at the level of the masses you will find agreement.

Nasser went on:

> We want to keep our people out of the inferno of war. If a global war did start, and Egypt became involved in it through belonging to the sort of pact you suggest, you might send planes to aid us, but that would be all. I must tell you in all frankness that I can't see myself waking up one morning to find that the Soviet Union is our enemy. We don't know them. They are thousands of miles away from us. We have never had any quarrel with them. I would become the laughing-stock of my people if I told them they now had an entirely new enemy, many thousands of miles away, and that they must forget about the British enemy occupying their territory. Nobody would take me seriously if I forgot about the British.

Dulles returned to the theme of the need to defend the Middle East and said that this should be done primarily by the people living in this area because they had most at stake. He said America was ready to give the Middle East countries military and economic help. Nasser told him, very politely: 'If that is so, and we are to be responsible for the defence of the area, why do you come here with a ready-made plan of defence instead of listening to us so that we can tell you how we see the problem of our defence?' Nasser ended by saying: 'Yes, we may see our future lying with the West, but this is something that can only be said openly by a truly independent Egypt.'

Nasser got the impression that their discussions had left Dulles, if not convinced, at least better aware of the Egyptian point of view. Nasser was not certain that Dulles had understood what he meant when he described Israel as an 'internal problem' — only a threat because of the weaknesses and divisions in the Arab world. He told Dulles that if the Arabs could solve their internal problems the existing balance in Israel's favour could be overcome and a reasonable settlement with Israel could be found. One figure which Nasser gave Dulles seemed to create a considerable impression on him — that in the current budget the estimates for the army were £5 million lower than in the last budget under the monarchy. This money had been transferred to development.

But Dulles obviously was not going to give up his pet project of some sort of Middle East defence arrangement. NATO was a flourishing concern; the Southeast Asia pact was coming along nicely. Something similar in the Middle East might have to be delayed — great patience might be required — but the final goal must not be abandoned. Before leaving Cairo he sent a polite note of thanks (addressed to Neguib who was still nominally in charge) in which he said, 'My discussions and observations here have been of material assistance in giving me a fuller understanding of Egypt's point of view on many problems. With respect to the Suez base problem, I firmly believe, as I said to you during our conversations, that a fair and equitable solution is of paramount importance not only to Egypt and the United Kingdom but to the rest of the free world.' There was no mention of pacts or bases, but they were implicit in this last sentence.

On the whole Nasser felt that his exchanges with Dulles had gone well, and augured well, at any rate for the short term. In a cabinet meeting which he attended, still as Deputy Prime Minister, he explained the situation as he saw it:

The Americans are very energetic. I continually ask myself what they really want, and sometimes wonder whether their aim may not be exactly the same as that of the British, but to be accomplished in a different style and by different means. In any case, the British and American approaches seem to be diverging, and may actually conflict. So we should have some time in which to manoeuvre between the two. The best that could happen is that it could turn out the Americans actually mean what they say; the worst is that it could turn out they mean what we suspect them of meaning. But if we manage to exploit the gap between the two we shall have achieved something.

Nasser aimed at making maximum use of the Americans. He sometimes referred to them and the British as the 'coming' and the 'going' – *el gayin wa el rayin* — and he thought the coming could be used to put pressure on the going. He hoped they could also be used to supply aid and especially arms. But he remained suspicious. 'I hope there are no booby-traps,' he always used to say.

The British were naturally eager to find out what had been discussed at the Nasser-Dulles meetings, and no doubt the Americans gave them an edited account. Nasser gained the impression that the British felt a particular antipathy towards Dulles — the most dangerous interloper yet to force his way into their bailiwick.

This was, in fact, the heyday of cooperation between Egypt and the United States. Some American aid got through the pipeline, and numerous invitations to send Egyptians, civilians as well as military, on training missions in America were proffered and accepted. The American diplomatic presence in Cairo was increased, or, rather, it was supplemented by a strong CIA representation. William Lakeland, a shrewd young diplomat, was already there, and may already have been working for the CIA, as he certainly was later, though this was not suspected at the time.

Roosevelt now brought in James Eichelberger, a pleasant enough person but someone who gave the impression of always trying to do several things simultaneously, and Miles Copeland, an advertising man, a nonstop talker in a permanent state of agitation. These two, though nominally members of the embassy staff, spent most of their time at the houses they had taken in Zamalek and Maadi, or at a flat in Badrawi Buildings in Zamalek which was rented in the name of Frank Kearn, the CBS correspondent, and became to all intents and purposes the CIA headquarters. It became apparent that the CIA was running a separate operation from that of the embassy and, it seemed, a more effective one.[5]

Strangely enough, many of the Egyptians closely involved with the Americans during this almost honeymoon period were later to be known as men of the Left, or even of the extreme Left. On their side, the Americans went to big business for their intermediaries — men like John McCloy, John Anderson, Eric Johnston, E. J. Chase, and David Rockefeller. They have their present-day counterparts in the Weinbergers and Shultzes.

Egypt's relations with the United States were certainly one of Nasser's main preoccupations as the first anniversary of the revolution drew near, but they were far from being the only one. On the domestic front, he was now contemplating a much more comprehensive programme of development. Although the High Council for Production and the High Council for Services had performed well, he felt there was also a need for a new High Council for Planning to supplement and coordinate their efforts.

In foreign policy, Nasser was giving a great deal of attention to the wider Arab world that lay beyond the frontiers of Egypt. He had realized that his ideas were being echoed by people in many other Arab countries and it was in order to reach this constituency that he had set up the Voice of the Arabs. Over the next three years its influence was to become immense. Perhaps the most telling tribute that could have been paid to its success was the fact that its transmitters were among the RAF's main targets when the British began to bomb Egypt in November 1956.

For although the Egyptian revolution had aroused enormous curiosity and enthusiasm elsewhere in the Arab world 'at the level of the masses', to use the phrase that Nasser himself used to Dulles, the ideas which inspired its leaders were not always congenial to those in high places – or to the British and French advisers who stood at their elbows. It must be remembered that, with the exception of Saudi Arabia, which had already cemented its 'special relationship' with the United States, the Arab world was still divided, *de facto* if not *de jure*, into spheres of influence within which the two colonial powers continued to ensure that their interests predominated.

Algeria, Morocco and Tunisia were still French colonies; and although Syria and Lebanon had been granted their independence in 1943, French influence remained strong in both countries. In Aden and the Gulf, British rule was as yet unchallenged. In Jordan, the Arab Legion had a British commander, Glubb Pasha, and many British officers; the RAF maintained bases at Amman and Mafraq and the country was still dependent upon grants from the British Treasury. In Libya there were both British and American bases. In Iraq, Nuri Said, who made no bones about his role as Britain's man in the Middle East, would become Premier for the twelfth time the following year. The British themselves would, of course, have had no hesitation about adding Egypt to the list of Arab countries that remained within their sphere of influence. It was because the Voice of the Arabs proclaimed to Arabs elsewhere that this was not so that it would, in due course, earn a place on the RAF's target lists.

One bone of contention had, however, been removed from Anglo-Egyptian relations at the beginning of 1953 with an agreement on the future of the Sudan. The old regime had insisted that King Farouk must be acknowledged as king of the Sudan as well as of Egypt. Nasser and his fellow officers knew that this was nonsense — and in any case Farouk was no longer there. They would have to grant the Sudan the same freedom of choice that they claimed for themselves. This agreement removed one of the two issues which had been the theme of all Anglo-Egyptian negotiations since the war, but it left the other — the British military base in the canal zone — as far from a solution as ever. Nasser stepped up pressure on the troops in the base as part of his campaign to compel a British withdrawal.

A report by the Conservative MP, Charles Mott-Radclyffe, dated 4 May 1954, vividly described conditions in the base, 'the biggest base in the world' as he pointed out.

> No other troops in the world [his report began] would show such discipline and restraint, in face of such provocation, as the British troops in the canal zone. . . . Life is extremely monotonous. There are few amenities. Accommodation is very poor, with no prospect of improvement in view of the uncertain future. Some men are doing guard duty every other night; the luckier ones every third

night. All vehicles have to travel in pairs; all senior officers have a jeep escort, and, except in a few places, even bathing parties are accompanied by an armed escort. . . . To sit in a sandbagged post, illuminated at night by arc lamps, with a village 100 yards away from which shots are fired every night and quite often during the day, without the slightest prospect of being able effectively to return the fire, is quite an ordeal for the old sweat, let alone for the National Serviceman.

It is not easy to explain to the troops the reason for this monastic and uncomfortable existence which has all the disadvantages and none of the advantages of active service. They see the base disintegrating before their eyes. They know that at any time the Egyptians could sabotage the canal if they wished to do so. In short, 80,000 troops are neither guarding the base nor the canal. They are merely guarding each other. . . .

All the senior officers to whom I talked agree that the canal zone is a very convenient location for a base, since it is astride the back door (the Red Sea) and the front door (the Mediterranean), *provided that the population is reasonably friendly and can be relied upon to supply local labour as required*. Without this proviso, all agree that the base is a useless white elephant. . . . The fact that no Egyptian has been near the base to look at the problems on the spot is the subject of some comment. The attitude of the American ambassador, Mr Caffery, is doubly difficult to understand. When I asked him how he could advise the State Department about the problem in the canal zone without ever having been there, he replied rather lamely that a visit would have prejudiced his position.

Mott-Radclyffe went on to discuss the possible future of the base. The military saw four possible courses of action: to reach an agreement with Egypt which would allow civilian technicians to work the base; to tell the Egyptians that there could be no negotiations under present circumstances and that Britain's forces would be redeployed in their own time; to stay put till 1956 (when the Anglo-Egyptian Treaty expired) and see what happened; to do nothing. 'The soldiers to a man are in favour of the first course,' the report said, and, it went on, the diplomats agreed that the only hope of getting a stable government in Egypt depended on reaching an agreement in the canal zone. 'If negotiations were to be reopened we could get an agreement tomorrow, including Turkey in the availability formula, if we were prepared to drop the request for uniforms.[6]'

Mott-Radclyffe had met Nasser and some of the other RCC
leaders, including Neguib,

> no longer in control but for the time being, at any rate, indispensable
> to Nasser. . . . As an admirer of Dr Buchman and as an ascetic, he
> presents a certain respectability in an otherwise singularly disreput-
> able gang. . . . Some of the men round Nasser are very bad indeed.
> He himself admitted to me in conversation that the communists had
> succeeded in penetrating certain sections of the Army. . . . Nasser is
> a dynamic figure of considerable personality. Fawzi does not count
> for much. He is merely a shock-absorber. What interested me was
> Nasser's admission that, if an agreement were reached and the
> British finally evacuated the canal base, a vacuum would be created
> in Egyptian political life which would have to be filled by drastic
> internal reforms, since no party in the future would be able to use the
> occupation by British troops of Egyptian soil as the universal
> whipping boy.

A year later an agreement on the future of the base was to be
signed precisely on the lines that both the military and the
diplomats were contemplating. Two years later the universal
whipping boy was voluntarily to present himself on Egyptian soil.

As Nasser's reputation grew, a steady stream of foreign politicians
and journalists made their way to Cairo, eager to meet this rising
star of Arab politics. Nasser usually enjoyed such encounters and
found the exchange of ideas rewarding. He was an omnivorous
reader and a good listener. At meetings with political leaders from
other Arab countries and every school of thought, or with journalists like Kingsley Martin and Walter Lippmann, or politicians such
as Aneurin Bevan and Barbara Castle, he would probably not speak
himself for as much as a quarter of the time, leaving the running to
his interlocutor. He particularly enjoyed Bevan's company and was
not put out when once Bevan said to him: 'Colonel Nasser, why do
you talk about revolution? With all due respect, what you have
done is provide a revolutionary façade. You haven't changed
Egyptian society.' On his return to England Bevan sent Nasser a lot
of books, including *Socialist Thought* by G.D.H. Cole, and his own
autobiographical work, *In Place of Fear*.

Rather surprisingly, one of the dialogues Nasser most enjoyed was with the British Labour politician, Richard Crossman. Despite the fact that Crossman was known to be a strong Zionist sympathizer and had played a leading part in concocting the ill-fated report of the 1946 Anglo-American Commission of Enquiry on Palestine, Nasser admired his force of mind and the vigour with which he argued his case. It was characteristic of how things were at the time that after Crossman had failed to obtain an interview with Nasser through the British ambassador, he turned to the American ambassador, who spoke to William Lakeland, and it was he who managed to set up the meeting which took place in December 1953.

Crossman was an aggressive character, with little time for diplomatic niceties. After Nasser had expanded his thesis that only after a complete evacuation of British forces and when Egypt was fully independent could there be any serious discussion of the next stages ahead, Crossman interposed, 'Colonel Nasser, I want to try to talk to you without any inhibitions. May I be allowed to call you by your first name?' Permission was granted. 'Well, Gamal, I understand what you've been saying, but I feel it misses the crucial issue. The only real question is are you prepared to drive the British out of the base by force? They won't go unless you do. Egypt is so important in the defence of the Middle East that we are only going to give it up if you make it impossible for us to stay there. Are you ready to fight us — to kill us? If you aren't ready to do that, don't bother to talk about anything else.'

Whether Crossman had come to the Middle East with the idea of playing the role of a mediator in the Arab-Israeli conflict is not clear, though most probably he had. Nasser explained the view that he was to put forward consistently, to Dulles among many others, that Israel was an internal problem, and that the root of the trouble was Egypt's underdevelopment. Without telling Nasser what he intended, Crossman went off to Israel and came back five days later via Cyprus. Another meeting between the two was arranged. Crossman told Nasser he had been to see Ben-Gurion and had told him that the Egyptians didn't want a war because they wanted to concentrate on developing their country. Ben-Gurion had begun scratching his head, and then said: 'Dick, this is the worst news I have ever heard.' He meant that a properly developed Egypt would be more than a match for Israel.

Israel was indeed watching events in Egypt with growing

anxiety. It seemed more than likely that an agreement was going to be reached which would result in the withdrawal of British troops, and, if this was done, Egypt's relations with Britain could well become as cordial as they already promised to be with America. Moreover, as has been seen, Ben-Gurion regarded the prospect that the new rulers of Egypt were going to concentrate on development as the worst possible news. A strong Egypt, closely associated with the West, was a prospect most unwelcome to Israel.

When Crossman went to see Ben-Gurion, he had recently given up the Premiership and retired to his desert retreat at Sdi Boker in the Negeb, though remaining the dominant figure in Israeli politics. He was succeeded by Moshe Sharett, with Pinhas Lavon as Minister of Defence, and the young General Moshe Dayan, a favourite protégé of Ben-Gurion, becoming Chief of Staff a month later. Ben Gurion had always regarded anything to do with defence as his preserve, when he was out of office as well as when he was in office. Whether, before he retired, he had personally given orders for what came to be euphemistically called in Israel 'a security mishap' is not certain. Preparations for it must have been quite far advanced when Sharett took over. Lavon claimed he was never told about it; Dayan said that, on the contrary, he had briefed his minister.

Whatever the truth may be, Ben-Gurion's fears of the way Egypt was going, particularly in its relations with America, were the motive behind an undercover operation by Israeli intelligence which was to provoke a cabinet crisis in Israel and a long-running political scandal the echoes of which can still be heard. It was to sour relations between Israel and America, and, for the Jewish community in Egypt, to prove little short of a disaster.

At 6.30 in the evening of 24 July 1954, a man called Philip Natanson was found with his clothes on fire at the entrance of the Rio Cinema in Sharia Fouad in Alexandria. A phosphorous bomb he had intended to plant in the cinema had gone off prematurely in his pocket. Investigations showed that he and several others were involved in a plot to place incendiary devices in American Information Offices in Cairo and Alexandria, in the main post offices in the two cities, and in British-owned cinemas. It was hoped that these acts of sabotage would be attributed to the Moslem Brotherhood or other extremist groups, and that thereby the Egyptian government would be discredited, and the British and Americans alarmed at an apparent breakdown in security reminiscent of the chaotic months immediately preceding the revolution. Bombs had in fact already gone off in the American Information Offices and the post office in Alexandria before Natanson was caught.

Some of the saboteurs, all of whom were Jews and most of them Egyptian citizens, were shown to have been trained in Israel and France. After trial by a military tribunal two of them were condemned to death and others to long terms of imprisonment. An enormous campaign to save the two from the gallows was mounted in the United States and other countries, Eisenhower, among many others, pleading personally with Nasser on their behalf. But as six members of the Moslem Brotherhood had only a few months before been hanged for complicity in an attempt on Nasser's life, this was understandably not an occasion for clemency. They were executed on 31 January 1955.

Just a month after Natanson's arrest, at the end of September 1954, Israel tried to bring the question of navigation through the Suez Canal to a head by sending an Israeli ship, the *Bat Galim*, through it. The ship had been stopped and its crew arrested, but there was no wish on the Egyptian side to make a major issue of the matter, and the crew had been released on 1 January. But when the British ambassador brought up the question of Israel and the canal, Dr Fawzi had to point out that ships controlled by a government which planned acts of sabotage against Egypt were bound to be regarded as bad risks in the canal.

The Jewish community in Egypt was an old and respected one, which had played an important part in the life of the country. One member of the wealthy Kattawi family, for example, had been a senator, and his wife one of the ladies in waiting to Queen Nazli, wife of King Fouad. Before the creation of the state of Israel in 1948 there was little awareness in Egypt of what Zionism meant. Most Egyptians regarded the migration of Jews from Europe to Palestine as essentially a humanitarian question, and a committee, not all of its members Jewish, was set up to help them. Some immigrants travelled via Egypt, and the left-wing Hashomer Hatzair (Young Watchmen) set up a training camp in Egypt.

In 1948 the community had numbered about 65,000, but after the creation of the state of Israel more than half had emigrated, leaving only 27,000, mostly in Cairo and Alexandria. The Chief Rabbi of Cairo, Chaim Nahum Effendi, was an extremely shrewd man. He was not a Zionist, and he did not want his flock to get involved in the affairs of the new state, realizing that they would be the first to suffer in any crisis concerning Israel. In 1949 he met Sassoon, Oriental Secretary in the Jewish Agency, and reached an agreement with him that Israel would not interfere in any way with the Egyptian Jewish community or try to make use of it. The conspiracy, of course, wrecked this agreement. Those implicated were not small fry, but included one of the doctors at the Jewish hospital, a professor of engineering, a wealthy businessman, and so on. The tragedy for what was left of Egypt's Jewry was that from now on inevitably they became looked on as potential traitors.

Despite these problems, 1954 was a year of considerable success. At home, the revolution was being consolidated. Neguib was finally removed from all his offices in October, leaving Nasser in name as well as in fact the unchallenged leader of the revolutionary regime. That same month also saw the culmination of Nasser's efforts to end the British presence in Egypt. Heads of Agreement between the two governments had been initialled in Cairo on 27 July 1954, whereby all British forces were to leave Egypt by stages within twenty months of the conclusion of the agreement. Thereafter the canal base would be maintained by not more than 1,200 British civilian contractors for seven years, and during that time it could be reactivated, and British troops return to it, if an attack was made on Egypt or on any country signatory to the Arab Mutual Security Pact, or on Turkey. The final signature of the agreement took place in Cairo on 19 October. 'The ugly page in Anglo-Egyptian relations has been turned,' said Nasser. 'There is now no reason why Britain and Egypt should not work constructively together.'

On 26 October a member of the Moslem Brotherhood, which had denounced the agreement as a capitulation to Britain, attempted to assassinate Nasser as he was addressing a large public meeting in Alexandria.

Nasser had also decided that he would go on the *haj* in 1954. He had headed the official delegation which went from Egypt to Saudi Arabia to offer condolences on the death of King Abdel Aziz on 9 November 1953, and had got to know his successor, King Saud, who seemed pleased that the new radical leaders in Egypt were anxious to establish good relations with him. Nasser had spoken in his *Philosophy of the Revolution*, written in 1953, a year after the revolution had been successfully accomplished, of the three circles of which Egypt was a part — the Arab, the African, and the Islamic – and in it he argued that the pilgrimage 'should have a potential political power' and become an occasion when heads of Islamic states and leaders of opinion should 'assemble to draw up the broad lines of policies to be adopted by their respective countries and lay down the principles ensuring their close cooperation.'

King Saud liked this idea when Nasser put it to him, and when he had intimated his intention of going on the *haj* Saud invited him to come some days in advance of an official visit. As can be imagined, Saudi hospitality pulled out every stop to make its guests welcome. Nasser was installed in the Nasiriyeh Palace in Riyadh, and when I went to see him there I found him in an enormous room, in the middle of which was an equally enormous bed, nine metres long and nine metres wide, ornamented in gold, standing on a pedestal. The bed was hung with quilted silk drapery, and the walls of the room were covered in more quilted silk, with elaborate picture designs. Nasser was sitting in his pyjamas on the edge of the pedestal, looking forlorn. But in spite of this inappropriate setting the meeting between him and Saud went well, and the King became a genuine friend of the new Egypt.

---

[1] A popular pastime at Cairo diplomatic gatherings in those days was the exchange of lists of names of the new men: 'Have you got X? Is it safe still to include Y?' Any evidence of their supposed pecking order was as carefully scrutinized as the appearance of the Politburo members at May Day or Revolution Day parades are by Kremlin watchers in Moscow. This often led to absurd mistakes. Thus, a few days after the coup, a military parade through the streets of Cairo was arranged, and it was natural to ask Ahmed Shawqi, commander of the Cairo garrison, to head it. For several days he was credited with being one of the most senior of the Free Officers, with whom, in fact, he had no connexion.

[2] Roosevelt had been a familiar figure in Cairo before the revolution, having contacts with many leading figures in King Farouk's circle. It was as a result of his initiative that, between 1949 and 1952, several people, mostly from the police, were sent to America to be trained in countering communism and subversion.

[3] The full text of this letter is given in Appendix 2.

[4] A master plan for the distribution of the waters of the River Jordan among all riparian states, including Israel, prepared by the Tennessee Valley Authority and explained to governments on the spot by President Eisenhower's special representative, Eric Johnston, President of the American Motion Picture Corporation.

[5] The CIA was the peacetime successor of the wartime Office of Strategic Services (OSS) which combined both intelligence-gathering and subversion, but unlike the British and French secret services it also had a more straightforward function as the political arm of the President in the making and implementing of foreign policy. The State Department and CIA have continued to conduct separate, and often contradictory, policies, but it has to be said that unofficial emissaries, not necessarily secret ones, have often proved their worth in diplomatic exchanges in the Middle East. In the eighteenth and nineteenth centuries, when diplomacy was a far less institutionalized affair than it is today, there was a fairly frequent coming and going of unofficial envoys between Middle East governments and the principal courts of Europe.

[6] A reference to the two issues which were still outstanding between the British and Egyptian negotiators at this point. The first concerned the circumstances under which the base might be reactivated: the British were anxious that they be permitted to return in the event of an attack on Turkey or Iran, as well as, of course, a threat to Egypt or another Arab country. The second issue was the question of whether, as the Egyptians insisted, the maintenance staff who remained behind should wear civilian clothes or, as the British demanded, military uniforms.

❧5❧

THE DIVISIVE
PACT

THE BRITISH AND AMERICANS had failed in all their efforts to persuade Egypt to join in some sort of military partnership. Whether described as 'mutual defence' or 'regional defence' it had always come down to the same thing — committing Egypt (and other Arab countries if they followed the Egyptian example) to an unequal alliance which would certainly perpetuate the stationing of foreign troops on Egyptian soil and very likely involve Egypt in a war with Russia. The only agreement which the two governments had been able to concoct for the area was the so-called Tripartite Declaration of May 1950, whereby America, Britain, and France expressed their readiness to supply the Arab states and Israel with arms for internal security and self-defence, and to take action 'both within and outside the UN' to prevent the violation by force of any Middle Eastern frontier or armistice line. But this was aimed almost entirely at trying to stop a fresh flare-up of the Palestine fighting.

However, the idea of a regional defence pact had by no means been given up. It remained a standing offence in Washington and London that the Middle East was not covered by the sort of alliances which were supposed to protect Western Europe and Southeast Asia against the threat of communist Russia, and a new idea began to gain ground. If most of the Arabs obstinately refused to participate in their own defence, a protective screen might still be erected without them. This was the so-called 'northern tier', in which Turkey, Iran, and Pakistan, supported naturally by the Western powers, were to play leading parts. It was the implementation of this idea which was to provoke a fatal division in the Arab world and do more than anything else to aggravate suspicion between Egypt and the West.

The first blocs in the 'northern tier' were fitted into place in February 1954 when Pakistan and Turkey signed a mutual defence pact. But a far more significant development, from the Arab point of view, took place on 2 August, when Nuri Said returned to power as Prime Minister of Iraq. A veteran of Hussein's revolution against the Turks, Nuri was an established bulwark of the Hashemite monarchy and a fervent advocate of a strong and continuing British connexion. He felt that the time had now come when Iraq, and he personally, could play a role in mediating between Egypt and the West, reconciling their divergent ideas about how the defence of the area should be organized. The time had passed, he argued, for bilateral arrangements, so Iraq would make no more attempts to revise its 1930 Treaty with Britain. It proposed instead to move on to something more in keeping with the realities of the existing world situation — a collective security agreement.

Before going to put his ideas to Nasser, Nuri had sounded out the Saudis but found them unresponsive. The founder of the kingdom, Abdel Aziz ibn Saud, had died the year before, and his son and successor, King Saud, was still feeling his way. But as far as protection of his kingdom was concerned he was certainly not going to exchange the American umbrella for an embryonic alliance controlled by the Hashemites, the traditional enemies of his house.

Nuri arrived in Cairo on 15 September, Nasser going to the airport to greet him. They agreed that their first meeting should be in private, and so, after a dinner at the house of the Iraqi ambassador, Nejib el-Rawi, the two men were left alone. Nuri started the discussion by saying that the Arab countries would have to organize themselves. Nasser did not dispute this, but said that in his opinion the framework within which they should organize was already there, in the shape of the Arab League Mutual Security Pact. All that was needed was for the pact's forces to be properly equipped and trained, and given a coherent objective. That led on to a long argument about who was the Arabs' real enemy. Nasser insisted that it was Israel; Nuri that Russia provided an equal or even greater threat. Russia was only 30 kilometres away from Iraq's northern border, he said, and Russian troops had penetrated to Rowanduz in Iraqi Kurdistan at the end of the First World War. Nasser repeated the arguments he had used with Dulles — that the only way in which the Arabs were likely to find themselves fighting the Russians was in the event of a global war. The communist danger was not going to take the form of a military attack but of internal subversion, and that was something which could only be met by each country's improving the conditions of the masses.

While they were drinking coffee Nuri suddenly leant across to Nasser and said: 'Your Excellency, I have something positive to suggest. What would you say if I was to bring a hundred million people and twenty mechanized and infantry divisions to join us in our battle against Israel?' Nasser said: 'Take my hand on your back [If you're being serious. . . .] Where are they?' 'Pakistan and Turkey,' said Nuri.

> This is something I had not meant to reveal to you. When I have been talking about the Russian danger and the need to go into a military pact with the West, the real target I have in mind has always been Israel. We can't say that openly, of course, but suppose Pakistan and Turkey were allied to us, and we became involved in a war with Israel, do you think Turkey's twenty divisions would keep out, or that the hundred million Moslems in Pakistan would remain neutral? What do you think of my offer?

After a time the two joined the other guests, and the discussion continued. Nuri called for some maps he had brought with him to be produced. He tried to spread them out on a table but could not find one big enough, so he had to use the floor. He went down on his hands and knees, put on his spectacles, called to Nasser to join him, and spent some minutes scrabbling around trying to find the locations on the maps that would support his argument. It was a strange sight, but contributed nothing to a better understanding. Nuri went back to Baghdad with the two governments' points of view as far apart as ever.

After his return Nuri continued his negotiations with the Turks, and the 'northern tier', so dear to the heart of Dulles, seemed well on the way to realization. Nasser grew increasingly concerned over the fundamental split in the Arab world which he saw developing. Iraq was not only determined to pursue its own course, but was inviting other Arab countries to join with it, and not without success. Lebanon and Jordan were sympathetic, and Syria, though undecided, was being subjected to tremendous pressure to come in. Nasser feared that if this new northern alliance took shape it would divide the Arab world in two, being welcomed by the Americans as part of the anti-communist crusade and so rewarded with arms. Egypt would then find itself isolated, deprived of any prospect of getting arms, and left to face the threat of Israel alone. He decided to make a last effort to prevent a disastrous split, and invited the heads of government of all independent Arab countries for a meeting in Cairo, which duly opened on 22 January 1955.

Nasser's invitation was accepted by the governments of Saudi Arabia, Syria, Lebanon, and Jordan. The Iraqis had been invited, but Nuri sent a telegram saying that unfortunately he was too ill to attend.

Nasser, as host, opened the first session[1] by suggesting that the agenda should cover, first, a general discussion; second, questions of foreign policy, including the Mutual Security Pact, the Arab League, and any other relevant issues anyone liked to introduce; and, finally, the pact now in preparation between Iraq and Turkey. He said that there was no intention of putting Iraq in the dock, but that following the recent visit to Baghdad by Celal Bayar, the Turkish President, when all Arab countries had been called on to join the proposed pact, it was proper that they should consider what response to make. Nasser said he had received a telegram from the Lebanese Foreign Minister intimating that the Iraqi Foreign Minister, Fadhel Jamali, was then in Beirut and ready to come to Cairo in place of Nuri Pasha, should those present be willing to accept him. It was generally agreed that it would be helpful if Jamali came, though they would want to know whether he had power to negotiate or simply to expound the by now well-known Iraqi point of view. An invitation was duly sent.

Faris el-Khoury (Prime Minister of Syria) asked what had happened at the last meeting of Arab Chiefs of Staff. Nasser told him that unfortunately nothing of value had been decided and nothing could be hoped for until the states signatory to the Mutual Security Pact could agree on who the enemy was. He said the real trouble was that as a result of the Palestine war the people everywhere had lost confidence in their leaders. It was their task to rebuild that confidence. The Emir Feisal (Prime Minister of Saudi Arabia) commented that journalists often asked him why the Mutual Security Pact was so ineffectual. What, he asked, would be Nasser's answer. Nasser repeated that it was a matter of trust. 'Let me give you an example,' he said. 'If Israel attacked Egypt tomorrow, what use would this piece of paper be to us? But it would be a different matter if we could be sure that in the event of

an attack every Arab country would come to Egypt's aid.' He said
that he was convinced that the only way to prevent the threatened
division in the Arab world was for all countries to base their policy,
as did Egypt, on complete cooperation through the Arab League
and the Mutual Security Pact. He said he had hoped that Nuri's visit
to Cairo would have resulted in agreement, but unfortunately this
had not proved to be the case.

At the second session the delegates had before them a telegram
from Nuri saying that Jamali would not be coming to negotiate but
only to explain the Iraqi point of view. Faris el-Khoury thought
that perhaps they might wait to see whether Nuri would come after
all, though he himself would only be able to stay in Cairo for a
week. Tewfiq Abul Huda (Prime Minister of Jordan) said he could
not stay for more than another two days, at which Faris suggested
adjourning the meeting. This led to an explosion by Nasser:

> All right [he said], if Egypt has to go ahead alone it will do so, but I
> shall tell the Arabs that the rest of you are not willing to cooperate
> with us. Egypt will not be intimidated. We shall carry on even if the
> Arab necklace is broken and all the beads scattered. Egypt will
> continue to champion the cause of the Arabs even if the rest have
> become slaves of the West and the Turks. I negotiated with the
> British for a long time, and I could have signed an agreement for the
> evacuation of British troops much earlier than I did if I had been
> willing to go into a pact with them, but I always refused, and
> eventually got evacuation without a pact. All Arab countries should
> maintain their independence and not be seduced by false rhetoric [He
> was probably thinking of Nuri's specious arguments about Turkey
> and Pakistan.] If we don't keep the ideas of Arab nationalism alive
> [he went on], we shall find ourselves back under foreign domination
> for another hundred years.

The next day the talks continued their desultory way. Faris
el-Khoury said that Syria had no intention of joining a pact
sponsored by the West, but he could speak only for his own
government; there might be a new government in Damascus which
would think differently. A telegram came from Nuri saying that he
was going to have a medical check-up, and only after he had heard
its results could he decide whether or not to come to Cairo. Sami
Solh, the Lebanese Prime Minister, said he couldn't see what all the
fuss was about. There was nothing new in Iraq's having a treaty

with Turkey; they were both signatories to the four-power Saada-
bad Pact of 1937 and to a bilateral treaty of friendship in 1948.
Nasser retorted that the creation of Israel had changed the situation.
If the sort of pact the West wanted came into existence Israel would
be openly or covertly associated with it. From time to time an
attempt was made to bring the discussion back to basics. Nasser
asked Feisal if Saudi Arabia would agree to join the pact and got the
emphatic answer, 'By God's heaven, never. We are not going to
agree.' But Lebanon remained unconvinced, Sami Solh claiming to
have received fresh information from Beirut that America was
threatening to cut off all aid unless the Arab countries toed the
line and joined the pact, while Tewfiq Abul Huda explained
Jordan's peculiar position, with a foreign country dominating its
political and economic life and its army commanded by foreign
officers.

Eventually Fadhel Jamali came to Cairo, bringing with him a
message of regret from Nuri and his assurance that anything Iraq
did was in harmony with the best interests of the Arabs. He said his
country's policy was based on three principles. The first was to
work for the liberation of all Arab countries and their security. The
second was to live in friendship with its neighbours, and the third
was to take account of the overall international situation. Jamali
went on to recapitulate Nuri's view of recent Middle East history
— what a pity it was that the other Arab leaders had not been
prepared, as he was, to welcome the 1939 British White Paper on
Palestine; what a pity that Egypt had rejected the proposal in 1951
for a Middle East defence pact without consulting the Arab
countries, and so on.

Jamali went on to say that war might break out tomorrow. The
international situation was extremely tense, particularly in Asia.
Russia constituted a real threat to Iraq. Iraqi Kurds were being
trained in subversion at a school in Tiflis. If Iraq was to defend its
northern borders it would have to get arms from the West. He had
told Dulles that Iraq was anxious to stand by the side of the West in
its resistance to communism, but in return he had asked that
America should end its bias in favour of Israel, and should help
Egypt to solve its problems with Britain.

Nasser asked Jamali if he would show them a text of the
agreement they were planning to conclude with Turkey, but this
was not available. Jamali claimed that it was only because the

Turkish President had not been invited to Cairo, as he wished, that he had gone to Baghdad instead. He said the Iraqis had thought this was just intended as a friendly gesture, and had no idea that Bayar meant to negotiate a new treaty with them. Bayar had then told them that he couldn't go back to Ankara empty-handed. When the Iraqis tackled him over his relations with Israel, Bayar had said, 'Try to persuade us to make a change. Help us to change.'

Jamali was asked if negotiations with Turkey could be held up, to which his answer was an emphatic, 'Never! Never!' Nasser felt the meeting needed calling to order. He said that as far as he could see he had three choices: he could wind up their deliberations immediately; he could terminate the Arab League Mutual Security Pact; or he could tell the press that, in view of the impending signature of a treaty between Iraq and Turkey, Egypt was going to cancel all its undertakings with all other Arab countries. This threat produced a telegram from Camille Chamoun, the Lebanese President, suggesting a meeting with Nasser and Nuri in Beirut. When Nasser said he could see this serving no useful purpose, Sami Solh produced another telegram from Chamoun suggesting that signature of the treaty between Iraq and Turkey should be put off for four months, and that in the interim Nasser and Nuri should have more private talks, followed by a reconvened Cairo conference. This was too much for Nasser. 'We have been talking for fifty-five hours without reaching agreement on a single point,' he said. 'Do we or do we not agree that a country which is signatory to the Arab Mutual Security Pact has no right to join another defence pact without the consent of the other signatories?' This produced resolutions agreeing, among other things, that no country would join the Turko-Iraqi Pact, that the Arab League and the Mutual Security Pact should be strengthened, and that the joint command not only should coordinate plans, training, arms, and so on but should decide what forces each country should commit to the pact's command.

Nuri eventually sent a message to Cairo to the effect that the discussions there had constituted interference in the internal affairs of Iraq. He said all these questions had been thrashed out at the meeting he had had the previous August in the northern Iraqi hill station, Sarsank, with the Egyptian representative, Salah Salem. (Salah Salem had discovered that the room in which they talked, as well as his bedroom, was bugged, which did nothing to improve the atmosphere.) This did not prevent the meeting from passing a resolution that a committee would be sent to Nuri for further negotiations. But of course nothing came of it.

---

[1] All the exchanges in this chapter are extracted from the official minutes of the conference, the meetings of which were held in camera.

BEGGARS AND
PRINCES

IF THE JANUARY CONFERENCE of heads of government had not achieved anything of much value, the next month, February 1955, was to be productive, for good or evil, of matters that were to fuel the Suez crisis. It was a month in which Nasser was to greet Nehru and Tito, two of those who were to be his closest political allies on the international stage, as well as Anthony Eden, the man who was to become his bitterest opponent. It was also the month that saw a Troika takeover in the Soviet Union — Khrushchev, First Secretary of the Communist Party, Bulganin, Chairman of the Council of Ministers, and Zhukov, Minister of Defence. Nearer home, on 17 February Ben-Gurion returned to the Ministry of Defence, and eleven days later Israel mounted, in Gaza, its most destructive raid yet against Egypt. It was this last event that was, in Nasser's words, to convert Egypt's search for arms from something important to a vital necessity.

On 5 February Tito passed through the Suez canal on board his presidential yacht *Galeb* (Seagull) on his way back from a state visit to India and Burma. Nasser was invited aboard and the two men had a five-hour talk, at the end of which a communiqué was issued stating that they had 'noted with satisfaction the identity of views on the fundamental questions of the present international situation'. Not mentioned in the communiqué was a message brought by Tito from Sharett, via Nahum Goldmann, to the effect that he thought a compromise settlement between Israel and the Arabs was a real possibility. But Sharett's influence was by then almost at an end, and Nasser had had to explain to Tito his conviction that Israel had no wish for peace.

Sir Anthony Eden, the British Foreign Secretary, was to attend a meeting of the SEATO Council in Bangkok and had decided to stop off in Cairo on the way to meet Egypt's new rulers. A dinner party was arranged for 20 February at the British embassy at which the ambassador, Sir Ralph Stevenson, would be host.

Nasser looked forward to this meeting. He was then still a believer in the value of personal contacts, perhaps having fallen into the error, as is so easy for those new to power, of overestimating the ability of others to control events in their own countries. He had still to learn how much policies are determined by the constants of history and geography, and how relatively little by the wishes of the man temporarily in command.

When the cars were heard coming into the embassy drive the ambassador went to the top of the steps to greet his guests, who included, besides Nasser, some of his revolutionary colleagues and Dr Fawzi, the Foreign Minister. Nasser, Amer, and Baghdadi were in uniform, Dr Fawzi in a civilian suit. A little behind Stevenson, at the entrance to the salon in which drinks were to be served, Eden was standing dressed, like the other men in the embassy party, in a dinner-jacket, and as Nasser approached he held out his hand and greeted him in Arabic: '*As-salamuh aleikum, wa rahmat ullah wa barakatuh*' (Peace be unto you, and the mercy of God and his blessing). Nasser was taken aback. A great many position papers had been prepared in advance of the dinner, touching on every subject which might be expected to crop up, but at no point had anyone mentioned that Eden knew Arabic. 'Ah,' said Eden, 'I have surprised you. You didn't know that I could speak Arabic?' 'No,' said Nasser, 'nobody told me.'

They moved into the large salon where fires were burning in the two fireplaces. Eden and Nasser sat on a sofa in front of one fire and the foreign secretary explained that he had read oriental languages when an undergraduate at Oxford. Persian had been his main language, but Arabic the other. He said he had read the Koran, and he thought it was a pity that most people in the West derived their ideas about Islam from what the orientalists said about it rather than from the original source. He asked if Nasser and his colleagues had any specifically cultural programme, and said he had noted the reference to Egypt as part of the 'Islamic circle' in *The Philosophy of the Revolution*. (This was before he equated that small volume with *Mein Kampf*.) He went on to talk about Islamic civilization in general and the special contribution made to it by Egypt and Persia.

This unexpected conversation, which Nasser felt to be friendly if not particularly relevant, continued while drinks were served. Nasser, of course, drank only fruit juice, and in answer to a question from Eden explained that he had once tried beer, while he was in the Sudan, but had not liked it and had never touched alcohol since. When the butler made an attempt to take away Eden's glass to refresh it, this gave him another opportunity to display his expertise. '*El agla min esh-shaitan*' (haste is of the devil) he said, quoting an Arab proverb. Each time he broke into Arabic Eden looked, not at Nasser, but at his wife, as if seeking her approval. She, very elegant in her long blue dress, was sitting on a sofa on the other side of the fire, and could be seen studying Nasser carefully.

Eden said he thought there was a lot of wisdom in many of the old Arab proverbs, and then went on to talk about the times he had spent in the embassy building during the war. 'Is this the first time you have been here?' Eden asked. Nasser said it was, and it was interesting for him to see the place from which Egypt used to be governed. 'Not governed, perhaps,' said Eden, 'advised, rather.' Nasser mentioned the ultimatum to King Farouk of 4 February 1942, which had been planned in the embassy. This gave Eden a cue to express his admiration for Killearn, to talk about Farouk and Nahas and the old-time politicians who, he thought, had been victims of their own propaganda. He reminded Nasser that it was he who had signed the 1936 Anglo-Egyptian Treaty, and that was why he had sent him a specially autographed copy of the new evacuation agreement.

Eden asked Nasser about the recently concluded meeting of the Arab heads of state. What was the explanation of the division in the Arab world? Was it perhaps something to do with the age-old rift between 'Shatt el-Arab' and 'Shatt el-Nil' (the Valley of the Twin Rivers and the Valley of the Nile)? Nasser said it was not really that, and began to explain his feelings about the Baghdad Pact. He said that, with his military background, he could understand the need for a proper defence for an area like the Middle East, which was so important for others as well as for those living in it. The difference between him and Nuri was what threat the area was to be defended against. He thought the main danger facing the countries of the Middle East was an internal not an external one.

This gave Eden his chance. 'But my dear Prime Minister,' he said, 'you have only a few months ago signed an agreement with us whereby the Suez base can be reactivated in the event of an attack on Turkey as well as if any Arab country is attacked. How do you fit this agreement into your concept of the way in which the Middle East should be defended?' But at this point, it now being a little after 9 o'clock (the guests had arrived at 8.15) all moved into the state dining-room.

The preliminaries had gone well. The atmosphere had been relaxed, with Eden doing his best to please and, if possible, to charm the Egyptians. At dinner Nasser and Eden were seated facing each other, and to begin with there was some talk about Egyptian food, but then Field Marshal Sir John Harding, the Chief of the Imperial General Staff, and one of those in Eden's party, held forth for nearly a quarter of an hour, giving an exposé of the international situation as seen from London. He said it was true, as Nasser had mentioned earlier, that the advent of nuclear weapons had radically altered all strategic conceptions, but it was not possible to rule out the possibility of a war confined to conventional weapons and such a war involving the Middle East.

Nasser replied that even if a war started non-nuclear it would be certain to become nuclear. He then answered the question about the recent Anglo-Egyptian agreement which Eden had asked him just before they went into dinner. He said that in fact he had been unhappy about the clause in the agreement providing for the reactivation of the base in certain circumstances and had only agreed to it because it seemed to be the point on which the agreement was going to break down. But he still felt that, whereas there was a real chance that Russia might use force against some of the countries with which she had a common frontier, like Czechoslovakia, there was no such likelihood of her making a thrust against any of the Arab countries. To do this Russia would first have to invade Turkey and Iran and that would surely mean a global war.

Eden said that the Iraqis saw things differently, and repeated the arguments which Nasser had heard from Nuri about the Russian frontier being only 30 kilometres distant from Rowanduz. He appreciated that Egypt, being 2,000 kilometres further off, felt less threatened, but the Iraqis thought that Nasser, by insisting on this point of view, was interfering in their internal affairs. Nasser said that if Nuri had confined his opinions to Iraq he would have had no objection. By sending invitations to the Cairo meeting to other

Arab governments he had not been trying to force any line on them. His only aim had been to try to preserve unity among the Arabs, but he had much evidence that since the meeting ended Iraq had been exerting enormous pressure on Syria, Lebanon, and Jordan to get them to join the Baghdad Pact. Eden asked if the enemy he really had in mind was Israel. Nasser said it was, and rehearsed once again, as he had to Dulles and others, the crucial fact of how the advent of Israel had split the Arab world in two.

After dinner they all went back to the large salon for coffee and liqueurs. Something Harding said about Israel gave Eden the chance to produce another Arab proverb — 'No, no,' he said, 'remember *el-lisanek husanek* — your tongue is like your horse, if you take care of it, it will take care of you; if you treat it badly, it will treat you badly.' He made a reference to 'certain rivalries in the area' which Egypt would be well advised not to get involved in, probably referring to the Hashemites and Saudis. He also said that, knowing as he did the former rulers of Egypt, people like Farouk and Nahas, the revolution had come as no surprise to him. He said he had warned the old lot not to play with fire by whipping up popular feeling with propaganda — no doubt this was intended as an oblique warning to the new lot. On the United States, he said that they and Britain had certain fundamental interests in common, which determined their policies, and it would be a mistake for anyone to pay too much attention to the arrogance of certain local representatives who might like to think they could ignore this fundamental community of interest. That was no doubt a reference to some of those in the American embassy who had the reputation of being anti-British.

Finally, before the party broke up, Eden said he would like to get clear in his mind the conclusions he thought they had reached: 'First, you appreciate the importance of the defence of the Middle East. Second, you have no objection to what Nuri is proposing to do provided he keeps it to himself.' Nasser said yes to both. For all his sophistication and expertise Eden had throughout given the impression of being on the defensive. He was dealing with an entirely new breed of Arab leaders — revolutionaries who owed nothing to his country or government, single-minded in their aims and confident in their ability to implement them. It was obviously going to be quite an undertaking for Eden and his colleagues to take the measure of these new men.

Eden walked to the door to say goodnight to the guests, and the ambassador escorted them to their cars. As he drove away, Nasser's first reaction was amused astonishment at the sartorial contrasts. He and his party had been in uniform or lounge suits, their hosts in dinner-jackets or, in the case of the ladies, in long gowns and jewels. 'What elegance!' he exclaimed. 'It was made to look as if we were beggars and they were princes!' But he felt the occasion had been a useful one and that Eden was the sort of person with whom it might be possible to do business. This was confirmed when, after Eden's return to London, shortly before he took over as Prime Minister (6 April), Nasser received a message from him suggesting that if Egypt stopped its propaganda against the Baghdad Pact, which now had reached a very intense pitch, Eden would guarantee that there would be no more attempts to recruit new members of the pact. Nasser thought that this idea of a moratorium was a good one and that it showed that their meeting had borne fruit.

If there was some prospect of improving relations with the old enemy, no such hopes could be held out where the new one was concerned.

Ben-Gurion had returned to office at the Ministry of Defence determined to arm Israel for the war with Egypt which he regarded as inevitable and necessary, but which would have to be fought at a time of Israel's choosing and after appropriate military and diplomatic preparation. This would have to be carried out before Egypt had been able to develop industrially or exploit its political and geographical position as the hub of the Arab world. He saw little prospect of getting the arms he needed from either America or Britain, but there was a third source which offered better prospects — France. French Jews had played a leading part in several Resistance organizations, and much of the network then established had not been disbanded after the end of the war but had been retained as part of the machinery for the clandestine transfer of European Jews to Palestine. The French ambassador in Israel, Pierre-Eugène Gilbert, was a Resistance hero and had energetically fostered links between the two countries.

The French were becoming increasingly worried by the rebellion in Algeria, and the Israelis knew how to play on this preoccupation. They heard about a meeting of Egyptian army commanders and ministers, a sort of embryo National Security Council, which had been addressed by Nasser, in the course of which he had repeated his thesis that Egypt could never be really secure as long as the Arab world was divided in two by Israel. This was easily blown up by Israeli propagandists as a secret meeting at which a master plan for Egyptian domination of the Arab world had been promulgated. So when Shimon Peres, Ben-Gurion's deputy at the Ministry of Defence, was sent to Paris in July 1954, the ground had already been well prepared. His mission proved eminently successful, France agreeing to supply Israel with Ouragon jets, tanks, guns, and radar. A later agreement provided for Mystère II jet fighters. The Americans did not approve these transactions.

Eden left for Bangkok on the morning of 21 February. Two days later the Turkish Prime Minister, Adnan Menderes, arrived in Baghdad, and the next day the Turko-Iraqi Alliance was signed. During the night of 28 February the Israelis attacked in the Gaza Strip, killing thirty-six soldiers and two civilians, and wounding eighty. On 2 March an agreement was signed in Damascus whereby Syria and Egypt became formal allies, the armies of the two countries being merged. Saudi Arabia joined the Alliance a few days later. Between 18 and 24 March Nasser was at the first Afro-Asian conference in Bandung. All these events were interconnected; all were stepping stones on the road to Suez.

The Gaza raid was an action of unprovoked aggression for which Israel was condemned in a Security Council resolution. It was also an action carried out with deliberate brutality, mortars, bazookas, hand grenades, and Bangalore torpedoes being used as well as automatic weapons; many of the dead were bayonetted while they slept. No mercy was shown. The raid was intended as a message from Ben-Gurion to Nasser, and Nasser understood the message. This was that building hospitals and schools and steel mills was not going to protect Egypt from a ruthless neighbour who was set on ensuring that it should not be allowed to prosper. Only arms could do that. Nasser realized that if things went on as they had been going he would find that he had developed Egypt only to hand it over to the Israelis. All the messages that had been passed on to him via well-meaning intermediaries were designed to lull him into a state of false security. Israel was determined to challenge the rising star of Egypt by every means at its disposal, and primarily by force.

The army was, of course, profoundly shaken by the raid, and since the army was the mainstay of the regime something had to be done to restore its morale. In the order of the day which Nasser issued to the army he promised it that aggression would be repelled, that an eye for an eye would be exacted, and that retaliation would take a political as well as a military form. Nasser immediately ordered a substantial increase in the budget allocation for the army. He also summoned Henry Byroade, the newly appointed American ambassador in Cairo[1], and presented him with a long list of all the times when they had asked America to supply them with arms, starting with the visit of William Foster. 'Up till now,' he said, 'we have been asking for arms so that our army could be properly equipped. Now we are asking for them to save our lives. The situation has changed completely. Now I can't wait.'

It is noteworthy that it was after the Gaza raid that the new team in the Kremlin first came out with a positive statement about the Middle East. This commended Egypt's attitude towards the Baghdad Pact, which it said was inspired by a genuine spirit of independence, and condemned acts of hostility by Turkey against Syria. (There had been a number of frontier incidents and overflights by Turkish planes, clearly designed to intimidate the Syrians.)

Nasser and General Amer went to Gaza a few days later. They found everyone in a state of extreme, though understandable, nervousness about security. Nasser and his party went up close to the Israeli lines, and one of the intelligence officers who were acting as guides approached me and asked if I had taken all necessary precautions. I asked him what precautions he meant. He said, 'Have you destroyed all the papers you were carrying? We might meet an Israeli patrol at any moment.' I told him that if a patrol found itself in a position to capture the Egyptian President and the Commander-in-Chief of the Egyptian army they would not be likely to worry about the papers in my pockets.

The alliance with Syria was another natural reaction to the Gaza raid. The merger of the two armies was called a 'resurrection', harking back seven centuries to a time when Saladin's army, composed mainly of Egyptians and Syrians, had crushed the Crusaders. Constant comparisons were made between the Crusaders and the Israelis, both examples of alien peoples from the West who had tried to settle in Arab lands, but whose position there was always precarious. The effective Crusader presence had lasted a hundred years; was it unreasonable to think that the effective Israeli presence might last a shorter time than that?

Saudi Arabia's adherence to the alliance was welcome, helping to counteract the unfortunate impression created by the Turko-Iraqi Pact. Less welcome was the telegram Nasser received from the Imam of Yemen[2] who, in those days, could be guaranteed to inject an element of farce into the political scene. 'I have spent three days studying the stars and see that your star is in the ascendant. We have therefore, with God's blessing, decided to join you.'

The discussions that took place during the visit to Cairo by Nehru, the Indian Prime Minister, in February were largely concerned with plans for the Afro-Asian summit in Bandung which was to take place the following month. There had been a preliminary meeting in Colombo at which U Nu, the Burmese Prime Minister, had argued that Israel, as an Asian country, ought to be invited. Egypt had protested against this on the grounds that Israel was not really an Asian country at all, but Nehru supported U Nu. Nasser told him that if Israel did attend he was quite certain that none of the Arab countries would be there. Nehru never liked absolutes, and this uncompromising statement by Nasser left him unhappy. He and U Nu were looking for something more positive and asked Nasser what was his solution for the problem. Nasser replied that Egypt was prepared to accept the UN resolution on partition, with the modifications included in the Bernadotte report. This pleased Nehru and U Nu and they approached the Israeli government to see if it would reciprocate. But the Israelis turned the idea down flat and so confirmed their exclusion from Bandung, where the UN resolution was adopted as the Afro-Asian position.

The Americans were very anxious that Nasser should not go to Bandung, and Kermit Roosevelt paid another visit during which he pointed out what bad company Nasser would find himself in there (China, for example). He said it would be a mistake for Egypt to waste its energies on talks about national liberation movements and Afro-Asian solidarity, all of which would probably lead nowhere. More subtle means of persuasion were also used. It is easy for a country with such advanced technology as the United States to give the impression of omniscience, and to imply that it is very anxious to help and that it knows a great deal that is of vital concern to whoever is being talked to. This is a technique that is used particularly in questions of security. So hints were dropped that it might be dangerous for Nasser to make the journey; he was told that the Moslem Brotherhood had plans to assassinate him, either in Karachi or when he got to Indonesia.

However, Nasser was determined to go, so he hired an Air India plane. He stopped off in Karachi, because he wanted a chance to talk to the Pakistani leaders before they irrevocably committed themselves to joining the Baghdad Pact, as then seemed likely. But he found the Prime Minister, Mohamed Ali, adamant. He said Pakistan needed arms to defend itself against India, and the only way to get them was from the West, and that meant joining the West's pact. Mohamed Ali was a short man, and rather stout, and he became quite excited while talking to Nasser. Leaping to his feet he shouted: 'Yes, I don't want to get involved! Noninvolvement, yes — but not now! Noninvolvement, yes — but not now!'

Nasser's next stop was in Rangoon. There he met Chou En-Lai, also en route to Bandung, and took the opportunity to sound him out about a possibility which, however remote it might seem, now had to be explored. Did Chou think, Nasser asked tentatively, that the Russians might be prepared to sell arms to Egypt? He expected the answer to be No, because he thought the boundaries marking the spheres of influence between East and West were so clearly defined that the Russians would be unwilling to step over them. But Chou said he thought they might be willing, if properly asked, and asked Nasser, 'Do you want me to explore?' Nasser said 'Yes.' So Chou made a report to Chairman Mao, who passed it on to Moscow via the Soviet ambassador in Peking.[3]

---

[1] Caffery's failure to persuade Nasser to see the world through State Department eyes was, it seems, attributed in Washington to his age and his style, which was that of an old-fashioned Southern gentleman. Whether or not this belief was justified, there is no doubt that Caffery was by this stage something of a spent force. The State Department had apparently decided that a younger man, with more specialized knowledge of the area and, if possible, a background similar to Nasser's, might enjoy greater success. Byroade, who had had a career as an army officer and had subsequently served as Assistant Secretary of State for Middle Eastern Affairs, seemed tailor-made for the part.

[2] On 2 April 1955 there was an attempted coup against the Imam. As he told the story later when he and Nasser were guests of King Saud in Jeddah, one of the senior army commanders, Colonel Ahmed Ben Tellaya, arrested the Imam and had him locked up in a cell in his own palace. The Colonel came in and demanded that he should hand over the ring which was the seal of his office (the Imams being spiritual as well as temporal rulers, and the idea behind the coup being to instal the Imam's brother Seif el-Islam Abdullah). He refused, there was a struggle and he bit the colonel's hand, who said no matter, they would do without the ring. Later one of the women in the harem managed to get in touch with the Imam and told him that they were all being mistreated, accused of passing messages to people outside Sana'a, and so would have to be searched every time they went in or out of the palace. Shortly afterwards the Imam heard a woman screaming and recognized her voice. He shouted as loud as he could, 'The women must never be allowed to be searched.' A guard heard him, apologized for what was going on, and opened the door of his cell. The Imam ran into the guardroom shouting '*allahu akbar!*' and soon was followed by several of the guards also shouting '*allahu akbar!*' He seized a machine gun and went to the minaret of the mosque in the grounds of the palace. After firing some rounds and proclaiming from the minaret 'The Imam is victorious! *allahu akbar!*' the conspiracy was at an end. Thirty-nine of the conspirators were arrested, their heads cut off and hung on branches of trees in the palace grounds for forty-two days. Members of the mission which was sent from Egypt to congratulate the Imam on his victory were appalled by the smell.

[3] See *Sphinx and Commissar* by M.H. Heikal (London 1978), pp. 58 ff.

ARMS AND THE
MEN

NASSER CAME BACK from Bandung via Afghanistan. While he was away, Eden had taken over as Prime Minister from Churchill and it was reasonable to hope that the moratorium that had been agreed on between them (as Nasser thought) would hold. But not all the indications were good. Nasser found a message from Sabri el-Asali, the Syrian Prime Minister, reporting a virtual ultimatum he had received from Nuri who maintained that the military alliance between Egypt, Syria, and Saudi Arabia amounted to an act of aggression against Iraq. This, combined with pressure from Turkey, was making the Syrians extremely nervous. It was thought that Turkish moves had the backing of the Americans.

In fact, the Americans' attitude was full of contradictions. They had encouraged Britain to join the Baghdad Pact, but assured Nasser that they had no intention of joining it themselves. American oil companies, with no opposition from the State Department, were planning what amounted to a coup d'état in the oasis of Buraimi, on the disputed frontier between Saudi Arabia, Abu Dhabi and Muscat, which would inevitably bring them into conflict with Britain, who championed the claims of the two latter. The situation in Gaza was still extremely tense and Nasser suggested setting up a demilitarized zone 1 kilometre each side of the frontier. The Israelis, who always preferred engagement to disengagement, countered by suggesting a zone only 50 metres wide.

But on the arms front there were signs of movement. A message came to Nasser from Chou via the Chinese ambassador, saying that his report has been well received in Moscow and was regarded as a positive step, and soon afterwards signals began to come in directly from Moscow.

The Russians did not immediately agree that they would supply arms, but they did send word that they were going to insist that the Middle East should be included on the agenda for the four-power summit meeting that was due to open in Geneva on 18 July. Further encouragement was also forthcoming indirectly. Nehru had passed through Cairo on his way to Moscow and Nasser had told him of his conversations with Chou. Nehru was non-committal, and said he had no idea what the Russian reaction would be. But he spent a day in Cairo on his way back, after visiting other European capitals, and told Nasser, 'I think you will get what you asked Chou about.'

On 19 May the Soviet ambassador in Cairo, Daniel Solod, told Nasser he had had a reply from Moscow. They wanted to be given a clear idea of exactly what was required from them and what should be the channels for future negotiations on this subject: 'How can details be worked out?' So far, so good, but Nasser still had his doubts. It seemed certain that the Russians were in favour of sending him arms, but none had actually materialized, and he could not forget that the Americans had in the past talked a lot about giving Egypt arms but that in the end nothing had come of it. He wanted to move on from agreement in principle to agreement on details. Moreover, he wondered how firm the Russians would be if the going became difficult at the summit meeting in Geneva.

Nasser felt it would be only fair to give the Americans some sort of warning of what was in the wind, so on 1 June he asked Byroade, with whom his personal relations were always friendly,[1] to see him. At their meeting he recapitulated his old grievances about arms and said plainly that if he did not get them from America he would have to get them from some other source. Byroade asked him, 'What other source?' Nasser said from wherever he could find them. Byroade said, 'Do I take it you are referring to the Soviet Union?' Nasser said, 'Why not?' 'But do you think they would sell you some arms?' asked Byroade. Nasser said, 'I can't tell. But I would not have raised the subject with you now unless I had grounds for saying what I have said to you. I am not going to beg for arms from you again. This is the last time you will hear me talking about arms.' Byroade could see that Nasser meant what he said, but told him that, with the Geneva summit meeting due to start work so soon, he thought it unlikely that the Russians would do anything that might prejudice an agreement there.

Two days later, Nasser had a meeting with Sir Ralph Stevenson, who was due to leave in four days' time. Byroade had obviously told him about his talk with Nasser, and Stevenson said that as this was to be his last meeting, he felt excused for talking frankly. 'I have been in Egypt over four critical years in its history,' he said. 'You have told my American colleague that you are even prepared to buy arms from the Soviet Union. My advice to you, as a real friend of Egypt, would be against taking such a risk. It could prove very dangerous.' This made Nasser extremely annoyed, and he showed it. Stevenson hastened to add, 'Please be assured that my advice was well meant. I am not speaking on instructions from my government. I am not even sure that you are going to do what has been suggested. I am simply speaking as a friend of Egypt.'

A delegation was sent to Geneva, headed by Dr Mustapha Kamel, later to be ambassador in Washington, to monitor the four-power conference. But he had an almost impossible task. Only a very small part of the negotiations had anything to do with the Middle East, and nobody was prepared to leak information about what was going on, so for most of the time the best they could do was to read the newspapers and glean what they could from them.

But on 23 July Dmitri Shepilov, the editor of *Pravda*, came to Cairo for the annual ceremonies commemorating the 1952 revolution. He was known to be particularly close to Khrushchev, who was later to make him Foreign Minister. He told Nasser that details of the deal were being worked out, but one thing was still worrying the leadership. When news of the deal got out the Americans would be certain to apply enormous pressure to sabotage it. If they succeeded, and Egypt backed down, the Soviet Union would be humiliated and left looking foolish. Nasser could now see that the Russians were really serious, so he gave Shepilov every assurance he could. He said that once the agreement had been signed, there was no force on earth that could make Egypt back down. It would have to be somebody else who did it, not him. Shepilov warned Nasser of the difficulties that would be faced by the army which had been trained on Western weapons and would have to get used to completely new ones.

Bulganin sent Nasser an invitation to come to Moscow, but he preferred to wait until the arms deal had been finally signed. In any case, there was too much happening in the area to claim his attention. A general election in Israel on 26 July had shown a swing to the right, but had confirmed Ben-Gurion in power, and a few days later the news leaked out that six squadrons of Mystère IV planes, earmarked for NATO, had been switched to Israel (America had approved the switch of three squadrons but the French had doubled the number). On 31 August Israel staged another bloody raid in the Gaza Strip, this time attacking the town of Khan Yunis, leaving thirty-nine dead. Nasser felt that Israel was trying to provoke him into war, so he made the unilateral gesture of establishing a demilitarized zone 100 metres wide on the Egyptian side of the border only, as the Israelis still refused to make any similar concession on their side.

Syria continued to be the ground on which the battle of the pacts was being fought. Beirut was now the focus of activity, having become the Middle East capital of the CIA as well as being the oil and banking centre of the area, and the playground for all its rich. Enormous sums — estimates put the figure at not less than £S100 million — were being spent by the Americans on buying newspapers and radio stations as well as politicians. Corruption was rife in Damascus itself, where a new President was due to be elected. Saudi gold reinforced Egyptian influence in favour of the veteran nationalist Shukri Quwatli, who had already been the first President after Syria won its independence from France in 1943. The election was made by the Chamber, with the result that there was an open market for deputies' votes, the going rate being £S100,000, rising to £S500,000 on election day, 18 August. Quwatli duly received ninety-one votes on a second ballot and became President again.

The French were showing increasing indignation at the help Egypt was giving to the Algerian revolution, which had broken out on 1 November the year before, and to the nationalist movements in Tunisia and Morocco. They objected strongly to the office which had been set up in Cairo, in which nationalists from all three countries were represented. The French demonstrated their resentment by giving increased aid to Israel, but when they withdrew troops which had been allocated to NATO and sent them to Algeria Nasser took this as in effect an act of aggression by the whole of NATO against the Arabs. Since, as he always said, he preferred to talk to the head rather than the tail, he asked Byroade to come and see him.

As soon as Byroade came in he said:

Mr President, you have scooped me. Just before I got your message, I received instructions from Washington to ask for a meeting. They think we shall get nowhere if we go on dealing with every subject separately. We must try for an overall settlement. This is something that I myself worked on when I was in the State Department. The lines we are thinking on are these — why not raise an international loan to help Israel to provide compensation for the refugees? Why not work for security measures between you and Israel in which the United States and others would take part? Why not try to agree final frontiers?

The meeting was on 19 August, and Nasser thought the American ideas were quite unrealistic. Two days later came the Khan Yunis raid, which showed just how unrealistic they were.

The next time Nasser and Byroade met was on 26 September, the day before the arms deal was announced. It was a routine visit connected with the Johnston Plan and Nasser intended to keep off the subject of arms. However, Byroade brought it up, saying that there were a lot of rumours going round about what Egypt was going to do. He said he personally didn't believe them (though probably he did), and added, 'What a pity you never signed the Mutual Security Pact. If you had, you might have got your arms from us.' Nasser just said, 'It's too late for that now.'

One of those working with Harry Kearn[2] on *Newsweek*, and like him connected with the CIA, was a journalist of Lebanese origin. He saw Zakaria Mohieddin[3] at the Ministry of Interior on the evening of the same day, 26 July. He was told nothing specific but came away convinced that the deal with the Russians had been concluded, and reported as much. By midnight all the lights were burning in the American embassy and in the Zamalek headquarters of the CIA.

I had become so close to Nasser, especially in matters concerning foreign policy, that some observers had started to call my office the 'Shadow Ministry of Foreign Affairs'. It was this involvement on my part which led to my being woken by the telephone at 1.20 on the morning of Tuesday 27 September. It was Eichelberger, who sounded rather drunk and very agitated. He said they had had confirmation that Egypt had signed a deal with the Soviet Union, and that Kermit Roosevelt was hurrying to Cairo from Washington. He thought the situation was very dangerous. I waited until I knew that Nasser would be awake, and then reported my exchange with Eichelberger to him. He thought it was essential that the news should now be declared, but this would have to be done before Kermit Roosevelt arrived. 'I'm not going to let him question me about it,' he said. Nasser was not due to make any public appearance that day, but he found an invitation to an exhibition of photography organized by the army public relations department, and that had to do. The press was told that Nasser would be opening the exhibition and then the announcement was finally made there.

Kermit Roosevelt reached Cairo the same evening. He had, in fact, been in Cairo only a week earlier, but the subject of Russian arms had not then been discussed. Instead, there had been a rather embarrassing dinner party at which Byroade had uncharacteristically lost his temper. This had taken place at the house of Dr Said Shukri, father-in-law of Ahmed Hussein, in Giza. Kermit Roosevelt and Eric Johnston were there, and Nasser was the guest of honour. Byroade was clearly in a very agitated state. When he arrived he went straight up to the bar and helped himself to a large whisky (he had obviously had a few already). It seemed as though he was bursting to get something off his chest, and soon after Nasser arrived it came out. 'Mr President,' he said, turning to Nasser, 'one of my men has been savagely beaten up today.' Nasser, who had already received a report about the incident, said, 'That was because he was spying and provoked some of the workers in Suez.' Byroade grew still more agitated. 'One of my men is badly beaten, and you try to make excuses for those who did it. I don't understand it.' That annoyed Nasser. 'All right,' he said, 'if you don't understand it we had better leave you until you do.' He threw away his cigarette and left the house.

What had happened was that the Labour Attaché at the embassy, Finch, who was in the habit of going round the country investigating working conditions and unions, had been in Suez and met the head of the oil workers union, Anwar Salama. He was accused of trying to interfere in the union's affairs, there was a quarrel, and he was beaten. But no doubt Byroade was already in a nervous state. The air was full of rumours, and he felt that the truth about what was going on was being kept from him, not least by his own people.

None of this augured particularly well for Roosevelt's return visit. He saw me soon after his arrival and said that Dulles was furious. Eisenhower had had a heart attack three days before and was in hospital in Denver, allowed to see nobody except briefly his Chief of Staff, Sherman Adams. Dulles and his brother Allen, Director of the CIA, were in effect running the government. 'This is very serious, Mohamed,' he said. 'I want Gamal to understand just how serious it is. Dulles is not going to let Eisenhower, when he recovers, hold him responsible for a major policy defeat.'

Roosevelt said there were four countermeasures which America would probably take if the deal went through. All Point Four aid would be stopped; all economic and cultural links between the two countries would be severed; diplomatic relations might be broken off, and, finally, a blockade of all Egyptian ports to prevent the Russian arms' coming in could not be ruled out. I took the message to Nasser in his office, but he was not impressed. He probably felt that this gave him the chance to prove to the Russians that he was perfectly capable of standing firm under American pressure. What did American aid amount to, he asked. Not much. And cultural exchanges? 'A troupe of jazz musicians.' As for the threatened blockade, that was a problem for the Soviet Union, because it was their ships that could be transporting the arms.

Roosevelt had asked for an interview with Nasser, but this was refused. The refusal led Washington to rethink its tactics. Eisenhower, the soldier, had an almost mystical faith in the efficacy of covert operations, especially after events in Iran and Guatemala had demonstrated what the undercover warriors of the CIA could do. But in this case the covert messenger had been rebuffed. It may be that Roosevelt was thought to be too soft and too friendly with Nasser. At all events, Dulles now decided to see what could be achieved by the big guns of orthodox diplomacy. Accordingly, George Allen, Assistant Secretary of State in charge of Middle Eastern Affairs, was despatched to Cairo with what amounted to an ultimatum.

Intrigue and rivalries among the Americans in Cairo had, in the meantime, reached an almost Byzantine pitch. Roosevelt and Johnston, realizing they had failed, were busy trying to shift the blame onto Byroade. Roosevelt, in particular, felt he would lose face badly if he had to report he had been unable to gain access to Nasser, so I arranged for them to meet unofficially at my house. He had to give an undertaking that he would not discuss the American reaction to the arms deal, but he tried to get round this by describing at some length the 1948 communist coup in Czecho-slovakia and how it had led to the suicide of Jan Masaryk.

The next day, Thursday 29 September, I called in at Eichel-berger's house, where I found Roosevelt and Johnston drafting a telegram to Dulles. They were cagey about its contents but read me the first paragraph. This contained their joint assessment that because Byroade no longer had access to Nasser his usefulness was at an end: 'Hank is no longer fit to stay in Cairo.' When I saw Nasser a little later I told him about this telegram. He could see that there was a campaign under way to break Byroade and he was already infuriated by another CIA-inspired operation involving the ambassador.

Nasser told me to see Byroade and to tell him that he refused to meet Allen unless he received an official request from the embassy and from the ambassador, himself, to do so. He was not going to have any more meetings with the covert channels. I went round to the American embassy where I found Byroade a broken man. Whether or not he had got wind of the Roosevelt-Johnston telegram he certainly knew that he and his embassy were by now more or less isolated. When I told him that I had a message from the President, which was that protocol must be observed, and that if Allen came to see him it must be in the company of the ambassador, his eyes filled with tears. 'Really?' he said. 'I will never forget this. Tell the President I will never forget this. I understand what this means.'

Immediately Byroade became the active diplomat again, setting in train all the preparations for a meeting with the President. 'My friend,' he said to me. 'I made a terrible mistake — something I should not have done. [He was referring to the dinner at Dr Shukri's house and the Finch affair.] But you know how I love and respect the President. I don't know what is happening to me these days. I'm very tired. Everything I have tried to do in Egypt seems to be slipping away from me.'

Allen was due to arrive in Cairo on the morning of Friday 30 September on what was being disingenuously described as a routine trip. Early that day, Nasser, who had been reading the agency messages about the visit, told me of an AP report which said that Allen was bringing an ultimatum to Egypt – that Nasser was to be told in no uncertain terms to stop playing his dangerous game with the Soviets. By now, of course, Nasser knew that the Russians had rejected protests about the arms deal by America, Britain and France, so he was confident there would be no weakening there. He instructed me to tell Byroade and Roosevelt that he was prepared to receive Allen, but that if the word *ultimatum* was uttered he would summon the head chamberlain in the presidency and instruct him to throw his visitor out. He would then meet the journalists and personally give them an account of what had happened. This was a matter of principle, he said, involving the national dignity of Egypt and he was not prepared to compromise.

Byroade and Roosevelt went separately to the airport to meet Allen. It would be for Byroade to board the plane to greet the visitor, but Roosevelt managed to use his intelligence connexions to get a message sent from the airport control tower to the plane, begging Allen to be extremely cautious in anything he said before he had a chance to brief him. Byroade conveyed the same message, so Allen's remarks to the assembled media men were entirely noncommittal. He said they should not dramatize the situation, and he would meet them later; it was all a part of the normal process of consultation between the two governments.

Back at the American embassy, Allen was given a full briefing. He duly saw Nasser the next day, but on the advice of Roosevelt and Byroade did not hand over the letter he had brought. They talked in general terms about their mutual relations, and there was no mention of the word *ultimatum*.

Reactions to the news of the arms deal, when it came out, were largely predictable. There was an outcry in the Western press. Nuri felt himself obliged to add his voice to the chorus of congratulations from other Arab leaders, but privately felt this provided fresh justification for trying to build up the Baghdad Pact. One complicating element was the Prime Minister of Libya, Mustapha Ben Halim. His government had for some time been asking America for arms, without success, and he now came out with a statement that he had told the British ambassador that if these arms did not arrive before 15 November he would ask not the Russians but President

Nasser to supply them! This stampeded the British and American governments into conceding that Libya should be given a battalion of armoured cars.

Ahmed Hussein had been on leave in Egypt when the deal was made public, and was full of forebodings about its consequences. He immediately hurried back to his post in Washington and sought an interview with Dulles, which was not granted until 18 October. It often happens that diplomats who have special knowledge of the country to which they are accredited find it easier to explain that country's point of view than to put over the views of their own government. Ahmed Hussein was a case in point. He naturally felt at home in the country where he had been educated, and concentrated his efforts on trying to win sympathy for Egypt from the world's most powerful nation.

Ahmed Hussein reported his meeting to Dulles in a long telegram. He had opened on an almost apologetic note, maintaining that the Israeli general election had shown their aggressive intentions, as had actual incidents of aggression, and this had made a purchase of arms from the Soviet Union a necessity. But he insisted that it was a purely commercial deal to meet an emergency and to fill gaps in Egypt's armaments, and that Egypt would never allow the communists to infiltrate or to influence its policies. Egypt would continue to resist communism with all its might.

Dulles thanked Hussein for the clarifications he had offered but said he could not conceal the fact that Egypt's purchase of arms from the Eastern bloc was an exceedingly disturbing matter, particularly in view of the fact that the United States had in the past year done all it could to help Egypt and to demonstrate its friendship in every way. 'You seem to have forgotten,' said Dulles, 'the assistance we gave you in reaching an agreement with Britain, the impartiality we have shown as between the Arabs and Israel, and the restrictions placed on the sale of American cotton so as not to harm Egyptian exports.' He added that they had also tried to intervene with the Sudanese on Egypt's behalf on the question of the Nile waters, and they had shown the importance they attached to Egypt as the centre of the Arab world when they instructed Eric Johnston to start his mission in Cairo, even though Egypt was not directly involved in the distribution of the Jordan waters. As an example of his government's even-handed approach, he quoted the freezing of aid to Israel after it had defied a Security Council resolution and started up operations in the demilitarized zone at Lake Tiberias. Indeed, Dulles claimed that their friendly gestures to the Arabs had lost the Republicans votes in the midterm Congressional elections.

Dulles said the United States had promised to give Egypt economic and military aid once the agreement with Britain had been signed, and many of its promises had already been fulfilled. 'We still trust your President,' said Dulles, but went on:

> I always tell my people he is the most important man in the Middle East, and that we can count on him and have confidence in him. But I must tell you in all frankness that what you have done has been a great shock to the American government and to its foreign policies Some Congressmen have been saying that it represents the biggest defeat to American policy since China. This has provided many of our opponents here with ammunition they were looking for, and it has strengthened the standing of the Israelis. All those people who opposed Britain's withdrawal on the grounds that the Egyptians couldn't be trusted now feel themselves justified, as do those who have all along been saying that Egypt was going to be a source of trouble.

Dulles said he did not think the Israelis were going to wait until the Arabs had completed all their preparations before they pounced. He himself had been placed in an extremely awkward position, because without any doubt Israel was now going to ask America for more arms and for guarantees, and would use every means available to it to get what it wanted. From his long experience of the Russians, and from a thorough knowledge of the way in which they operated, he could assure Ahmed Hussein that Egypt was going to be no match for them. 'I trust Nasser's good intentions,' he said, 'and I know he does not want to give the communists a chance to interfere in his country, but, with all respect, you can never be cleverer than they are, and you will never get the better of them.'

Dulles ended by sketching the scenario of what he expected to happen if the arms deal went through. It would give the communists a foothold in the Middle East and this would mark the beginning of a thrust aimed at denying Arab oil to the West. The arms deal had a much wider purpose than simply to oblige Egypt. It would now become impossible to ask Congress for a penny of help for Egypt, because not only the influence but the prestige of the United States was at stake. Everyone was going to say that the way to get American aid was to blackmail them.

Ahmed Hussein said he could not agree that American prestige had been damaged, and he asked Dulles what suggestions he had for improving the atmosphere between their two countries. Dulles said that time would be needed to make further analysis of the crisis. He hoped that America's relations with the Arabs would not suffer any drastic deterioration, and he would do all he could to avoid anything in the nature of an act of revenge.

Nine days later, on 27 October, Ahmed Hussein saw Kermit Roosevelt, who said he was alarmed at reports that Egypt was encouraging other Arab countries to buy arms from the Russians and was even acting as an intermediary in this. He said that the Egyptian government was in control of the situation, and could check communist infiltration, but other Arab countries might not be so well placed. He said he had Saudi Arabia and Syria particularly in mind. Did Hussein know, he asked, that Yemen had asked Russia for arms?

Roosevelt said that Europe's oil needs were increasing because of the high cost of coal and nuclear power, and the Russian aim was to control all the countries which produced oil or through which oil passed to reach its markets. This was part of a global strategy, stretching from Indonesia to Venezuela, and represented a threat to Europe which the United States could not permit. He said that if Syria got arms from Russia that was something Turkey and Iraq would resist. He thought it quite possible that Israel would now start a war, or provoke some Arab country into starting a war, and this was a matter that had been discussed at the last meeting of the National Security Council — how such a war might start, and how it could be stopped once it started. The NSC had also discussed the possibility that, if war did break out, there might be rioting in Cairo which would put American lives at risk. Emphasizing the gravity of his words, Roosevelt said that many people in Washington, both inside and outside the State Department, were beginning to wonder whether Egypt had any wish to maintain a friendly attitude towards America or to cooperate with it. Egypt's friends in Washington would have liked to be able to defend its actions, but nobody was going to buy the theory that the arms deal was purely a commercial transaction.

Egypt's friends, said Roosevelt, were now placed in an extremely awkward position, especially in the light of attacks on America and the West generally in the Egyptian press and radio. This made Americans feel that the Egyptians were being deliberately mobilized against them. He said he had had a talk with Hoover, then acting Secretary of State, the previous day and he had said that the State Department was coming to believe that Egypt now regarded the United States as an enemy. Hoover had said with a laugh: 'The only man who disagrees with this is someone called Roosevelt.' It was all extremely embarrassing for him, said Kermit, but, quite apart from personal considerations, if things went on as they were, the United States would come to the conclusion that Egypt was an enemy and would base its policy accordingly. He begged Hussein to send a plea, personally from himself, to Cairo to stop the propaganda campaign against America. If this was not stopped, the first victims would be Egypt's friends in America, next Egyptian interests there, and finally relations of every sort between the two countries. Hussein argued that the real source of all the trouble was Israel; if Israel had not put pressure on America, none of this would have happened. Roosevelt said that was something that could only be discussed when the Egyptian propaganda campaign had ended.

In fact, the attitude in Washington was far from being as negative as Dulles and Roosevelt implied. Obviously there had to be a reassessment of policy towards Egypt, but when this was done in a more sober spirit officials were reluctant to write Egypt off after all that had been achieved there and abandon it to the Soviet Union without a struggle. The former Alpha committee was wound up and a new committee, the Omega, was constituted, headed by Raymond Hare, who was to succeed Byroade as ambassador in Cairo. The new aim was to isolate Egypt from the rest of the Arab world, particularly from Syria and Saudi Arabia, the first being regarded as Egypt's front line outpost and the second as the holder of its purse-strings. It was decided that the best way of achieving this isolation would be to encourage Egypt to concentrate on its internal problems — in other words, to concentrate on development. They recalled what Nasser had said about development in his first contacts with the Americans, and this was of course something where they were well qualified to help. They were naturally aware that from the beginning of the year the Egyptian government had been engaged in serious negotiations with the World Bank over finance for building the High Dam at Aswan, and decided that their best bet would be to join in so prestigeful an undertaking. Some time later Dulles epigrammatically characterized this new policy: 'Russia is helping you in death, but we are going to help you in life.'[4] A public announcement that the American and British governments, together with the International Bank for Reconstruction and Development, were going to finance the building of the dam, was made by Dulles on 16 December.

Ahmed Hussein was told by a senior State Department official that the decision to help Egypt over the dam had been taken only after much consideration and long discussions. Immense opposition had had to be overcome, and Congress would have to be asked to authorize the necessary bills, because a long-term financial commitment like this was more than the President could sanction on his own. Hussein was left in no doubt about the favour that was being done to Egypt. He was told that, though help over the dam was being given willingly, it would have been very easy for a completely different decision to have been arrived at. Already Iraq and Pakistan were complaining that they saw that the best way to get American help was not to go into an alliance with them, but to join the other side. The Israelis too had been bombarding Washington with demands for arms, but they were not going to get them — not yet at any rate — because this would only encourage the extremists in Israel who were spoiling for a war. But the ambassador was told that a real programme of development depended on a settlement of the Arab–Israeli problem, and America was now preparing a new initiative which, it was hoped, would pave the way for such a settlement. If the Arabs played their part, the Americans would be prepared to twist Israel's arm to get them to cooperate.

Two other telegrams concerning Israel came from Ahmed Hussein about this time. In the first he recorded a talk he had had with Herbert Hoover, who had recently breakfasted with Sharett and Abba Eban, the Israeli ambassador. Sharett had said that all attacks against Egypt were personally ordered by Ben-Gurion, who assumed that Egypt was going to attack Israel when the chance offered. Unfortunately, said Sharett, those people in Israel who thought that the only way to treat the Arabs was with an iron fist were gaining ground as a result of the arms deal. He did not know what exactly Ben-Gurion was planning, but he did not trust him an inch.

A 'well-informed source' gave Hussein a rather different picture. He said he thought that Ben-Gurion meant what he said when he asserted that keeping the peace was better than winning a war. He thought that Ben-Gurion would wait for some months to see whether Western efforts to reach a settlement between Israel and the Arabs within a fixed period achieved anything, and to see whether Israel got its arms. Only when he was certain on these two points would he resort to war.

The second telegram was in answer to a report emanating from the Syrian Prime Minister, who said he had heard that the Americans had agreed to sell Israel arms, to give a guarantee of Israel's frontiers and to allow American volunteers to join the Israeli army. The ambassador saw both Hoover and Dulles and was able to report that, as far as he could make out, no decision about selling arms had been reached. Certainly, Israel had submitted a huge list of its requirements, and might get limited quantities. America would be prepared to guarantee Israel's frontiers only if these had previously been agreed with the Arabs, and legislation would be needed before American citizens could join a foreign army.

Byroade came back to Washington for consultations, and saw Ahmed Hussein on 15 January. They spent three hours together. Byroade said he could at last breathe freely again, because Dulles seemed to have got over his initial shock over the arms deal. He had asked Byroade to talk to congressmen, and he had had three sessions with the Foreign Affairs Committee, as well as talked at the Press Club. 'God knows what I've suffered as a result of being accused of being your man,' he said. He said he couldn't rule out the possibility of Israel's starting a war, because they were all furious over the arms deal, and Ben-Gurion had become so senile that his thought processes were upset.

Although the offer of American financial aid towards construction of the High Dam represented a new policy line, old policies had not been abandoned. The Americans were still furious at the arms deal and the hostile propaganda emanating from Cairo. The Omega Committee in Washington was working on ways of isolating

Egypt from the rest of the Arab world, concentrating its efforts on
Syria and Saudi Arabia, one to be the political and the other the
financial spearhead of the attack. But the CIA, by now the main
executant of American policy in the area, was itself divided. Kermit
Roosevelt had moved from Cairo to Beirut, where he headed the
bureau which operated in Syria as well as in Lebanon, under cover
of a consultancy agency. He had brought Eichelberger and Copeland with him, and he was now assisted by an American citizen of
Arab origin with diplomatic cover called Ghosein Zoghby, and
Eugene Trone, who was later to be active in Cairo.

Roosevelt still hoped that a more positive role might be found for
Egypt, but others at CIA headquarters in Washington, led by James
Angleton, had come to the conclusion that nothing was to be
achieved through the Arabs and that much the most promising
country for the agency's endeavours was Israel. He had worked
with Zionist groups during the war and later, after the creation of
Israel, with Mossad, and was to be responsible for passing on to
Israel much of the information which enabled it to develop its
atomic programme so successfully.

Radio propaganda, directed largely against Egypt, was being
stepped up. There was a clandestine station run by Americans in
Rhodes which sent out messages on the lines of those transmitted
from London during the war to Resistance groups in occupied
Europe: 'Group One — mission confirmed', 'Group Two — be
careful. The camel [Gamal?] is soon to take the desert road to
Alexandria. Your instructions confirmed.' 'Inform Group Three
that Mahalla el Kubra [the industrial complex near Cairo] is ready
for what is planned.' And so on. It was psychological warfare
obviously conducted by professionals and, though probably entirely a work of the imagination, designed to have an unsettling effect.
There were several other American stations in the area, and the
British had stations in Cyprus and Aden which were easily heard in
Egypt. Said Ramadan, formerly prominent in the Moslem Brotherhood, acted as adviser to the station in Cyprus, while the Abel Fath
brothers, well-known Cairo journalists now in exile, organized a
so-called 'Free Egypt' radio which broadcast from the French
station Europe Number One. At their peak, there were no fewer
than ten stations beamed at Egypt, not counting long-established
overt broadcasts like the Arabic service of the BBC.

But at the same time America was keeping help for the High

Dam very much to the fore. Abdel Moneim Kaisouni, the Finance Minister, was in Washington in December for discussions with the administration and the World Bank and on 9 December Eisenhower announced that he would be asking Congress for $200 million over a ten-year period for the dam, and four days later Eugene Black sent Kaisouni a letter indicating that the World Bank was in principle prepared to advance a similar sum for the same purpose. Dulles had earlier asked Nasser for an assurance that the first arms deal with the Eastern bloc would be the last, which was of course an undertaking Nasser felt nobody had a right to demand of him, and one which he would not give.

The Russians had less reason to equivocate. They had achieved an important breakthrough, and for the moment were content to wait and see how the situation would develop. Their only fear was that Nasser might back down as a result of the enormous pressure he was under from the West, particularly from the Americans. They felt that if the Americans did go ahead with finance for the High Dam this would give them very considerable leverage on Egypt, which they would know how to exploit. But there was no suggestion of their replacing the Americans as backers for the dam. The only hint of that sort came in November when Daniel Solod, the Soviet ambassador, was talking to Nasser. He assured Nasser of his country's support against any attempts by other powers to put damaging pressure on him, in connexion with either arms or the economy, and he added, without elaborating: 'The High Dam is a very important project, and Egypt needs it.' Nasser made no attempt to pursue the conversation. For one thing, he felt that this was not a subject which should be discussed at ambassadorial level, and for another he was satisfied with having achieved a satisfactory diplomatic balancing act — arms from the Russians at a reasonable cost, and the prospect of Western funds for the High Dam.

The British government was also pursuing contradictory policies. Anthony Eden, Prime Minister since the spring, devoted most of his traditional speech at the Lord Mayor's Banquet in the Guildhall on 9 November to the Middle East, bitterly attacking the Soviet Union as fomenters of trouble and presenting himself as a messenger of conciliation.

Between Israel and Egypt lies an area of dangerous tension. . . . Now, into this dangerous situation, the Soviet government has decided to inject a new element of danger and to deliver weapons of war to one side only. It is fantastic to pretend that this deliberate act of policy was an innocent commercial transaction. It is no such thing. It is a move to gain popularity at the expense of the restraint shown by the West. . . . We have tried for a long time past [he concluded] to find common ground for some kind of settlement. . . . If, for instance, there would be accepted an arrangement between [Israel and her Arab neighbours] about their boundaries, we, and I believe the United States, and perhaps other powers, would be prepared to give a formal guarantee to both sides that would bring real confidence and security at last. . . . If there is anything we can do, we will gladly do it for the sake of peace.

But meanwhile most of Britain's energies were devoted to strengthening the Baghdad Pact. On 11 October Iran had joined the two original signatories of the pact, Turkey and Iraq, which led Russia to warn the Shah that he was playing with fire. On 21 November the permanent council of the pact met in the Zuhur Palace in Baghdad, with representatives of Britain, Turkey, Pakistan, Iran, and Iraq present. Harold Macmillan, the Foreign Secretary, attended on behalf of Britain and was urged to use his country's influence to persuade Jordan to join. He was quite willing, and at the beginning of December General Sir Gerald Templer, Chief of the Imperial General Staff, was despatched to Amman. His mission was to warn King Hussein that he must stop wavering and cast his country's lot in with his British ally and his Hashemite cousins in Iraq.

The failure of the Templer mission was a humiliation for Britain which in many ways foreshadowed the greater humiliation which was to be enacted a year later. It was symptomatic of Britain's diminished stature in the area that its top soldier should be sent to perform a task which, not so very long before, would have been left to someone in the embassy or to a word in the royal ear from Glubb Pasha. The King was told, as he was later to recount, that the British had information that Egypt was planning to overthrow the monarchy and set up a Jordanian republic with the ex-Mufti of Jerusalem, Haj Amin el-Husseini, as president. That was fiction, but Nasser certainly regarded the attempt to expand the pact as a violation of the understanding he thought he had reached with

Eden. He did not so much mind when the pact recruited Iran and Pakistan, but recruiting an Arab country was different. He felt absolved from any restraint which had been placed on propaganda to the Arab world, and the Voice of the Arabs now went into action with deadly effect. The streets of Amman were filled with demonstrators; the Arab Legion and the police refused to fire on them. Templer went back to London empty-handed, and Hussein saved his throne only by installing a caretaker government which would prepare for new elections in which, it was now clear, the nationalist forces which looked on Nasser as their mentor would sweep the board.

Syria was never regarded seriously as another candidate for membership of the pact, but America and Britain had designs on it of a different nature. The new President, Shukri Quwatli, was to prove not much more than a figurehead, and the government of traditional politicians over which he presided lacked authority. Real power rested with the army, where many of the younger officers demonstrated openly Nasserist sympathies, and in particular with the chief of military intelligence, the *Deuxième Bureau*, Colonel Abdel Hamid Sarraj. The enthusiasm generated in the army — and among civilians — for Egypt's arms deal was largely responsible for the signature of a military alliance between Egypt and Syria on 20 October 1955. Britain, however, hoped that, with Iraqi support (Damascus having throughout its Arab history been torn between the rival pulls of Baghdad and Cairo) the Quwatli regime might be toppled and the former military dictator, Colonel Adib Shiskekli, ousted in February 1954, brought back. The Americans had different plans, their protégés lined up and paid for by the CIA office in Beirut.

---

[1] The cordial relationship that grew up between Nasser and Byroade is illustrated by the incident of the Nail of Goha (Goha being a character who is the subject of many legends and sayings in Arab tradition). The story is that one day Goha sold his house and asked the new owner if he could go on making use of a

nail in the wall of the house for a few days. The new owner consented, and every day Goha came and hung some fresh object on the nail — a basket, a stick, a coat, and so on. Goha's nail accordingly came to represent the process by which a minor concession can be exploited into a major privilege.

There was one occasion when Byroade had mentioned to Nasser the request by the British civilians left in the canal zone after the 1955 agreement for restrictions on their movements to be relaxed. Nasser said he feared that any relaxation would be used like Goha's nail. Byroade looked puzzled. 'Do you know Goha?' asked Nasser. 'Oh yes,' said Byroade, 'I know him. I think I met him at a cocktail party.' Nasser roared with laughter: 'You met Goha at a cocktail party!' 'Yes,' said Byroade, 'but only once, I think.' Nasser went on laughing but did not explain. Afterwards Byroade, who thought Nasser had been talking about a Colonel Gowar who was a liaison officer in the Truce Commission, made some enquiries and so learned about the real Goha. He got hold of a book about Goha in English and sent it to Nasser with a note: 'Mr President, I think you took me by surprise the other day. I was mistaken about Goha, but I have educated myself since, and to prove that I now know about him I send you this book.'

[2] Kearn was Middle East correspondent of *Newsweek* and spent a great deal of time travelling all over the world. His CIA connexion was revealed in a Congressional enquiry. Every time he came back to Cairo he had a great store of confidential information which he was eager to impart. 'What an extraordinary person he is,' said Nasser. 'He seems to know more than any ambassador.'

[3] Zakaria Mohieddin got to know Nasser when they were both cadets in the Cairo Military Academy in 1937. He too fought in the Palestine war and was one of the early recruits to the Free Officers movement. He was in command of the troops which, on 26 July 1952, surrounded King Farouk in Montazah Palace in Alexandria. In 1953 he became Minister of the Interior.

[4] The first person to suggest the idea of the High Dam to Nasser was, oddly enough, neither an engineer nor an irrigation expert, but a Greek, resident in Egypt, called Daninos, who was interested in agriculture and used often to travel to the south. In 1953 he wrote a two-page manuscript letter in Arabic, addressed to Nasser, headed: 'Subject: The building of a huge dam on the rocky area south of Aswan.' He went on to argue that if the existing Aswan dam could store water for a year, a High Dam could store it for a century. Nasser passed the letter on to Gamal Saleh, a member of the RCC, who met Daninos, but with no results. Daninos wrote Nasser another letter, the two met, and the proposal was passed on for serious study. When the High Dam project was eventually adopted Daninos was given £E10,000. At first he said he wanted no cash reward, but would like the highest decoration in the land. But later he accepted the money.

The original Aswan Dam, completed in 1902, stored water for use in the Spring, when the Nile flow is normally low, but it could not store water for use from one year to another. The purpose of the High Dam was to provide long-term storage of the Nile waters, and thereby bring a million and a quarter more acres of land under cultivation. The dam was to be 2.5 miles long and 365 feet high, and would create a lake 344 miles long upstream, 124 miles of which would be in the Sudan. This, the largest artificial lake in the world, would involve the flooding of many towns and villages, including Wadi Halfa, and mean that 50,000 people would have to be resettled. The original estimated cost of the dam was $1,300 million.

❧ 8 ❧

MORE VISITORS

AT THE BEGINNING of December 1955, the Americans made a final effort to gain control over events. A new and extremely high-powered emissary was sent to Cairo, and Kermit Roosevelt begged Nasser to give him maximum attention and cooperation. This was Robert Anderson, one of Eisenhower's most intimate friends, a wealthy Texan businessman who, though he had no previous experience of the Middle East, would, it was said, bring to its problems an open and eminently practical mind. Nasser was, of course, prepared to listen carefully to any proposals that might be put to him by anyone with such credentials.

Anderson duly arrived, and on 18 December had his first meeting with Nasser. He proved to be an amiable man, but somewhat out of his depth. His main claim to fame was that, when he had been at the Treasury, it was his signature that appeared on the dollar bills. He liked to produce a bill and show it: 'That's me!' — and he would then add his signature in ink and present the bill to whomever he was talking to.

At his first meeting Kermit Roosevelt was present also, and Anderson began the proceedings by speaking uninterruptedly for twenty-five minutes. Nasser nodded his head, and Roosevelt said, 'It seems to me that my friend feels you are showing you agree to what he is saying.' But in fact Nasser's nods were nods of incomprehension; he was almost completely baffled by Anderson's Texan accent, and had to ask Roosevelt to act as interpreter.

After his introductory remarks, Anderson asked Nasser to explain to him what the problems were. Nasser agreed to do so:

> I will try to set them out in a businesslike fashion. There are two basic problems. The first concerns the rights of the people of Palestine. Most of them are refugees from their own country, often living in miserable conditions. They ought to be able to return to

their homes, and that is what the majority will certainly want, or, where this is impossible, they ought to receive compensation. And a fixed frontier must be drawn between the Israeli state and the Palestinian state.

The second problem is a strategic one. Israel forms a wedge between the two halves of the Arab world, the Arabs of Africa and the Arabs of Asia. When the Israeli army occupied Umm Rashash, the southernmost tip of Palestine on the Gulf of Aqaba, which they have now turned into the port of Eilat, they completed this separation, which now runs from the Mediterranean to the Red Sea.

Anderson expressed astonishment. This was a fact of geography of which he was ignorant, so Nasser took a piece of paper and drew a rough map for him.

Anderson then asked if Nasser had any message for him to convey to Ben-Gurion. This was the first time his intention to go to Israel as well as Egypt had been mentioned, or that his role was to be that of a mediator. Nasser said: 'Let me make this absolutely clear. I am not going to negotiate with Ben-Gurion by proxy.' And when Anderson asked permission for the special aeroplane which had brought him to Cairo to fly direct to Israel, this was refused. He was told he must go via some neutral country, and he decided to go to Athens.

After about ten days Anderson was back in Cairo again. It was by now nearly the New Year, and he complained about being kept away from his family over the holiday season, which made it seem as though he had expected to solve all the Middle East's problems in a day or two. He had seen Ben-Gurion, who had advanced his political education with a particularly rough lesson. Israel could not yield an inch on its southern frontiers. Israel would accept no refugees back. Israel would never agree to the closure of the Suez Canal or the Gulf of Aqaba to its shipping. There could be no demilitarization on Israel's borders with Egypt (something Nasser had suggested), and he wanted a ceiling on the number of troops kept by Egypt in Sinai. Finally, he wanted a peace settlement and the complete normalization of relations to be achieved according to a fixed timetable within a period of five years. Nasser told Anderson that all this was quite unacceptable, and Anderson returned to Washington.

In the middle of January he was back in Cairo again, bringing

with him a message from Dulles to the effect that the United States
would continue to be neutral between the Arabs and Israel and that
they would never join the Baghdad Pact themselves or encourage
anyone else to join it. But in the interval the State Department must
have been working overtime, because Anderson brought with him
two highly original, not to say extraordinary, proposals.

The first was the draft of a letter which, it was suggested, Nasser
should send to Eisenhower, to which was annexed a memorandum
covering the points at issue between Egypt and Israel and the lines
along which they might be settled. There was also the draft of a
letter for Nasser to send to the World Bank about the financing of
the High Dam.

The language of the Eisenhower letter was high flown and
frequently ungrammatical. Was that intended to give it an air of
verisimilitude? Who it was who thought that the President of Egypt
— or of any other country for that matter — would be prepared to
let words be put into his mouth, and sign on the dotted line, is not
known.[1]

One sentence in the Eisenhower letter spoke about 'permitting
the Arabs of Asia and Africa to be joined together by a continuous
and substantial land area under Arab sovereignty and peopled by
Arabs' which produced the second surprise. Apparently what was
intended was an enormous bridge, linking Sinai and Jordan, a huge
flyover, which would be under Arab sovereignty, Israel retaining
sovereignty over the underpass. Anderson insisted that there would
be no problem from the engineering point of view — this was the
sort of project that was being undertaken every day. Nasser could
hardly conceal his astonishment, or rather his indignation. 'So we
are to have the overpass?' he asked. That was so, he was told. 'But
supposing,' Nasser could not resist the temptation of suggesting,
'one of our soldiers wanted to piss, and did so from the overpass
onto some Israelis in the underpass — wouldn't that start a war?'
Anderson said that some arrangement might be made whereby for,
say, six hours every day the Israelis would stop all activities in the
underpass, during which time Egyptians and Jordanians could use
the overpass, and then for another six hours the positions would be
reversed. The discussion between the two was serious and prolonged, but unfortunately Nasser's patient explanation of historical
and geographical realities did not make the impression he had
hoped. Anderson, true to his background, continued to treat the

whole matter as a commercial proposition which could be resolved by tough pragmatic bargaining. Finally, Nasser was given the draft of a letter he was to send to Eugene Black about finance for the High Dam.[2]

Nasser told Anderson politely that the documents brought for his signature were quite unacceptable, whereupon Anderson said, 'Why not turn them over to your experts for them to redraft?' But this Nasser declined. Anderson then took himself off to Ben-Gurion and showed him the draft letter and draft treaty, only to be told by him too that the idea was a nonstarter. 'If you really want to further the cause of peace,' said Ben-Gurion, 'what you ought to do is to arrange a face-to-face meeting between Nasser and me, either in Jerusalem or Cairo or anywhere else.' Anderson brought this proposal back with him at the beginning of February, to be told that it was out of the question. 'If I agreed to it,' said Nasser, 'my people would prevent me from going. Or, if I did arrange to go, they would kill me when I got back.'[3]

All the evidence is that, in spite of the letter Nasser was supposed to send to Eugene Black, the Americans had by now given up any idea of financing the High Dam. They were not going to make this decision public, preferring to let the project die a natural death, and so informed neither Eugene Black nor the British, though the subject came up when Eden and Selwyn Lloyd, appointed Foreign Secretary on 22 December 1955, met Eisenhower and Dulles in Washington at the end of January. It was then, according to Selwyn Lloyd, 'we learned, I think for the first time, of doubts about the Aswan Dam project. Dulles told us that Black, of the International Bank, had said that his talks with Nasser were almost at breaking point. Black felt that the dam was too grandiose for Egypt's fragile economy and shaky political base.' So all the responsibility was to be shifted onto Eugene Black, with Dulles left the dispassionate observer.

Shortly after their meeting two events took place which fuelled Eden's growing obsession with Nasser as a personal enemy who must be destroyed — the dismissal of Glubb and Selwyn Lloyd's visit to Cairo.

General Sir John Bagot Glubb, who had served in Jordan for twenty-six years and was Chief of Staff of the Arab Legion (the Jordanian army), had naturally seen the failure of the Templer mission as a personal rebuff. At the beginning of February he submitted to Felah Pasha Medadha, the Minister of Defence, the names of eleven officers who should be dismissed from the army and of a further thirty-four officers who should be transferred from the army to the police or other civilian departments. He was unaware of the fact that King Hussein, thoroughly alarmed by the crisis which had nearly cost him his throne, had been in contact with the so-called Free Officers group, headed by Ali Abu Nuwar, his principal ADC, and had held several secret meetings with them.

At noon on 1 March King Hussein drove to the office of the Prime Minister, Samir Rifai. There were several ministers there, and their surprise at seeing the King was considerable. The King went into the Prime Minister's office and handed him a piece of paper containing a couple of lines in his own neat handwriting, to the effect that Glubb's services were to be dispensed with and he was to leave Jordan immediately. It was signed Hussein ibn Tallal. Samir Rifai's jaw dropped. 'Sayida, what is this?' he asked. 'Those are my orders,' said the King. The Prime Minister wanted to discuss the possible consequences of the action but the King told him that everything had been taken into account and he would have to carry out his instructions.

As the King drove off the street was filled with armoured cars from the Arab Legion carrying portraits of the King and Jordanian flags. Felah Medadha was told to summon Glubb, which he did. When Glubb arrived he was shown the paper containing the royal order. 'Is there anything I have done wrong?' he asked. He asked if he could see the King, but was told that this would not be possible, though Hussein hoped to see him later when he was on one of his visits to England. He would have to leave the country within two hours. This produced a brief outburst of anger on the part of Glubb. 'I'm not a dog with rabies, to be expelled like this after twenty-six years of service,' he said. It was finally arranged that he was to leave by a special air force plane at 7 a.m. the next morning, 2 March.

From the moment he took office as Foreign Secretary, Selwyn Lloyd gave the Middle East priority. Two weeks after taking over he summoned all Britain's ambassadors in the Middle East for two days of discussion at the Foreign Office, as a result of which it was agreed that the Baghdad Pact should be strongly supported, but without trying to bring any other Arab countries into it, that America should be urged to take some initiative for settling the

Arab–Israeli dispute, and that one more attempt should be made to come to terms with Nasser, and that this should be done by Lloyd himself.

Lloyd arrived in Cairo on 1 March and spent the afternoon in talks with the Egyptian Foreign Minister, Dr Mahmoud Fawzi. That evening Dr Fawzi was host at a dinner for him, which was held in the Tahira Palace because Nasser wanted to attend. Also present were two of his colleagues, the British ambassador, Sir Humphrey Trevelyan, and Sir Harold Caccia of the Foreign Office who was travelling with his minister. The dinner seemed to pass off amicably, though there was some quite straight talking. Lloyd complained about the propaganda emanating from Cairo attacking Britain and its friends and suggested that there should be a return to the moratorium on propaganda which was supposed to have been agreed at the meeting between Nasser and Eden. He assured Nasser that no attempt would be made to persuade any Arab country to join the Baghdad Pact.

Nasser complained strongly about the Templer mission. It was that which had been responsible for breaking the understanding with Eden, and so for breaking the moratorium. It was that which had obliged Egypt to react. He said he had welcomed Eden's Guildhall speech, but it was a great pity that he had listened to people like Glubb. Nasser elaborated on this, taking Glubb as representative of the conservative elements in the Middle East who were out of touch with the new progressive forces there.

Towards the end of the meal Trevelyan was called out to see one of the embassy staff who was there with an urgent message for him. He put the envelope in his pocket and went back to the dinner. It was only on the way back to the embassy in the ambassadorial Rolls Royce that he showed Lloyd the message — Glubb had been dismissed and was to leave Jordan at 7 o'clock the next morning. Lloyd immediately got in touch with London, where a furious Eden told him to seek immediate clarification from Nasser, who, it was assumed, must be behind the dismissal. When he talked it over with Trevelyan they were sure that Nasser must have known what had happened before he came to the dinner, and had been playing cat and mouse with them. The way in which he had harped on Glubb as an anachronism in the Middle East proved that.

But as a matter of fact Nasser had known nothing about it, any more than I or any other journalist had. The news was officially embargoed in Jordan until after Glubb had left the country, and it was only because Glubb had told the British ambassador in Amman, who had alerted London, that the news had got back to Trevelyan and Lloyd.

Lloyd was due to have a second and final meeting with Nasser at 9 o'clock the next morning, 2 March. A little before that I received a telephone call from Tom Little, the general manager of the Arab News Agency, asking me if I had any comment to make on Glubb's dismissal. I asked him what he was talking about. 'I'm talking about Glubb Pasha,' he said. 'He's been sacked. He left Jordan half an hour ago.' I did not know whether Nasser had heard the news, so I telephoned him. He was just finishing dressing and Selwyn Lloyd's car was at that moment drawing up in front of the house. 'Are you joking?' he asked. I said no, it was true. 'It's just as well you told me,' he said. 'I must go and see this man.' It never occurred to Nasser that the sacking might have been done on the King's own initiative. He assumed that it had been engineered by the British and that the timing had been arranged as a gesture of goodwill to coincide with the visit to Cairo of the Foreign Secretary[4].

When Nasser came into the room he found two tense and unsmiling figures, Lloyd and Trevelyan. 'Are you aware, Mr President,' said Lloyd, 'of what has happened in Jordan?' 'Yes,' said Nasser, adding in all innocence, 'it's good, isn't it?' Lloyd went extremely red in the face. 'What's good about it?' he asked. Nasser said he thought it showed that Britain at last appreciated that these out-of-date figures, like Glubb, no longer served any useful purpose in the area. But then, looking at Lloyd's face, it suddenly dawned on him that they were talking at completely cross-purposes.

After Lloyd had left Nasser spoke to me on the telephone again. He was laughing, and I asked what had happened. 'It's absurd,' he said. 'He thinks that we engineered the Glubb business, that we knew about it before the dinner started and that it was done deliberately to humiliate him.' During dinner Nasser had tried to explain about the nationalist movement and why it was strong everywhere in the Arab world. They must not think, he said, that he was responsible for everything that happened — that he only had to press one button on his desk and a demonstration erupted in Amman; another button and there was a riot in Aden. 'Now the man will be convinced I've got all those buttons,' said Nasser. 'We shall have to be cautious.'

Nasser decided that the whole incident should be played down. He did not want any fresh attacks in the press or radio on the British at a time when their anger was certain to be extreme nor did he want Glubb to be attacked personally. He did not want any specific position by Egypt to be adopted, or any positive action, like sending congratulations to King Hussein. 'These people are furious,' said Nasser. 'They think we are all involved in a conspiracy against them. This morning to begin with I had difficulty in prevent ing myself from bursting out laughing because the situation was so ludicrous, but Selwyn Lloyd's face had nothing comic about it. It was a very tragic face and it can mean real trouble. We must watch our step carefully.'

King Saud and President Quwatli of Syria arrived in Cairo on 5 March for a conference to discuss the financial help they could give to Jordan, which, as a result of Glubb's dismissal, would be deprived of the grants it had hitherto been receiving from Britain.

The next visitor to Cairo was Christian Pineau, Foreign Minister in the cabinet of Guy Mollet, who had become Prime Minister on 1 February 1956. Shortly before he came, on 14 March, the French ambassador, Couve de Murville, left and was replaced by Count Armand du Chayla. De Murville, a future Prime Minister, had never managed to get onto easy terms with Nasser, and his farewell audience, during which he spoke about France's 'traditional role' in the Orient and her predominant position in Europe, was far from cordial. No doubt he, like all French ambassadors in Egypt, was conditioned by the all-pervasive influence of the Suez Canal Company.

This was not a helpful preliminary to Pineau's visit. Nasser was determined that there was going to be no repetition of the Selwyn Lloyd mix-up — no dinner parties. 'Something is said at dinner, and then something happens. I don't want to have to contemplate another of these tragi-comic farces.' So on this occasion the meeting took place in Nasser's office.

Pineau had two principal subjects he wanted to talk about — North Africa and the Suez Canal Company — and Nasser, of course, was going to raise the question of France's supply of arms to Israel. Algeria had become the main concern of Mollet who had visited Algiers a few days after assuming office, only to be pelted with garbage by a mob of infuriated French *colons* who feared that he, a socialist, would betray them and hand the country over to the Moslem insurgents. They need not have worried. A chastened Mollet assured his attackers over the radio that he understood their emotions, had been greatly moved by them, and could assure them that France would remain present in Algeria. His revised sentiments were shared by his Foreign Minister.

Pineau complained that Egypt was giving aid and comfort to the Algerian insurgents by way of arms, training, and propaganda. Nasser pointed out that Algerian nationalism had become militant long before he appeared on the scene, and tried to explain the obligations which Egypt felt towards Algeria as one Arab country to another. He admitted that Egypt was helping the Algerians, and gave his opinion that, though the theory that Algeria was an integral part of France was plainly untenable, he thought that the nationalists would be found open to negotiation. 'Why not find out for yourself what they want?' he suggested. 'I can't speak for them. We hold no mandate on their behalf.' It was arranged that if France sent a delegation to Cairo, Nasser would arrange for an Algerian delegation to meet it. About a week after Pineau left the two delegations did in fact arrive and had one meeting, but the French flew back to Paris without telling anyone, and a projected second meeting never took place. So that particular initiative got nowhere.

Regarding the Suez Canal Company, Pineau spoke of what he called France's 'historical interests'. Nasser asked him what he meant by 'historical'. Pineau did not openly claim that the Suez Canal Company was French, but that was the implied interpretation of the adjective. But Nasser pointed out that whereas the company was making an annual profit of about £39 million, the only direct benefit Egypt derived from its operations amounted to £800,000. Egypt was pressing hard on the company to invest more in the country from which it derived its profits. It was being squeezed by new legislation affecting local taxes and the conditions under which local labour was employed, but its real anxieties were about what was going to happen to it when the British base was wound up. Pineau's final statement was that good relations between France and Egypt would depend on an end to the arms being sent to the insurgents in Algeria and Egyptian propaganda on their behalf, and on how the Suez Canal Company was treated. But he left optimistic for the future.

Nasser had now been visited by most of those who were to be leading actors in the drama of the coming months — Eden, Selwyn Lloyd, Dulles, Pineau. Those he had not met (and was never to meet) were Eisenhower, Mollet, and, of course, Ben-Gurion.

---

[1] The full text of the messages is given in Appendix 2. The same technique — drafting documents which were then given to an Egyptian President to sign as if they were his own — was employed in the negotiations which led up to the Camp David agreements.

[2] See Appendix 2.

[3] Neither he nor anyone else could have imagined that only twenty-two years later his successor would make precisely that journey.

[4] It is less surprising than it may seem that neither Lloyd nor Nasser considered, even for a moment, the possibility that the King might have acted on his own initiative. In retrospect, it is true, he can be seen to have had motives enough. He had been left badly shaken by the aftermath of the Templer mission, and a dramatic gesture like the dismissal of Glubb was clearly a means of restoring his credentials with his own subjects and establishing his reputation as an Arab nationalist, perhaps even a rival to Nasser himself. But it was — and still is — hard to imagine how Hussein brought himself to burn his boats with the British so conclusively without some form of outside encouragement. Certainly, the only person on the Middle Eastern political scene who seemed unsurprised by the development was Kermit Roosevelt — by now installed in Beirut and actively implementing the CIA's new policy which was aimed at isolating Egypt from her Arab neighbours.

DOUBT IS REPLACING CONFIDENCE

DURING THE SPRING of 1956 tension on Egypt's frontiers was increasing. On 14 March Israel sent a protest to the Security Council giving a list of 180 alleged acts of aggression against Israel in the Gaza Strip area between 5 December and 9 March, but a meeting of the Council was not asked for because, as General Burns, the Chief of Staff of the United Nations Truce Supervision Organization, put it, 'of course the Egyptians could have produced a similar list of complaints of Israeli aggression.' On 4 April, in retaliation for mortar shells directed against an Israeli settlement which caused a few casualties, the Israelis bombarded the centre of the town of Gaza, killing 56 and wounding 103 civilian men, women, and children who had been going about their normal business. The UN report on the incident called it a shocking outrage of extreme gravity for which Israel must bear full responsibility.

Dag Hammarskjöld, the United Nations Secretary-General, was sent on a mission to the Middle East and saw Nasser in April. After nearly a month of continuous diplomatic activity he succeeded in arranging an effective ceasefire between Egypt and Israel.[1]

Later in the month came a meeting which afforded a certain amount of unexpected light relief. Imam Yehya of Yemen had been anxious to see an agreement for the defence of his country concluded with Egypt and Saudi Arabia. This was arranged and the ceremony of signing was fixed for 20 April. Nasser flew to Jeddah on 20 April, and the Imam greeted him with embarrassing enthusiasm. He was a short man and Nasser a tall one, and when the Imam flung his arms round Nasser's neck to embrace him he was left with his feet dangling in the air. When he had been returned to terra firma he started to feel Nasser's biceps. 'How strong you are,' he exclaimed, 'How young!'

When the company was all seated the Imam's first question to Nasser was: 'My brother, has Omar Sharif really married Fatin Hamama?' Nasser was somewhat taken aback, as he had not been following the love lives of Egyptian actors and actresses, so he passed the question over with a laugh to Sheikh Ahmed Bagouri, the Minister of Waqfs, who was unfortunately equally ill-informed. But it appeared that the Imam spent much of his time in his palace in Taiz reading the gossip columns in Egyptian magazines, particularly those items which concerned stage and film stars.

Later, when the text of the agreement was brought for signature, and the Imam was asked to sign first, he looked around him, pen poised over the document, but then declared that he would not sign until the other two had. 'But you are our guest; it is for you to sign first,' said King Saud. The Imam still refused. So first Nasser and then Saud signed, and finally it was the Imam's turn. He scrutinized the other two signatures, and seemed to approve them, then took his pen and wrote one letter of his name, after which he looked slyly around him, whether for reassurance or in complicity it was hard to decide, added another letter, gave the bystanders another look, and so eventually came to the end of his name and the treaty was signed. It had been known that the Imam was an eccentric figure, but until the Jeddah meeting the degree of eccentricity had not been realized.

At about the same time, on 18 April, the new Soviet leaders, Bulganin and Khrushchev went to London. Eden was anxious to get Russia to become a signatory to the Tripartite Declaration of 1950 by which Britain, France, and the United States were supposed to ration the supply of arms to Middle Eastern countries. The Americans were not keen on the idea, because they felt it would legalize the Russian presence in the Middle East, but the British realized, as not all Americans did, that, as the massive flow of arms from France to Israel was continuing, Egypt's first arms deal with Russia was not going to be the last. Nasser thought it was not impossible that Khrushchev would agree to the British proposal, which might affect the supply of arms to Egypt, and this was one of the main considerations in his decision to recognize the Peking government on 16 May. Communist China was not then a member of the United Nations, and Khrushchev before leaving had spoken at a press conference of a possible UN agreement to halt arms shipments to the Middle East. So Peking could be an alternative source of arms.

The Russians kept Cairo informed of those parts of the London exchanges which concerned Egypt. When the question of the arms deal came up, Khrushchev insisted that the countries of the Middle East were perfectly at liberty, as sovereign states, to deal with anybody they liked; nobody could claim a monopoly. He was annoyed when Eden said that Middle East oil was so important to Britain that it would, if necessary, go to war to protect it. 'Look at the map,' said Khrushchev. 'The Middle East is much nearer to the Soviet Union than it is to you, and if there was a war over it the sparks would reach us before they reached you.'

London was also the setting for another April meeting which provided a further ingredient in the Suez macedoine. After Cairo, Selwyn Lloyd had gone on to Bahrain, where he had been met by a hostile crowd (which of course he attributed to the malign inspiration of Nasser) and then to India and Pakistan, coming back to London via Iraq, Iran, Turkey, and Israel. He had been criticized by Britain's allies in the Baghdad Pact, whom he visited on the grounds that more help was being promised to its enemy, Egypt, than to its loyal friends. Lloyd hinted that perhaps this would turn out not to be the case. Two special committees of the pact were set up, one dealing with security and the other with propaganda, on both of which America, though not a signatory of the pact, was represented. The pact's propaganda target was to be Nasser, and member countries were to make their own attacks on the target but to coordinate their efforts.

Earlier, towards the end of February, there had been a meeting in London attended by representatives of the American and British intelligence services, James Eichelberger for the CIA and John Young for the SIS (MI6). Young said that in Iran the Americans had played a major part in the overthrow of Mossadeq, but Egypt was Britain's parish; dealing with Nasser would be its prerogative. Young spoke with a frankness which horrified his American colleague. He talked openly about the possibility of assassinating Nasser, instead of using a polite euphemism like *liquidating*. He said his people had been in contact with suitable elements in Egypt and in the rest of the Arab world, and, though he did not mention this, with the French, who were thinking along the same lines. Eichelberger was so alarmed by what was said at this meeting that he leaked much of it back to Cairo. This was perhaps the last useful contact Egypt was to have with the American undercover organizations. The message Eichelberger sent was that the British were now desperate and were determined to 'do a Mossadeq' with Nasser, but had been warned by the Americans that the two situations were quite different; in Iran there had been the Shah as an alternative focus of loyalty, but there was no comparable figure in Egypt. Nasser minuted the account of what Eichelberger reported: 'Is this intended to frighten us or to worsen our relations with the British?'

Assassinations apart, black as well as white propaganda against Egypt was now going at full blast. The main theme was that Egypt had become a communist puppet and so a threat to the West's oil supplies; it wanted to keep Middle East oil for itself and its communist friends. This line was backed up by a great deal of documentary evidence, made up either of selective quotations taken out of their context or of actual forgeries. One day Nasser was brought a tape which contained extracts from alleged broadcasts put out over the Voice of the Arabs, in which the speakers said that Arab oil was the property of Arabs everywhere, and the proceeds from its exploitation should be put into a central pool and shared out among all Arabs. Oil production in Arab countries should be put under centralized control. Another tape was supposed to contain a monitored conversation between Nasser and the Egyptian military attaché in Amman in which plans for overthrowing King Hussein were discussed. Trevelyan lodged an official protest.

A careful enquiry was made, and every broadcast that had gone out over the Voice of the Arabs was checked, and nothing like the alleged talks was discovered. The entire output was given to the Americans, who, since they had been involved in the operation from the outset, were obliged to admit the deception. Tapes of the fake broadcasts had been sent to the governor of every American state, to many delegations at the UN and to leading officials in some of the major oil companies. One of these was Elton Jones, chairman of Two Cities Oil Company, a close friend of Eisenhower and one of his regular golfing partners. His company was drilling for oil in Egypt, and he was naturally much upset by what he heard. Later a press conference was arranged in Cairo at which these lies were nailed, with a fair amount of success.

On 30 March Ahmed Hussein sent Cairo a telegram describing a meeting he had had with Herbert Hoover, Assistant Secretary of State. Hoover reported the British as being in an extremely nervous state, angry with America for not joining the Baghdad Pact, and regarding Egypt by now as being their open enemy. The propaganda war, they argued, could easily become a shooting war, because at a certain level propaganda can be equal to a declaration of war. The British were particularly sensitive about Egyptian broadcasts beamed at Kuwait and other areas in the Gulf, because if the Gulf was lost it would mean the end of Britain's dominant position in the Middle East. They also complained that Egyptian propaganda was pouring into countries which had nothing to do with the Arab world, like Kenya and Zanzibar. Hoover said that, to be frank, in his opinion the British complaint was justified. He begged us, said Hussein, not to provoke the British into a position where they could encourage Israel to attack Egypt. He said he could not rule out the possibility that the British and Israelis might connive at organizing assassination attempts against Nasser and other prominent Egyptians.

Ahmed Hussein said he had drawn Hoover's attention to the flood of articles in American newspapers and magazines highly critical of Egypt, which he thought must be prompted by Britain. The British had a lot of influence in certain American quarters, as had the Israelis, and he hoped that the American public would not believe all it read. Hoover said Egyptians would have to accept the fact that suspicion of their country was increasing daily, and that many of America's friends, such as the Philippines, Pakistan, Iraq, Turkey, and even Greece, were critical of the way America was going on giving Egypt aid even after the Russian arms deal.

On 19 April Ahmed Hussein reported a talk he had had with Charles Bohlen, the American ambassador in Moscow, who was in Washington to report after the Bulganin-Khrushchev visit to London. Bohlen said he thought the Eden government was in a very weak position and was desperately anxious to reach some accommodation with the Russians, and that the French would be delighted if Israel attacked Egypt and defeated it. In view of the state of feeling in Britain he would not be surprised if the government there came to share the French point of view. He thought both the British and the Israelis were trying hard to persuade the United States to line up with them against Egypt on the grounds that it had opened the door to communism in the Middle East, but so far their efforts had not been successful. The faction inside the State Department which argued that Israel was America's only real friend in the Middle East was gaining ground, and in the CIA James Angleton, who wanted to make use of Israel, was exerting more influence than Kermit Roosevelt, who still felt use could be made of some Arab countries.

Bohlen said he had warned those he had spoken to in Washington that they should expect Russia to adopt a much more aggressive policy towards the Middle East. For the first time the Soviets now had a positive Middle Eastern policy, and this was aimed at undermining Western influence in the area. Considering that they had really only become actively involved in the Middle East a few months earlier the Russians had come a long way, and he did not see how they could easily be checked. Hussein mentioned the fact that Molotov and Mikoyan had attended the independence day reception at the Israeli embassy in Moscow, and asked what significance he attached to that. Bohlen said Russian policy contained a lot of contradictions, but he thought that particular incident was more concerned with policy towards the Jewish communities in the Eastern bloc than with Israel.

About the same time Hussein reported growing concern in many of the principal oil companies, which were beginning to be influenced by the stream of propaganda alleging that Egypt was in the process of being sold out to the communists, Hoover and Allen of the State Department were claiming that the arms deal was really a much bigger transaction than had been admitted at the time and far beyond the true defensive needs of Egypt. They also complained about allegedly increased Russian activity in Libya. When Hussein said that Egypt could hardly be held responsible for what went on in Libya, the answer was that Washington had information that in many Middle Eastern capitals close relations had been established between the Egyptian and Russian embassies, presumably on instructions from Cairo. It was not surprising if doubts were growing about the real intentions of Egyptian policies.

Hussein went on to report a talk with James P. Richards, Chairman of the House Foreign Affairs Committee, who said he understood that Nasser was no longer interested in getting foreign backing for the High Dam because he was going to get control over all the Arabs' oil and could finance the dam that way. He had obviously been influenced by some of the faked broadcasts which had been distributed to congressmen, and Hussein warned him about the efforts that were being made by certain interested parties, including the Zionist lobby, to poison relations between Egypt and America. Richards said that though undoubtedly the Jews had a lot of power in the press, 'in the South, where I come from, they don't have that much importance.'

On 8 May Hussein reported that he had been given a dossier by George Allen of the State Department about the attacks which were being organized by the British on Nasser personally. He reported that Henry Luce, the owner of *Time* and *Life* magazines, had told Dulles that when he (Luce) was in London Churchill had said that if Nasser was going to lose Britain its Middle East oil, then Nasser would have to go. Hussein said that the British embassy was doing all it could to convince the Americans of the gravity of the threat to Western interests in the Middle East, and individual members of the embassy staff were making public attacks on Nasser. One of them, a Mr Hall, had given a talk to students at St James's College in which he had referred to Nasser as 'our public enemy number one'. Hussein had been told this when he too was asked to give a talk in the college. The Dean of the Faculty had then told him not to worry about an attack like that on his President: 'The British always use that sort of language when talking about the heroes of independence. Don't forget that at one time George Washington was their public enemy number one.'

Hussein said that Allen thought Britain was prepared to fight for its interests in the Middle East whatever the cost, and he warned that America might be obliged to give the British political backing to avoid handing over the area to the Russians. Hussein commented that suspicions of Nasser were growing in the State Department. Egypt used to have good friends there, but now 'doubt is rapidly replacing confidence'. Allen hinted that America's relations with King Saud were improving, and that Saud's continued support for Nasser could not be counted on, particularly in view of his dislike for the arms deal. Shortly afterwards Hussein was recalled to Cairo for consultations.

* * *

Nothing that occurred during May and June did anything to lessen the steadily rising tension in the Middle East or to reduce the suspicions that each side now harboured about the other's intentions.

On 6 May there was a meeting in Paris between representatives of the United States, Britain and France, the three signatories of the 1950 Tripartite Declaration which was supposed to regulate the supply of arms to Middle East countries and to prevent the violation of frontiers or armistice lines in the area. It was agreed that as far as its first aim was concerned the declaration was clearly not working, and shortly afterwards the Egyptian government received information from its embassy in Paris that the three had undertaken to provide Israel with more arms.

On 16 May Egypt recognized the government in Peking. As already explained, Nasser took this step largely as precaution against the possibility that the Russians might agree to some form of UN control over the supply of arms to the Middle East — but this was scarcely something that could be explained to the Americans. Inevitably, they saw it as a further provocation and the formal language in which Dulles expressed his government's regrets did nothing to conceal his anger.

On 29 May Hammarskjöld presented his Middle East report to the Security Council. The British delegate complained about Egyptian propaganda, and accused Egypt, together with Saudi Arabia and Yemen, of inciting the tribes against the Aden Protectorates.

On 31 May a boycott on the loading and unloading of French shipping in the Suez Canal was called in sympathy with the Algerians.

On 1 June Dmitri Shepilov, former editor of *Pravda*, who had been sent on a mission to Egypt the year before and got to know Nasser well, replaced Molotov as Russian Foreign Minister. His first journey abroad after his appointment was to Egypt, arriving on 16 June. His first meeting with Nasser lasted five hours, but there was no discussion of the High Dam. Although Nasser was by now convinced that Western backing for the dam would not be forthcoming he did not want to give the Americans an excuse to blame him for the breakdown in negotiations. He was happy for the Russians to be Egypt's arms supplier, and now also for them to help in Egypt's programme of industrialization. When he left the

President's office after this meeting Shepilov was asked by Western journalists whether they had talked about the dam, to which he replied: 'There are other projects which are as important for Egypt as the High Dam, and anyway we are cooperating with Egypt in its general development plans.' Dulles interpreted this as meaning that the Russians were not in a position to finance the dam as well as all the other undertakings to which they were committed in Egypt.

On 14 June a new government was formed in Syria, with Sabri el-Asali as Prime Minister, pledged to 'consolidate our ties with Egypt through immediate talks which we hope will lead to a common policy.' Popular support in Syria for a union between the two countries was growing in strength. It was a time when the crowds in the streets of Damascus were chanting *'bidna wahda baker baker, ma el asmar Abdel Nasser!'* (We want unity tomorrow, tomorrow, with the magnificent Abdel Nasser.) On 5 July, after Asali had seen Nasser in Cairo, the Syrian government adopted the principle of unity and appointed a ministerial committee of three, headed by the Prime Minister, to conduct the necessary negotiations. The Israelis responded by ordering partial mobilization.

At their meeting in February the representatives of the two main Western intelligence agencies had agreed that, in addition to 'a more responsible leadership' in Egypt, a change of regime in Syria was also desirable. Both had in mind something a good deal more dramatic than a change of premier — and, in any case, Asali clearly did not figure on either's shortlist of preferred candidates for that post. The British continued to cherish hopes that, with the aid of the Iraqis, they might be able to contrive the overthrow of President Quwatli and the restoration of the former dictator, Colonel Shishekli. But the Americans (working out of the CIA office in Beirut since Colonel Sarraj and the *Deuxième Bureau* made clandestine activity difficult in Damascus) had other ideas. Indeed, they already had a coup d'état simmering, as it were, on the back burner.

Among the many Syrians with whom the CIA had been in contact over the years was a landowner called Michel Ilyan. Back in the summer of 1954 he had met with a CIA representative at the Bristol Hotel in Beirut. Ilyan, who claimed to speak on behalf of a group of politicians and officers who were prepared to engineer a coup that would overturn the government, asked for £S500,000. Two weeks later another CIA man, William Evelan, travelling on a diplomatic passport, drove from Beirut to Damascus carrying the money in a briefcase. It seems, however, that Evelan, who was supposed to be masterminding the coup, did not have the guts to actually hand over the money in person: instead, he parked outside the New Umayyad Hotel and sent his driver inside to deliver it to Ilyan. Subsequently there had been several more meetings and the date of 29 October 1956, when President Quwatli was expected to be away from Damascus at the start of a state visit to Russia, had eventually been set.

Meanwhile, on 13 June, a few days ahead of the deadline, the last British troops left Egypt. Now that at last Egypt could claim to be independent in fact as well as in name, Nasser felt justified in assuming the office of President, which he did on 25 June after a virtually unanimous plebiscite.

On 17 July Nasser went to Bourg el-Arab for a few days rest. He was soon to embark on a trip abroad and had just had a strenuous few weeks, many election campaign speeches to make and many visitors from abroad demanding to see him. Ahmed Hussein, on leave from Washington, was hoping for a talk with Nasser before he returned to duty. I saw him in Alexandria and afterwards mentioned him to Nasser who told me to bring him along for lunch at Bourg el-Arab, which I did the next day, 8 July. Hussein described the climate of opinion in Washington, as he saw it, saying that he considered the position extremely dangerous and that something ought to be done at least to rescue the High Dam.

Nasser said, 'Hey! Wake up, doctor! There is no High Dam.' Hussein said, 'What do you mean? There is.' Nasser said, 'No. I've even read it in the paper, in *Al Ahram*, that the item in the American budget providing for the High Dam has been dropped at the end of this fiscal year, and is not going to be renewed.' Hussein insisted that the situation could still be saved if the few outstanding points, especially those relating to a limitation of the amount of Egypt's foreign debt and the right of the World Bank to keep a check on it, were settled. Nasser said, 'I can prove you are wrong. Go and see Dulles and tell him that I have accepted all the conditions he made.' Hussein said, 'If I told him this he wouldn't believe me.' He asked for it to be put in writing, so Nasser took a piece of paper and wrote on it that Egypt accepted all the outstanding conditions relating to finance for the High Dam and was ready to sign accordingly.

Hussein was delighted. 'This is fantastic! It's wonderful,' he said.

'This is going to solve everything.' But as he was leaving the rest-house at Bourg el-Arab after lunch Nasser said to him, 'Ahmed, do you know Egyptian history?' Hussein said he did. 'But do you know about the Suez Canal?' asked Nasser. 'Before you go back to Washington go to a bookshop in Cairo and buy a book about the canal.'

---

[1] Hammarskjöld was an old friend of Dr Fawzi and soon became on almost equally cordial terms with Nasser, who introduced him to Egyptian cooking. I recall one evening at the President's house when the principal dish was *melokhia*, the vegetable soup which is very popular in the Egyptian countryside.

✠ IO ✠

MASTER-STROKE OR
BLUNDER?

ON 12 JULY Nasser set out for Yugoslavia, where he was to make a
state visit, followed by a meeting on the island of Brioni with Tito
and Nehru.[1] Tito had recently been to the Soviet Union and met
the new Russian leaders and was anxious to discuss the changes that
were taking place there following the momentous Twentieth
Congress of the Communist Party in February, at which Khrushchev had denounced the tyrannical methods of Stalin.

Tito had sent Nasser a letter on 23 May in which he said (the
letter was in English):

> The complex situation has shifted from Europe to the Afro-Asian
> system, and this requires a serious analysis and caution on the part of
> all those who are interested in peace, and particularly on the part of
> leading personalities in that region of the world. The easing of
> tension in Europe has been, to a large extent, due to the new, more
> realistic, policies of the present Soviet leaders. . . . There are en-
> couraging signs that the Western countries are also more and more
> inclined to adopt such a method for the solving of international
> problems. (But easing the tension in Europe will not necessarily
> mean doing the same in the Middle East — it may aggravate it.)

Tito had also been in Paris where he discussed the Algerian
problem with the Prime Minister, Guy Mollet, and others. This
was obviously another subject which was going to come up in his
talks with Nasser and, as will be seen, their views were quite far
apart. The letter went on:

> I gave them [the French leaders] my impression of your country. I
> informed them about the constructive aims pursued by you and your
> colleagues. The French government does not agree to the Baghdad
> Pact . . . but they have their own problem which is plaguing them,
> viz. Algeria. . . . It would not be reasonable to expect the present

government and M. Guy Mollet to renounce the interests of France in Algeria and to agree to all the concessions demanded by the Algerian insurgents. M. Pineau [French Foreign Minister] and certain other personalities are ready to recognize the national character of Algeria, but they consider that this question can only be solved in a liberal manner within the framework of France, whereby Algeria would attain a certain individuality and the possibility of pursuing their national development. We are under the impression that they [the French government] consider that some suggestions to the insurgents made by you to this effect [ending the fighting] ought to be useful — if you considered it opportune. We understand, of course, the delicate character of this question, so I am mentioning it here more for the sake of information. In my view a realistic appraisal of the Algerian problem in the present period shows that the insurgents have no chance to attain today, through armed struggle, what they are demanding. . . The best course would be to proceed with the gradual solving of what can be solved, because, otherwise, I believe the French leaders are right in saying that someone else would probably take their place there, if they left, and this would not be useful for the Algerian population itself.

The Algerians thought the meeting at Brioni would provide a good opportunity for them to present their case to the three leaders of the nonaligned movement, and sent a delegation to lobby them. But this annoyed Tito, who had the Algerians stopped by the police at Pola, on the mainland, and prevented from crossing to the island. Nasser heard of their arrival and sent one of his aides to see them, but this was all that could be done.

Before returning to his post in Washington Ahmed Hussein had a meeting with Byroade, who by now knew that he was soon to be replaced, and almost certainly told him of the message from Nasser, withdrawing all reservations about the High Dam, which he was taking back with him. This information would have been sent on to Dulles, and so given him plenty of time to prepare his next moves. Hussein passed through London on 12 July and told reporters at the airport that he was going to Washington with fresh instructions which he hoped would lead to an agreement. Nasser and his party followed world events during his week-long tour of Yugoslavia through specially prepared bulletins based on agency reports. When Nasser read Hussein's London airport statement he said, 'That was a mistake; he should have waited till he got to Washington.'

Not that it would have made any difference. Nasser was now more than ever convinced that money for the High Dam would not be forthcoming. He paid particular attention to reports of a debate in Congress during which the influential Republican, Senator Knowland, had urged Dulles to give an assurance to the Foreign Affairs Committee that no funds would be allocated to the High Dam. Dulles had said that he could give no such pledge, but did promise that no allocation would be made without further reference to the committee. Nasser also received information from friendly ministers in Baghdad that when Selwyn Lloyd had attended a Baghdad Pact meeting there he had given broad hints that Nasser was not going to get his dam.

Nasser reached Brioni on the morning of Tuesday 17 July. Nehru arrived the same afternoon and discussions between the three leaders began on Wednesday morning. Brioni is a very pleasant island off the Yugoslav coast at the head of the Adriatic, which used to be a summer resort for rich citizens of the Austro-Hungarian Empire. Tito expanded on the impressions he had gained during his visit to France which he had touched on in his letter to Nasser, speculating that France might be the first Western country to join the nonaligned movement. He thought France was looking for a new role to play and might choose to become a broker between Russia and the West, and so develop a constructive *Ostpolitik* before the Germans did. The atmosphere was very easy and the discussions cordial. Tito had planted a vineyard at the mouth of a cave on the island which he looked after himself, bottling and labelling his own wine. At dinner on Wednesday evening this wine (grape juice was provided for Nasser) was served with a dish of quails. It was a relaxed and friendly meal, a suitable climax to a constructive meeting. The next day all were due to disperse.

As soon as Ahmed Hussein got back to Washington he asked for a meeting with Dulles, and this was arranged for 6 p.m. on Thursday 19 July, a time when the State Department would be almost deserted. Hussein told Dulles of his new instructions and said he thought that now there was a real chance to reach an agreement.

1. Eden and Nasser met just once, when Eden, then still Foreign Secretary, stopped off in Cairo en route to a meeting in Bangkok. A dinner party was given in the British embassy on the evening of 20 February 1955 by the British ambassador, Sir Ralph Stevenson, the figure on the left of the picture.

2A

2B

3A   3B

2A and B. On 15 August 1956 Eden gave a luncheon at 10 Downing Street for the leading figures at the London conference then in progress. Seen here, shaking hands with the Prime Minister on their departure, are John Foster Dulles, the US Secretary of State (above), and Christian Pineau, the French Foreign Minister (below).

3A. Krishna Menon, the Indian minister without portfolio who led his country's delegation at the London conference. Later, at the UN debate in October, his behaviour was to exasperate all parties.

3B. The Australian Prime Minister, Robert Menzies, entering Lancaster House, the scene of the London conference, shortly after receiving the news that Nasser was willing to receive the five-men delegation under his leadership.

4A

4A and B. Cartoonists reflected the Egyptian view of the developing crisis. Above, a typical reaction to Eden's reported statement that he did not trust Nasser: 'See how we take care of the people we trust' says Eden. The Suez Canal Users' Association (whose members are shown in the pram in the cartoon opposite) was devised by Dulles in an effort to keep peaceful negotiations going in the wake of the Menzies mission; the Secretary of State was, as a result, subject to severe attacks in the British press. Here an irate wife chastises her American husband for flirting with her Egyptian rival.

4B

5A. India, as both a member of the Commonwealth and a leader of world opinion, was a key factor in Egyptian policy. Here Nehru is seen as the sole dove at a meeting of otherwise bellicose Commonwealth leaders.

5B. This Egyptian cartoon provided a remarkably accurate forecast of the eventual outcome of the crisis. 'If you don't give it back,' Eden threatens, 'I'll shoot!'

5B

6A

6A and B. A striking convergence of views from the two sides of the Anglo–Egyptian divide. Both the British cartoonist Vicky and his Egyptian counterpart see Eden ensnared by the wiles of the French. In Vicky's case France plays the role of Eve. The caption to the Egyptian cartoon reads: 'France begins her piracy – the pirate and his wife.'

6B

7A. In Britain, the Anglo–French ultimatum and the subsequent bombing of Egypt divided public opinion into two fiercely opposing camps. As the cloth caps and bowler hats in the Giles cartoon suggest, the division ran largely along party lines: 'As Eden says, "This is not a state of war, simply armed conflict." '

7B. The Trafalgar Square demonstration of Sunday 4 November, called to protest against the Anglo–French action, was one of several indications of British public opinion which did much to confirm Nasser in his view that Eden would not be able to resist the pressures that were building up.

8. Nasser leaving the Al-Azhar mosque on 2 November, after delivering his speech to the Egyptian people. The people who crowded the streets of Cairo that day were unequivocal in their support for his decision to fight.

9A. Pictures of the havoc wrought by British air raids did much to arouse world opinion against the Anglo-French action. This photograph was taken after the bombing of the village of Abu Za'bal on 3 November.

9B. After the British attack on Port Said, the Egyptians sank block ships in the canal which was closed to traffic for six months.

A

B

10A and B. Almost as soon as the ceasefire had come into effect it became 11 clear that, apart from Nasser himself, the crisis had one clear victor – America. Although the Russian ultimatums to the three aggressors had contributed to bringing the conflict to an end, Russia herself was in an extremely equivocal position in the aftermath of her brutal suppression of the Hungarian revolution (above). And, in the immediate aftermath, Britain and France – the oil pipelines from Iraq to the Mediterranean having been blown up – were forced into the position of supplicants (below).

11. Israel appears unabashed before the court of world opinion – 'I'm a war criminal too!' says Ben-Gurion.

12A. Dr Fawzi, the Egyptian Foreign Minister, in conversation with the UN Secretary General, Dag Hammarskjöld, as both men prepare to leave Cairo for New York on 18 November.

12B. A British view – with Eden, Macmillan and Butler – of the motives that had determined American policy during the crisis. But American actions over the coming months would show that Eisenhower was no less intent than the British on imposing his own priorities on the Middle East.

Dulles replied that his government had been making a fresh evaluation and had come to the conclusion that the High Dam was too big an undertaking for Egypt, and they did not feel justified in committing the American taxpayer to it for perhaps ten years, or in asking Congress for the necessary funding, which, in the prevailing atmosphere, would in any case almost certainly be refused. The American government was therefore withdrawing its offer.

Dulles was polite but explicit. He said he would give Hussein an aide-mémoire on the subject. Hussein said he thought the United States was missing a great opportunity which others would be ready to avail themselves of. Dulles retorted that they would have no objections if this happened. (But it is not true, as has sometimes been alleged, that Hussein said he had a Russian offer to finance the dam in his pocket.) Two or three times Hussein asked if this decision was final, and Dulles assured him that it was. 'I am speaking for the President,' he said, 'and I am sure that I am also expressing the feelings of Congress and the country.'

Hussein was shattered by what he heard. He felt that everything he had been working for was now destroyed. When he left the State Department he found journalists waiting to interview him, all of them having been given copies of Dulles's aide-mémoire. He was asked what he thought of its wording, and it was then that for the first time he appreciated its offensive tone, and saw that insult was being deliberately added to injury. He had been too taken aback during his interview to make any notes, and all he felt able to do immediately was to send Cairo the text of the aide-mémoire *en claire*. He explained later that there was really no need for him to add any comment in view of the flood of news coming out of America.

There has been some argument about how and when Nasser received the news of the American action. It has to be remembered that the American press had been full of leaks for some time, and a cartoon in one newspaper that day had shown Nasser and Dulles playing chess, with the latter saying 'Check!' So Nasser had never expected anything to come out of Hussein's interview except a flat No. It was not the message, but the way in which it was phrased, which came as a surprise.

Nasser and his party had been due to leave for the airport at 5 p.m., but their departure was delayed because of discussions on the text of the final communiqué, and the plane, a Viscount, did not

in fact take off until 9.30. Nehru and his daughter Indira were on
the plane too, because they had arranged to spend two days in
Cairo, staying at the Indian embassy. He sat next to Nasser on two
of the front seats of the plane, Indira and Dr Fawzi on the other two
front seats. There was six hours' difference in time between Pola
and Washington, and so it was while we were still in flight that the
first flashes about the meeting began to come in. The pilot of the
plane and one of Nasser's secretaries were listening to the news on
the BBC and other stations, and sending written messages back to
Nasser. He showed all these to Nehru, who, as he read about the
rejection, exclaimed: 'There is no end to their arrogance! These
people are arrogant! Arrogant!' Then he turned to Nasser and said,
'My dear friend, I know that you have much on your mind. But
you will have to think about it carefully.'

When the plane landed in Cairo Nasser saw for the first time the
full text of the American rejection, which was handed to him by
Zakaria Mohieddin. As both Nehru and Nasser were arriving there
was an official reception for them, involving diplomats as well as
ministers. These had all come to the airport at the time when the
plane was originally supposed to arrive, but had stayed on when
they heard of the delay. There had been some angry scenes when
the terms of the American rejection were learned, and Byroade
found himself in an embarrassing situation. He was visibly shaken
when it was his turn to shake Nasser's hand. 'You have heard the
news?' Nasser asked. 'I have,' said Byroade. 'Perhaps I will have a
chance to talk to Your Excellency later.' 'Oh yes,' said Nasser, 'We
are going to have a lot to talk about.'

Before he left the airport Byroade asked me to see him at
11 o'clock the next morning, which I did. He was clearly anxious to
have a preliminary talk with someone before he met Nasser. I
found him extremely distressed, not just by what had happened the
day before, but by the reactions to it in America which were now
being reported. A State Department briefing had accused Egypt of
trying to blackmail America by threatening to 'go to the Russians',
and the official line was that Egypt could do what it liked; it could
go to hell. The version of Ahmed Hussein's interview which was
leaked to the press said that Dulles had not asked him to sit down,
while he delivered a lecture, warning him that anyone who was
foolish enough to get involved in building the dam would be cursed
for generations to come by the Egyptian people, who would have

to tighten their belts to pay for it. The accepted view was that Dulles had achieved a diplomatic master-stroke.

Whether Dulles's action was a master-stroke or a major blunder, it was quite consistent with the main lines of American policy. No doubt Dulles would have preferred the High Dam affair to fade gently out of the picture, but knowledge of the instructions Ahmed Hussein was bringing back to Washington with him, together with a misreading of Shepilov's comments when questioned in Cairo, had prompted him to make this more positive gesture. He thought that the Russians could not help Egypt both with the dam and with arms, and if they did undertake the dam it would make all the Eastern bloc states very angry. So, whatever happened, both Russia and Egypt were going to be made to look foolish. From his point of view this rebuff could not have been better timed. Dulles always believed any form of neutralism to be immoral, and the Brioni meeting, attended by the three high priests of nonalignment, was just the sort of occasion he most disapproved of. What a devastating curtain he had been able to drop on their deliberations!

He had managed to involve the British in this, too — as subordinate partners, of course, They still had some limited use in the area, and it was, for example, a good idea that Britain should be an open member of the Baghdad Pact and that America should keep in the background, but if the coup de grâce was to be given it would have to be America and nobody else that administered it. This was the pattern over the High Dam; and it was to be equally the pattern over Suez.

After greeting the ministers, diplomats, and others who had been waiting for him at the airport, Nasser went to his home in Heliopolis. It was there, by himself — his wife and children being away in Alexandria — and in a house where the builders had temporarily taken over, that he made, within a few hours, what was to be probably the most fateful decision of his career. Everyone was expecting him to come up with some dramatic response to Dulles's calculated rebuff, but virtually nobody was asking themselves the unanswerable question Nasser now posed: 'Why not a hundred per cent? Why not complete nationalization of the Suez Canal Company?'

¹ Some months earlier (December 1955) the Egyptian ambassador in Washington had received a message from what he called 'a very high-level source' (probably a senior official in the State Department) informing him that Tito was planning to visit Cairo to act as mediator in the Arab–Israeli dispute. The informant said he felt obliged to pass on what he knew about relations between Tito and the Jews. Tito, he said, was a puppet of world Zionism, which had been responsible for helping him to power in Yugoslavia. Tito had presented the marble for a statue to be erected in New York symbolizing 'The Rebirth of Israel'. All this made him unfit to act as a mediator. This surprising message was probably intended to drive a wedge between Tito and Nasser.

✠ I I ✠

CODE WORD
DE LESSEPS

NASSER WAS AT WORK in his office at 6 o'clock in the morning. 'I became a staff officer again,' he said afterwards. 'I sat down to write an appreciation of the situation from the point of view of our opponents — Eden, Pineau [the French Foreign Minister) and Ben-Gurion.' The appreciation for Eden covered five pages; Pineau's one, and Ben-Gurion was dismissed (mistakenly as it was to prove) in a couple of lines.

Nasser started from the premise that Eden was weak — weak in character, weak in his position in his party and government, and weak in his standing in the country. Nasser calculated that, like many essentially weak men, Eden was attracted by the idea of doing something violent, all the more so because he probably could count on the support of public opinion at home as well as on that of the American government, which would bitterly resent a slap in the face administered to its second most prominent member, Secretary of State John Foster Dulles. But if he was to take advantage of these favourable circumstances Eden would have to act very quickly. The period of maximum danger for Egypt, Nasser believed, would be in the first few days after nationalization of the Suez Canal Company had been proclaimed. He thought that up to, say, 10 August there would be a 90 per cent risk of an armed attack on Egypt; for the rest of August the risk would decline to about 80 per cent; in September it would be down to 60 per cent; in the first half of October to 40 per cent; in the second half to 20 per cent, and thereafter, thanks to the mobilization of world opinion which Nasser confidently looked forward to, the risk would virtually evaporate.

Nasser was planning to make the announcement on 23 July. That day, the anniversary of the 1952 revolution, had in recent years been the occasion for a major policy speech, and no occasion would be more fitting for making known to the world by far the most

revolutionary action the new regime had yet contemplated. But if
he was to be prepared for the inevitable repercussions, Nasser, the
staff officer, must first have information about the state of the
enemy forces.

The nearest British bases, for land, sea and air forces, were in
Malta or Cyprus, where Britain's Middle East headquarters had
been moved after the agreement to withdraw them from the canal
zone. During the years of confrontation in the zone close links had
been formed by Egypt with elements in both Britain's island
colonies, and special liaison offices had been opened in the Egyptian
consulates there, headed in each case by a senior officer in military
intelligence seconded to the Foreign Office, whose main task was to
monitor the strength and movements of the British forces. Relations with Archbishop Makarios and Colonel Grivas, then leading
the revolt against the British colonial regime, had become particularly cordial, and the Greek Cypriots had been helped in their
struggle for independence with training facilities in Egypt and with
large quantities of arms. The fact that Cyprus was the hub of
Western intelligence activity in the Middle East, and therefore a
constant source of threats to the Syrian regime, as well as being an
important centre for Israeli intelligence, had also led the *Deuxième
Bureau* to increase its presence at the Syrian consulates in Nicosia
and Limassol.

But in a matter of such supreme importance Nasser was not
content to rely on routine telegraphic exchanges with our consulates. He decided to send special emissaries to Cyprus and Malta,
and it would be on the basis of their assessment that he would make
a final decision.

Time was short. Dulles's rebuff had been delivered to the
Egyptian ambassador on 19 July; Nasser was due to speak only four
days later. Meanwhile everyone, not only in the Arab world, was
agog to learn what he would say. His traditional Revolution Day
speech was awaited with intense eagerness. The Egyptian newspapers had promised their readers an important speech, and the
Beirut newspapers carried banner headlines: 'Nasser to reply to
Dulles'. The speech was to be given at Mostorod, an industrial
complex five miles out on the road from Cairo to the canal, where
Nasser was to inaugurate a new terminal in which oil brought from
the canal was to be processed. But as the time at which he was to
speak, noon, drew close there was no news from any of the

emissaries that had been sent out, and so Nasser was obliged to improvise. He talked about the achievements of the revolution, and about the conspiracies being hatched against it, and he ended with a fierce denunciation of the American government: 'Let them die in their fury, for they will not be able to dominate us or control our existence. We shall continue our chosen road in spite of them, the road of honour, freedom and dignity.' But it was an anticlimax, and Nasser was very conscious of the fact, which meant he spoke under an artificial restraint.

The man responsible for the refinery — in fact, for all operations in the country relating to oil production — was a former army officer called Mahmoud Younis. He had lectured at the War College, where Nasser had been one of his class and had learned to appreciate what he called his 'organized mind'. Mahmoud Younis had been sitting in the front row of the audience as Nasser delivered his speech, and after it was over he escorted his former student to his car. He, like so many others, had been disappointed in the speech, and was surprised when Nasser told him to get in the car with him. When they reached the presidential office Nasser asked him a single question: 'Mahmoud, can you run the canal?' Mahmoud Younis looked blank. Nasser said: 'I have decided to nationalize the Suez Canal Company.' Mahmoud Younis exploded: 'Ach! Why didn't you say so this morning?' 'Just wait a bit,' said Nasser. 'Sit down.'

Nasser explained what was by then known only to a handful of his closest associates and one or two other members of the RCC. Younis, like the others, was sworn to the utmost secrecy. He was to choose two or three associates, whom he could trust absolutely, but who would have to be approved by Nasser, and with them he was to prepare plans for the takeover of the company's offices in Cairo and the canal towns. The Cairo takeover would have to be particularly carefully arranged. Nasser told Younis that he had rejected the idea of getting the army or the police to do this because they were more likely to bungle the job, which would give the company officials a chance to destroy vital papers. Younis was so overwhelmed by the responsibility now thrust upon him that he was left virtually speechless.

Tuesday 24 July passed without any news from the emissaries sent to Cyprus and Malta. Nasser went over and over his assessment of what was to be expected. He decided that however angry

Dulles and the Americans might be they could not resort to force because that would show them up as vindictive bullies, and in any case the Saudis would restrain them. The French were bogged down in Algeria and he did not think they would act unless the British did. He thought Israel would stay quiet because he knew that Ben-Gurion, though no doubt tempted to take some dramatic action, was still keen to be accepted as part of the Afro-Asian world — the role that had been denied him at Bandung — and would not wish to appear as the tool of Western imperialism. He calculated that Britain and France would certainly keep their distance from Israel for fear of fatally compromising their reputations in the Arab world.

At last, on Wednesday 25 July, news began to come in, one emissary arriving from Cyprus in the morning and the second at about 4 o'clock in the afternoon. The information they brought was precise and encouraging. Britain had one old aircraft carrier in Malta, one destroyer on patrol in the area between Cyprus, Haifa and Alexandria, with another destroyer in the Red Sea on its way from Port Sudan to Aden. British troops in Cyprus were reported to include the Third Guards Brigade, the Third Commando Brigade, and elements from a parachute brigade. Grivas reckoned that all these were geared to meet the Cyprus emergency and neither equipped nor trained for operations outside the island. The Syrians, on their own initiative, sent Cairo information about the small numbers of British troops in Jordan and Libya. Nasser thought that if the British were so foolish as to move any formations from Libya into Egypt that would be the end of King Idris and the Senussi monarchy.

The next day, Thursday 26 July, Nasser was due to deliver another speech. The custom had grown up of two commemorative speeches — the first on 23 July in or near Cairo, marking the anniversary of the revolution, and the second, three days later, on 26 July, in Alexandria, marking the deposition of King Farouk and his departure by sea into exile. Nasser was to go to Alexandria in the morning of Thursday, and would in fact be staying there all the summer because of the work being carried out at his house in Heliopolis. A villa had been rented near San Stephano overlooking the sea, and his wife and children were already living there.

Younis was reporting to Nasser every day. He had recruited those who were to be his closest collaborators. These included four army officers who were to head the teams that would take over the company's offices in Cairo, Ismailia, Port Said, and Suez. Each had under him teams which were to perform the actual takeover operation. Only the four officers in charge knew what was afoot, and even they did not know that nationalization was contemplated. They had been told only that the company's offices were to be seized, but not why or when. Each of their subordinates was given a sealed envelope containing instructions telling him what he was to do, to be opened only when the order was given. The main objective was to ensure that the operation of the canal continued without interruption. Employees of the company were to be treated with a mixture of firmness and conciliation, but they were to be left under no illusions. They would be operating under martial law, and Younis had full powers under martial law delegated to him by the President.

Nasser felt that before he made his speech he must inform members of the RCC and the Cabinet of its contents. It will probably seem extraordinary to Western observers that no ministers had been consulted before so momentous a decision was taken, but nobody in the Third World would find it strange. In these countries decisions in which security is in any way involved are almost invariably taken by the one man at the top whose fate depends on them. In fact the RCC had been disbanded when Nasser had been elected president a month before, but he considered that in view of the importance of the decision and the short time that had elapsed since its disbandment, the RCC should be specially reconvened on this occasion. Its former members were summoned for a late lunch at his villa at about 3.30, but when they heard the news nobody felt much in the mood for eating.

Then it was the turn of the Cabinet. Ministers had been summoned for 5 o'clock, also at his villa, and though they had a feeling that something special was in the air they had no idea what it was. I happened that morning to be at the beach and was preparing for a swim. One of the senior ministers came up and suggested joining me — rather to my surprise, since I knew he was not a strong swimmer. After a good deal of puffing and panting on his part we reached a rock some way out from the shore, and sat down on it. Now, feeling that at last we were secure from eavesdroppers, he gasped out: 'Tell me: what's it all about?'

Nasser told assembled ministers that he could have followed a different course and asked them for their opinions, but he had rejected this idea, partly because he was absolutely convinced in his own mind that the decision he had come to was the right one, and partly because what he was proposing to do involved calculations outside the scope of their departments. Grave risks would have to be met, and it would have been unfair for anyone but him to be made responsible for them. He then told them that in a few hours time he was going to announce that the Suez Canal Company had been nationalized.

The Cabinet ministers were stunned. Many of them were graduates from Western universities, and this was not at all the sort of political game they had expected to take part in. When Nasser had finished speaking one minister applauded, but it was clear from their questions that most of them were thinking about the dangers they saw ahead. One asked whether it would not be better to proceed by degrees, taking, say, half the canal to start with, rather than all of it. Nasser said that 50 per cent or 100 per cent — the risk would be the same. Another minister suggested threatening nationalization rather than ordering it, withdrawal of the threat being conditional on the West's after all finding the money for the High Dam. Nasser's answer was that he didn't like ultimatums; in this context an ultimatum would simply give the Western Powers time in which to mobilize public opinion and their armed forces. Another minister was not happy about the idea of linking nationalization of the canal to the financing of the High Dam; it would, he said, make it look as if this was an act of political spite — revenge for the humiliation which Dulles had inflicted on Egypt. That was exactly the point, said Nasser. Dulles had made withdrawal of the offer to finance the High Dam a political act, not an economic one; Egypt must make its reply a political act also.

More than one minister mentioned Mossadeq; he had national-ized his country's oil industry, and this had proved a failure. Nasser said that was no real parallel. The success or failure of Egypt's act of nationalization would depend on two things: if, after twenty-four hours, two convoys, northbound and southbound, had passed freely through the canal; and second, if Egypt's friends in Asia and Africa gave their backing. In Mossadeq's case, his opponents had managed to prevent others from using Iranian oil, and so he had been robbed of the fruits of its nationalization.

There were, of course, some ministers who could not resist the chance for oratorical flourishes, but most of the discussion was severely practical. They wanted to know how the operation was going to be conducted, and Nasser explained the composition of the new authority he had set up, and how it was going to perform later that day. The possibility of an economic blockade came up. Nasser asked the Minister of Supply, Kamal Ramzi Stinou, about the state of food stocks in the country, and received a reassuring assessment. He asked Abdel Moneim Kaisouni, the Minister of Finance, if he thought it would be possible to rescue Egyptian deposits in London and Paris before action was taken against them. Kaisouni said he thought there might be a chance. The next day was Friday, and if no action was taken then there might be a respite over the weekend. (In fact most of Egypt's assets in Britain, held by the Midland Bank, were blocked two days later before they could be withdrawn.) Other questions covered civilian defence and the possibility of enlisting volunteers. Nasser said they must avoid giving the impression that Egypt was going to be the first to start military preparations of any description. After the meeting broke up, the ministers prepared to leave. 'Where are you going to, gentlemen?' asked Nasser. They said they were going to take their places in Menshiyeh Square. 'No,' said Nasser, 'It's too early. You will be confined to this house until we all leave for the square together.'

Younis went very early in the morning to Cairo. The team to take over the headquarters there was stationed in cars near Shepheard's Hotel, and as dawn was breaking he and the officer heading the Cairo team went carefully over the ground round the company's headquarters, checking every detail of the operation. He then went back to Ismailia. His next move was to summon the Governors of the three districts, Ismailia, Port Said, and Suez, to meet him in the office of the GOC Eastern Command, General Ali Ali Amer. The three officers heading the three takeover teams were also ordered to attend. The Governors received their orders with surprise and some resentment. Who was this oil engineer to give them orders? What did he want them for? Probably just a lecture. But as the order had come to them via Ali Ali Amer (though he too was unaware of its significance) they thought it better to obey.

Younis addressed his audience of seven men: 'I have an announcement of the greatest importance to make to you,' he said, 'and one also of the utmost confidentiality. If anyone breathes a word about it, I shall be obliged to shoot him,' and he slammed his revolver on the table in front of him. He then told them that the offices of the Suez Canal Company were to be taken over, though again the word *nationalization* was not mentioned. When he had finished speaking his audience cheered. General Amer was given an additional task. There were six hundred British technicians in the canal zone, stationed there under the terms of the 1955 agreement. They were in civilian clothes, but armed, and the possibility that some of these might cause trouble could not be ruled out. General Amer was ordered to deal with that contingency should it arise.

Younis had been told in the morning by Nasser that he regarded it as almost certain that everything would go ahead as planned, and he had been told to listen for a code word which was to be the signal for him and his teams to move into action. The code word chosen was, appropriately, the name of the Frenchman who had originally secured the concession for the canal and whose huge statue still dominated the entrance to it, 'de Lesseps'. For fear of a breakdown if he listened to the speech on one radio, Mahmoud Younis had surrounded himself with a battery of radios in Eastern Command headquarters.

Alexandria at the end of July is a holiday city, and, with its long palm-lined beaches, its brilliantly lit cafés and shops, a place of beauty and excitement. As Nasser made his way slowly along the sea road to Menshiyeh Square in an open car, picked out by a spotlight in the following car, thousands of Alexandrians and visitors lined the streets to cheer him. There was an electric feeling in the atmosphere, as though the people were all unconsciously preparing to be partakers in high drama. Nasser was caught up by the excitement of the adventure on which he and the whole of Egypt were so soon to be launched. When he spoke to the Cabinet and the RCC he had been grim and unsmiling. Now he was a different man, the popular leader, at one with his people, sharing their enthusiasm and showing that he shared it.

Nasser had not prepared the speech he was going to make, but only made a few notes. He began by looking back at Egypt's history, at the way in which throughout the ages its people had been exploited by one tyranny or another, foreign or native-born. After he had been speaking for about half an hour he told his audience that Eugene Black had reminded him of how the Khedive Said had given out the contract for the canal. 'But,' he said. 'de Lesseps imposed conditions on the Khedive. I am not the Khedive, and I am not willing to accept conditions.' The code word had been given.[1] Mahmoud Younis and his teams moved into action. 'Therefore,' Nasser went on, 'you should know of a decree that has been signed by the President of the Republic. Article 1. Compagnie Universelle du Canal Maritime de Suez shall be nationalized as an Egyptian company and transferred to the state with all its assets and commitments. Article 2. The administration of navigational traffic in the Suez Canal shall be taken over by an independent body.' There were four more brief articles filling in details.

There was a moment of silent incredulity, as the significance of what they had just heard sank into the quarter of a million people crowded into Menshiyeh Square. Then pandemonium erupted and scenes of wild excitement broke out in towns and villages through the length and breadth of the land where millions had been clustered round their radios to listen to the President's speech. Nobody in Egypt slept much that night.

Nasser had told Younis that there must be no hitch in the takeover operation, and there was none. It had been thought that the company's communications were centred in Cairo, and that there might be safes there containing a lot of confidential records and documents, but in fact Ismailia was the communications link with Paris, and when the company's employees there saw the jeeps and armoured cars surrounding their offices, not to mention the by now wildly cheering crowds thronging the streets, they realized that any resistance would be futile. Everywhere the sealed envelopes had been opened, the detachments had taken up their appointed positions, and occupation of the company's four principal offices was completed in a matter of minutes.

Younis immediately called a meeting of senior employees in the Ismailia offices. He mixed warnings with conciliation. They were, he told them, now under martial law, and he had replaced the board of directors in Paris as the source for their authority. Operations in the canal must be continued without any interruptions, and he was appointing a liaison officer to work in each of the three departments into which the company's activities were divided — Travaux, Transit, Administration. He hoped that amicable relations could be quickly established, but any attempts at sabotage would be ruthlessly dealt with.

The French among the company's employees made little attempt to hide their chagrin at what had happened, so Younis did his best to encourage the non-French employees, mostly Italians, Greeks, and Maltese. The senior French official in Ismailia told Younis that he could not recognize the act of nationalization or Younis's authority. Younis said he was not concerned about whether he was recognized or not; the only thing that mattered was that navigation in the canal should continue without interruption. 'Can I put it on record that I only obey your orders under duress?' asked the official. 'What do you mean by duress?' asked Younis. 'Under the threat of force.' Younis agreed that this was the situation, and gave permission for a written protest to be handed to him.

Some of the officials in Cairo claimed that their fundamental rights had been violated because they were unable to communicate with Paris either by telephone or cipher telegram, but the senior official there was allowed to send a letter to Paris via the French embassy in Cairo, and Younis assigned an official from the Ministry of Foreign Affairs to remain in permanent contact with the embassy.

After the conclusion of his speech, which lasted for about an hour and a half, Nasser asked me to go to Cairo. Almost all the top-ranking members of the government were now in Alexandria, and he wanted someone to watch events in the capital. I had no driver with me so I drove myself back, Anwar Sadat, who had some business in Cairo too, sitting beside me. It took a long time to get clear of Alexandria, every street being packed with rejoicing crowds, but once on the desert road we were able to listen on the car radio to the first foreign news bulletins in which, naturally enough, Nasser's speech took pride of place.

The next morning, back in my office at *Akhbar el-Yom*, I telephoned to Younis to ask him how things were going, and in particular whether we could tell our readers that convoys were passing through the canal normally. He said they were and that everything was going smoothly. Then I telephoned to Nasser, and he asked me if I had spoken to Younis. When I told him that I had, he told me I must on no account do this again. He was not going to call up Younis himself, and he had given strict instructions to ministers and members of the former RCC that they were not to do that either. Younis was not to be distracted. 'If he has any problems he can get in touch with me,' Nasser said, adding that he had instructed General Ali Ali Amer, in whose district the canal lay, to report on the flow of traffic in the canal, so that this duty would be taken off Younis's shoulders. In fact on this first day Younis had only one question to ask Nasser — the captain of a French ship entering the canal had refused to pay the tolls; what should be done with him? Nasser told him to debit the company to which the ship belonged with the charges due. These could be collected later. Much the most important thing was to keep the traffic moving. Other ships which refused to pay the tolls were treated likewise.

So, after the first twenty-four hours, the most momentous decision in Nasser's career had proved itself totally justified.

---

[1] In fact, to make certain that the code word was not missed, Nasser mentioned de Lesseps no fewer than thirteen times in his speech.

12

THE NEHRU FACTOR

THE WAY IN WHICH the world heard of the Suez Canal Company's nationalization has often been described. It was one of history's greatest ironies that Eden should have received the news while he was entertaining to dinner at No. 10 Downing Street King Feisal of Iraq, the Regent Abdul Ilah, and the Iraqi Prime Minister, Nuri Said. At first the dinner had been relaxed and cheerful. It was generally felt that the bumptious Egyptian leader, who had been causing those present such a lot of trouble, had been finally put in his place. But then a secretary came in and handed Eden a note. He read it and said: 'Nasser has nationalized the Suez Canal Company.' Nuri spoke: 'You must hit him. You must hit him hard, and you must hit him now.'[1]

Nuri went back to Baghdad convinced that his advice had fallen on receptive ears, and that now the Baghdad Pact, of which he had been the principal architect, was going to prove itself justified. He thought nationalization would be a nine days' wonder, and that then sober realities would take over. But not all members of his Cabinet were so optimistic; indeed, some of them, opposed to his unyielding pro-Western line, were secretly in contact with Cairo and passed on news of all the government's deliberations. It was, however, impossible for Iraq not to join all the other Arab governments in sending a message of congratulations to Nasser on his great national achievement, even though Nuri well knew that if Nasser pulled it off that would be the end of all that Nuri had been hoping and planning for — and would probably mean his own end too (as two years later proved to be the case). As a final irony, Nuri also knew that, if his British allies followed his advice and 'hit Nasser hard', he would have no alternative, in view of the state of Arab opinion, but to send the Iraqi army to help in repelling them.

* * *

As soon as the Iraqi guests had left, a meeting of senior ministers was called in the Cabinet room. 'The *mise en scène* will live in my mind,' Lord Kilmuir wrote in his memoirs.[2] 'Anthony Eden, Selwyn Lloyd, Salisbury, and I were, of course, in full evening dress for the Royal Dinner — Anthony and Bobbity [Salisbury] with the sash and knee breeches of the Garter. Then M. Chauvel, the able and acute French ambassador, came in a lounge suit. He was followed by Mr Foster from the American embassy, similarly clad. . . . Then Gerald Templer, the CIGS, and Dickie Mountbatten,[3] obviously prised from private dinner parties, both in dinner jackets. It was a remarkable gathering to discuss one of the most serious questions since World War Two.'

It soon became obvious that Britain was in no position to implement Nuri's advice to 'hit Nasser hard and quickly', and Eden received no encouragement from Washington to do so. Eisenhower's first reaction was, 'There is no reason to panic,' and he thought Eden's reported plan for an attack on Egypt 'a very unwise decision'. Dulles being in South America, Eisenhower sent Robert Murphy, Assistant Secretary of State, over to London on Saturday 28 July with instructions to 'hold the fort. See what it's all about.' Murphy had talks with Selwyn Lloyd and Pineau the next morning, and at dinner met Harold Macmillan, Chancellor of the Exchequer, and Field Marshal Lord Alexander, both former wartime colleagues in North Africa. Dulles arrived in London three days later, on the morning of Wednesday 1 August, and in his turn had talks with Lloyd and Pineau. The day before, Byroade had seen Nasser, for the first time since nationalization. He now felt justified in the warnings he had given Washington but which had gone unheeded. He told Nasser on this occasion that some political outlet was needed for the head of steam that was building up. He thought America would be prepared to give Egypt every political help.

Nasser was still in Alexandria, following the news on the agencies. Although by now it seemed most improbable that there would be any immediate intervention by force — indeed, the estimates Nasser was now receiving were that this would take at least six weeks to prepare — he was naturally extremely anxious to know what the three foreign ministers had decided on. I was in Cairo, following the news on all the tapes and listening to broadcasts, and telephoning to Alexandria every ten minutes or so, when there was anything to report. But at about 8 o'clock in the

evening on Wednesday I told Nasser that I thought there was little
chance of hearing more that night because people in London never
worked after 6 or 7 o'clock in the evening. 'Very well,' said Nasser.
'I'm not going to sit here biting my nails. I'm going to a movie.'
So, taking Amer and Baghdadi with him, he went off to the Metro
Cinema where they saw a film called *Appointment in Las Vegas*.

What the three foreign ministers had decided, it soon emerged,
was to call a conference in London to be attended by the principal
countries which used the canal. It would have been pointless to
summon the signatories of the 1888 Convention because the
Austro-Hungarian and Turkish Empires had ceased to exist, and
the United States had not been among those who signed. So this
idea of Dulles was adopted as a substitute.

At the same time Eden, in an atmosphere that was becoming
increasingly hysterical owing to his obsession with Nasser and
pressure from his own back-benchers for some sort of action,
instructed General Stockwell to prepare a plan for an Anglo-French
invasion of Egypt. This was code-named Musketeer I. Eden, who
never got on with Dulles, was always hoping to circumvent him
and get in direct contact with Eisenhower, with whom he had
worked closely during the war and had, he thought, a good
rapport. Though understandable, this aim was not so well-founded
as Eden believed. Eisenhower strongly disapproved of the nationalization of the Suez Canal Company, but there was a part of him
which admired what had been done, or rather of the way in which
Nasser had been prepared to take the sort of risk which he, as a
supreme commander in war, had had to take himself. As he said
later: 'No matter what you think of Nasser, at least he is a leader.'

Paradoxically, Dulles seemed at first to see things in much the
same light as Eden — after his arrival in London he had spoken of
the need to 'make Nasser disgorge his theft'. Such an apparently
robust attitude on the part of the Secretary of State had for a time
led Eden to believe that he might secure American backing for the
use of force despite Eisenhower's warning. But his optimism was
shortlived. Dulles's main aim, it became clear, was to defuse a crisis
which he was being widely blamed for having created. Realizing
this, Nasser decided that it would be in Egypt's interests to try to
assist Dulles in his efforts to restrain the British and the French.
This could be done by lending some verisimilitude to Dulles's
denials that it was he who had provoked the crisis by first

encouraging and then abruptly dashing Egypt's hopes for help over the High Dam.

So in his first press conference after 26 July Nasser said that nationalization was something that had been thought about for a long time — for at least two years — thus investing a body called the Suez Canal Management Committee, which had been set up in the Ministry of Industry and Commerce to prepare for a smooth transition when the company's concession expired in 1968, with a greater significance than it had ever really possessed. This was a deliberate political statement, designed to weaken some of the leverage which Eden was trying to apply to Dulles. It served its purpose, being widely quoted in the American press and used by the State Department in its briefings.

Nasser was playing for time, trying to mobilize support for Egypt both in the Arab countries and in the wider world opinion. The two key Arab countries were Saudi Arabia and Syria. The Saudis were not happy. King Saud was offended that, although linked to Egypt by a military alliance, he had received no prior warning of an action which, as he complained in a letter to Nasser, might involve his country in war. Like everyone else, he had simply heard the news over the radio, and this had been a considerable embarrassment. Nor could he ignore the fact that nationalization of the canal set a precedent which might be applied to oil. Everyone was making comparisons between Nasser and Mossadeq, in spite of the fact that there was no real similarity: Mossadeq's act of nationalization had brought his country's main industry to a halt, whereas Nasser's had resulted in no interruption to navigation in the canal.

Syria was still under tremendous pressure. Nasser's popularity there was now at its peak, and he could count on the active backing of almost all the younger officers. But the old guard, including President Quwatli, were afraid of what he might be letting them in for, and neither the CIA nor the British and Iraqis had given up their plans for subversion. They were now reinforced by the oil companies, fearful that they might be next on the list for takeover.

But during these early August days the whole Arab world was in a ferment. It might almost be said that nobody did any work, being far too preoccupied with listening to the news and passing resolutions in support of Egypt. There was a lot of talk about boycotts of Western goods, interrupting Western communications and oil

supplies, and other practical measures if Egypt was attacked. The
first Russian reaction came in a TASS statement on 29 July that the
Suez Canal was the property of Egypt and nationalization a
measure which would benefit the Egyptian people. Support from
China came a little later, on 4 August. On 7 August the Iraqi
government came out with a statement that Iraq stood by the side
of sister Egypt and would place at her disposal all possible material
and moral aid. A private message from Nuri to London explained
that this statement was the result of *force majeure* and represented no
change in policy. On 9 August came another Russian warning to
Britain and France against the use of force, and the same day
recruiting centres were opened in Egypt for the enrolment of
volunteers.

From the Egyptian point of view the principal target for diplomacy
must now be India. India was politically and numerically the most
important member of the Commonwealth, as well as of the
Afro-Asian community, and Nehru's international prestige was
second to none. If India proved hostile, or even lukewarm, Egypt's
chances of achieving a diplomatic victory would be much reduced.

The immediate outlook was not good. India, though not a
signatory to the 1888 Convention, was one of the major users of the
canal, and the Indian press was highly critical of Nasser's action.
Fears were expressed that tolls would be much increased to pay for
the High Dam, and that navigation in the canal might be interrupted, if military action resulted. And Nehru was being criticized
in the newspapers on the grounds either that he had known of
Nasser's intentions, in which case he had clearly been unable to stop
him, or, that if he had not known, this showed that he had not been
trusted.

Nehru had necessarily not been told in advance about nationalization and was in consequence both hurt and angry. Why had Nasser
not told him what he planned while they were both at Brioni, or
when Nehru flew back to Cairo with him? It was inconceivable to
him that a decision of this magnitude could have been reached
except at the end of prolonged deliberation, the weighing up of
evidence, the calculating of every contingency, and after protracted
consideration and consultation. If Nasser had really decided on

nationalizing the company on the spur of the moment, so to speak, in a fit of pique, this showed irresponsibility, and this was to Nehru incomprehensible, and left him, to his intense annoyance, exposed to the charge of being an accomplice to an action which threatened the vital interests of the West and, indeed, of his own country. The day after Nasser's speech the Indian ambassador hurried round to see Ali Sabri (as did so many others) to gather what further information he could. It was at least possible to reassure him that the decision to nationalize had not been taken while Nehru was in Nasser's company. Then, on 3 August, Nehru sent Nasser his first considered comment, in the form of a personal letter delivered by the hand of the Indian ambassador in Cairo.

Nasser had got to know Nehru well, and had an enormous admiration for him. But their natures and their approach to political problems were very different. Nehru was the intellectual, looking at things from every angle, hesitating, qualifying, reluctant to commit himself absolutely. Tito and Nasser used sometimes to speak with affectionate exasperation of Nehru's intellectualism and of the difficulty of ever pinning him down to a positive course of action.[4] In this letter it was Nehru the lawyer, the cautious elder statesman, who was speaking. Choosing his words with the greatest care, he gave a scarcely veiled warning that Egypt should not expect India's support in this crisis — a crisis of its own making — to be either automatic or uncritical. It was for Egypt to take the initiative in finding a peaceful solution to the crisis, preferably by itself calling for an international conference.

To His Excellency President Gamal Abdel Nasser from Jawaharlal Nehru, Prime Minister of India:–

1. Soon after my return to Delhi from Cairo and Beirut I learnt of your decision about the Suez Canal. As this had not been mentioned by you in the course of our talks at Brioni and Cairo, I thought that decision must have been taken after I left Cairo. Our ambassador in Cairo has confirmed this after a talk he had with Minister Ali Sabri. This has helped me to understand this aspect of the matter. I have today received from your ambassador in Delhi a copy of your statement of 31st July. Thank you for this. [This referred to the statement about the background of the legal position sent to Egyptian missions abroad and to some friendly governments.]

2. I have till now made no comments on these developments beyond saying in Parliament that this matter was not discussed

between us at Brioni or Cairo. I was hoping to have fuller information about the future to enable me to make a statement in our
Parliament. A matter of this kind has international repercussions. I
want my statement in Parliament to be as helpful as possible. Our
direct interest is as users of the canal like others but we are naturally
also interested in a friendly settlement.

3. We are in no doubt as to sovereign right of Egypt and note that
the position adopted by you in 1954 [at the time of the signing of the
Anglo-Egyptian agreement] is that 'the Suez Maritime Canal, which
is an integral part of Egypt, is a waterway economically, commer-
cially and strategically of international importance' and that you have
expressed 'the determination to uphold the Convention guaranteeing
freedom of navigation of the canal signed at Constantinople on the
29th October 1888.'

4. Recognizing the sovereign right of Egypt as above and welcom-
ing your statement of the 31st July that your present position 'does
not in any way or to any extent affect the international commitments
of Egypt' and that you are 'determined to honour all your international obligations and both the Convention of 1888 and the assurance
given in the Anglo-Egyptian Agreement of 1954', I venture to
express the hope that you will decide to take the initiative yourself to
call together all those interested in the international aspects of the
development and on the basis of Egypt's sovereignty. Such a step
would be fully in accord with your declared intentions and help the
consideration of such mutually agreeable arrangements consistent
with your law as well as international usage and to clear any
misconceptions.

5. I am sure you will appreciate that my suggestion is in no way
designed as an interference in Egypt's affairs or with your decision
but actuated by the desire to see that there should be as little
acrimony about this as possible and to assist in a peaceful and
conciliatory approach.

6. My own attitude and desire is only to see that all questions that
have arisen should be settled by peaceful means and I feel sure you
share this desire.

7. There have been repercussions and some of these might well
increase tension but it should be the wish of all parties concerned to
settle all problems and questions arising from these developments by
talks in a friendly way. Our own attitude will be governed by this
consideration and due adherence to our friendships and international
usage.

8. I trust you will give consideration to what I have said above and
take your own initiative or respond to any legitimate steps taken by

others which do not prejudice the sovereignty and dignity of Egypt.

9. I shall be most grateful to you for your views.

Sincere regards,

Nasser found Nehru's letter extremely worrying. If this represented the attitude that India was going to adopt it must be expected that many other nonaligned countries would adopt it too. In particular, it was more than likely that India's lead would be followed by the other two major Asian countries in the Commonwealth, Pakistan and Sri Lanka. Accordingly Nasser sent an oral message to Nehru through the Indian ambassador, in which he emphasized Egypt's wish for a peaceful settlement and mentioned that his government was thinking of taking the matter to the Security Council, where a new agreement to replace the Convention of 1888 would be presented and all interested parties be invited to sign. Almost immediately, on 5 August, a reply to this message came from Delhi:

1. I am grateful to you for your kind reply to my message and appreciate your assurances that you are doing everything to make conciliatory approaches. I would like to express the hope that your attitude would remain firmly conciliatory in spite of provocation. It is more likely that this would lead to the more satisfactory results and strengthen responsible positions.

2. We are studying your proposal and will send you a reply very soon. The proposal for a reference to the United Nations requires further consideration, but I welcome your readiness to execute fresh treaties with concerned nations on an international basis. This may well give an opportunity for others to find a common ground for coming to suitable arrangements.

3. With regard to my own position in regard to the British invitation [to the first London conference], we have sent them no reply and are considering the matter. We shall not in any event accept the invitation without reservations regarding the arguments and grounds stated in the joint communiqué [of the three foreign ministers making the invitations] and the composition of the conference, and certain other matters. We cannot also subscribe to any form of settlement without full consideration ourselves and consultations with you.

4. Our object would not be to weaken your position but, as you yourself have been doing, to work for conciliatory approaches. In

this way it may be possible to prevent the proposed conference from being a barrier to a settlement.

5. We wish to emphasize this aspect and not to support any unilateral action taken by any one nation or group of nations.

Yet another message of advice came the next day, 6 August. It read:

1. We have given further and careful consideration to your message of 3 August 1956 and to the ideas which you are considering for inclusion in your reply to the UK by way of your counter-proposals.

2. I appreciate your decision that you propose 'instead of rejecting the British invitation to make a counterproposal'. This readiness to consider with other governments proposals to resolve present diffi-culties can only improve the prospects of a settlement and the position of Egypt in this matter.

3. I would suggest that you express yourself surprised at the UK convening a conference on the Suez Canal issue without consulting, or even referring to, Egypt, and deciding on the countries to be invited as well as indicating further action in regard to this.

4. Your reply may say that Egypt is agreeable to a conference to be composed of an agreed list of invitees based on the Constantinople Convention and present concerned parties in the use of the canal and any other relevant considerations. It would be useful to add that it should not be difficult to agree on such a list.

5. The conference would be convened without requiring from the participants commitments on any basis for a future settlement, such as is set out in the joint communiqué. Egypt agrees, however, that the question should be considered on the basis of the Constantinople Convention of 1888 and the Anglo-Egyptian Agreement of 1954. [Nasser had always refused to accept that this agreement, which gave Britain a role in protection of the canal, had any relevance, but probably Nehru was here referring to the declaration of principle which accompanied the agreement.] Participants should not be required to abandon beforehand insofar as they are concerned any position they hold. It would be desirable not to put any restrictive conditions on anything.

6. Egypt would be willing either to execute a fresh treaty with all concerned nations or to agree to a convention which will guarantee the security of the canal, freedom of navigation, and safety of passage and other such matters as are covered by previous agree-ments. [This was going further than Nasser was ever prepared to

accept. There was all the difference in the world between the canal's being guaranteed by a convention and being guaranteed by Egypt.]

7. Egypt cannot agree to any challenge to her sovereignty and stands by her position in regard to the canal being an integral part of Egypt, and its being a waterway of international importance in terms of Article 8 of the Anglo-Egyptian agreement of 1954.

8. Such a conference would be convened by UK, France and Egypt, and this would be in conformity with the Constantinople Convention. The venue of the conference may also be fixed by agreement.

9. Egypt is willing to participate and cooperate in a convened conference to consider the internationalization of all international waterways, the Suez Canal included, if there is agreement to convene such a conference. This may be under United National auspices or otherwise.

10. We do not think it wise for you to suggest that the present problem should be considered by the United Nations. In the present state of the world the alignment of forces there may not be favourable. Further it can also lead to the interpretation of prior acceptance of international control. It is wiser to be cautious about bringing in the United Nations just now.

11. The Egyptian reply could usefully include the strong expression of Egypt's desire for the recognition of all legitimate rights and treaty obligations and for a peaceful settlement which would lead to cooperation. It might also state that all parties should strive to create a climate of peaceful approach and negotiations. Egypt has sought to do so by maintaining freedom of navigation and by making these proposals.

12. I have made suggestions in response to your kind request and in the belief that they would constitute a helpful approach to the problem.

This last message was an improvement on Nehru's first letter, which had so alarmed Nasser. Admittedly Nehru was still far from wholehearted in his backing for the Egyptian position (e.g., in paragraphs 6 and 7), but he was clearly attracted by the idea of an appeal to the United Nations (nothing came of this, which in a way was just as well: what, it was often asked in Cairo, would happen if Israel wanted to adhere to a new convention sponsored by Egypt?), and by the idea of placing all international waterways under international control — this being, of course, something the American government would never accept because of the Panama

Canal. It had not been a pose when Nasser begged Nehru to give him the benefit of his ideas, and the result was, as he had foreseen, that Nehru was well into his stride, doing what he enjoyed almost more than anything — that is, thinking and speaking on behalf of someone else.

It was on 9 August that Nasser received information which showed that volunteers might be needed sooner rather than later. This came from London, and reported that General Stockwell was preparing a plan for an Anglo-French force to invade Egypt. Already Mrs Pandit, Nehru's sister who was Indian High Commissioner in London, and who was particularly well informed, thanks partly to her friendship with Hugh Gaitskell, the Labour leader, had advised Nasser that he had better watch the activities of a certain General Stockwell. Now the reason for watching him was made clear. In fact, as became known later, it was on the following day, 10 August, that Stockwell submitted the plan for Musketeer I to Eden, who approved it.

It became obvious to Nasser that the London conference was going to take place, whatever he said or did, and this alone was enough to make him abandon the idea of an appeal to the United Nations. The immediate question was what answer should be given to the invitation to Egypt to participate in the conference. The argument in favour of accepting was that staying away would leave the field open for Egypt's critics and enemies, but the arguments against were stronger, and Nasser set them out in a telegram to Nehru. Although he did not mention it, he was also convinced by the hostility of the press and public opinion in England that an Egyptian presence there would be pointless. Eden's television address to the nation on 8 August, in which he branded Nasser as thoroughly untrustworthy, a dictator who would 'snatch and grab' — 'our quarrel is not with Egypt, still less with the Arab world; it is with Colonel Nasser' — was, as he hints, the clinching argument against going. His telegram read:

> I appreciate your kind message. After you sent it a joint communiqué was released from London containing not merely invitation to conference but stating arguments and grounds for invitation and almost laying down terms of reference of conference which, with convenient selection of states, makes imposing of international authority a foregone conclusion.

2. Canal Company never had anything to do with security of canal and freedom of navigation. They were never entrusted to company either by concession or by practice at any time.

3. Security of canal and freedom of navigation were provided for by Convention of 1888 and were recognized and guaranteed by us both in 1888 and 1954. Declared object of British occupation of canal zone was to ensure both and when they evacuated after Suez Base Treaty of 1954 they accepted that the guarantee by us in that treaty was enough and satisfactory. Disappearance of company, which would anyhow have happened in 1968, does not affect that guarantee and we have reiterated it.

4. I would have understood agitation over nationalization if we had been unfair over compensation and rights of stock or share holders to be protected (which would have been relevant). In absence of justification for any such objections and to mislead people unacquainted with relevant documents or real position and difference between concession and convention, nationalization issue is being mixed up deliberately with question of security of canal and freedom of navigation. No one asks who looked after these when British troops evacuated. Did the company do it? The canal passes through Egyptian territory and is recognised by 1954 treaty as integral part of Egypt and its security and freedom of navigation are the responsibility of Egypt which has guaranteed and continues to guarantee them. The guarantee itself would be meaningless if it has to be fortified by another authority and no such authority was ever thought of before as necessary.

5. British say we prevent Israeli ships from passing and blockaded ships going to Israel. This was done in state of war, and since 1949 and, with 80,000 British troops present in canal zone, British did not then think of protecting freedom of navigation.

6. All these arguments are baseless and used as excuses to foist a new domination on us so that, having got rid of one, we will now have three dominating us in our territory. If we accept British invitation to conference we will be accepting all the arguments in joint communiqué leading to invitation and this will not bear independent and impartial scrutiny. It is also against our sovereignty and dignity that three powers should, without consulting us at all, issue invitations, we being one of the invitees, and lay down future methods of controlling part of our territory. What will happen if we do not accept the recommendations of such a conference? Besides, choice of states for conference is conveniently such as to ensure majority for proposal for international control. We also see no reason why invitation should have been issued by Britain and why venue

should be in London, but these are comparatively minor objections.

7. I can see wisdom and statesmanship in all international waterways being brought under international regime of United Nations, not only the Suez Canal, and I propose instead of rejecting the British invitation, to make a counterproposal to that effect and express my readiness to discuss it within the United Nations at as early a moment as the organization may desire. There is no reason to single out the Suez Canal for such treatment and our acceptance of it would imply that we accept the discrimination and that even the friendly nations who use the Suez Canal are not content with our guarantee which till now was deemed sufficient even by British who evacuated the zone on basis of that guarantee. Besides, there is really no reason why, if this issue is so internationally important, it should be discussed outside the United Nations and only between countries which the three powers have selected by their own standards. We would also be willing to execute a fresh treaty with all concerned nations guaranteeing again the security of the canal and freedom of navigation, and that treaty can be registered with the United Nations.

8. I shall await your advice regarding this proposal before announcing it and would welcome any other suggestion you may have in view but I hope you will appreciate my reasons for not agreeing to respond to the British invitation, and I do sincerely trust that, in view of those reasons, you will also oblige us by not accepting it. I hope you will not mind my suggesting this, as acceptance of the invitation by you, particularly without any reservations regarding the arguments and grounds stated in the joint communiqué or regarding the composition of the conference or the anticipating beforehand and without our consent of an international authority over us, will seriously affect us and weaken our stand, and I thought therefore I should venture to make this request to you while also putting my alternative proposal for your consideration.

9. I assure you I am doing everything to make my approaches conciliatory and our embassy in London was in fact instructed to issue a statement reaffirming our desire for friendly relations with Britain. The response is not only to the joint communiqué but also to Eden's latest speech and announcement of military preparations by British and French to force us to accept their demands. This is not a peaceful approach, and force is threatened because we are comparatively weak and an oriental people. I thank you again for your message and advice.

Later it was agreed that it would after all be better if India was represented at the London conference, and Krishna Menon, the Minister without Portfolio, was sent. But India was not to be Egypt's only ally or advocate. Messages came to Cairo from friendly inclined governments asking what attitude Egypt would like them to take up — from the Indonesians, the Russians, and even the Spaniards and the Greeks. These formed the nucleus of a bloc which in London would be able to stand up to the continued pressure of Britain, France, and America (and always with Israeli influence in the background). It was decided to send Ali Sabri, Director of the Office of the President, to act as observer in London. He would stay at the Egyptian embassy, but might expect daily briefings from Krishna Menon and from Shepilov, who would be the Soviet representative.

All this time the French were continuing to cement their private alliance with Israel. Not only were they flooding Israel with more arms, but they were urging on it a more active policy. 'What are you waiting for?' they said in effect. 'This is your opportunity.' A further temptation was put in Israel's way since, faced by an imminent military assault by Britain and France, all Egyptian troops in Sinai had been withdrawn except for six battalions divided among three locations. General Burns, the truce supervisor, sent a message to Hammarskjöld expressing his astonishment, on passing through the Egyptian lines in Sinai, to find them unoccupied. He feared this might be a temptation Israel could not resist.

There was much discussion in government circles in Cairo about where, if an invasion took place, it was to be expected. Alexandria was the obvious target, the second city in Egypt with excellent communications to the capital. But it was felt that there were many considerations in favour of Port Said. A landing in Alexandria would be a bare-faced attack on the whole of Egypt, whereas a landing at Port Said could be presented as a limited action involving only the canal. Besides, it was known that the Suez Canal Company was lobbying energetically in favour of Port Said in the hope that, once the town was again in friendly hands, this would give the company a voice in any postwar settlement.[5]

[1] Almost everybody seems to have been taken completely by surprise by Nasser's action. One person who foresaw it was the French ambassador in Cairo, Count Armand du Chayla. Meeting a senior Foreign Ministry official at the Gezira Club the day before Nasser's Alexandria speech he said he expected the President to move against the canal, 'and against the company'. But it is not known whether he passed his suspicions on to Paris.

[2] Lord Kilmuir, *Political Adventure* (London 1964), p. 268.

[3] Earl Mountbatten, First Sea Lord, who was later to describe the Suez operation as 'a complete disaster. The reverse of everything I had tried to do in Southeast Asia and India after the war, and so I hated it.'

[4] Nehru was later to confess his admiration for Nasser's action, while adding that this was a decision he could never have taken himself.

[5] The company spent an initial £25 million on lobbying in Britain, France, and other countries, later supplemented by another £20 million. This represented almost exactly the amount it eventually received in compensation.

13

THE MENZIES MISSION

As a result of the discussions in London between Eden, Dulles, and Pineau, a communiqué had been issued which contained strong condemnation of Egypt and an assertion of the need to put the Suez Canal under international control. When he heard of this communiqué Nasser jotted down a few notes about Egypt's position, mainly to serve as an aide-mémoire for himself. The substance of these notes was as follows:

The Egyptian government cannot accept the declaration by the three powers which tries to invest the Suez Canal Company with a symbolic significance in order to provide an excuse for foreign interference with Egyptian sovereignty. Although the Egyptian government is prepared to endorse its adherence to the 1888 Convention, it cannot accept the implication that freedom of navigation in the canal can only be ensured by its internationalization. The 1888 Convention remains valid whether the canal is under the control of the Egyptian government or any other management. The Suez Canal Company has never at any time been responsible for maintaining freedom of navigation in the canal, which remains the concern of the 1888 Convention. Attempts to link the position of the Suez Canal Company to the question of freedom of navigation raise suspicions about the motives of those who do so. By representing the Suez Canal Company as an international authority with power to guarantee freedom of navigation, the three-power declaration represents a threat to Egyptian sovereignty and to the control by the government of Egypt over a part of its territory. The Egyptian government considers the proposal to internationalize control over the canal as being the equivalent of introducing international colonialism.

Coinciding with the three-power declaration has come an international conspiracy which aims at threatening the Egyptian people with starvation. The three governments have frozen Egyptian assets held in banks in their countries, which is a breach of international law and not, as is claimed, a normal exercise of national sovereignty. The three powers aim by this action to exert economic pressure, including the threat of starvation, against the people of Egypt, who built the canal at the cost of 120,000 lives. Moreover, Britain and France have made no secret of their intention to recover the canal by force, and are massing troops in Cyprus and Libya. The Egyptian government emphatically condemns such actions, which are intended to coerce the Egyptian people into submitting to the surrender of sovereignty over their own territory to an international organization, which would mean a return to colonialism.

The first London conference met at Lancaster House on 16 August. Egypt could hope for a strong first line of defence led by the Soviet Union and India, and probably Indonesia. India was vital, of course, particularly in view of its dominant position in the Commonwealth, which made it certain to be subjected to tremendous pressure from other Commonwealth countries, particularly Britain and Australia. That, and the fact that Nehru was still being accused in the American press of having been Nasser's accomplice, and that the Indian press was still giving vent to fears about increased canal tolls, meant that the Indian attitude would have to be watched very closely. The Soviet Union was a valued ally, but Nasser did not want it to become spokesman for Egypt.

It was not clear what line the Americans were going to take. In some respects they seemed as hostile as the British and French. They had blocked Egyptian assets and cut trade links, and Dulles had talked about the need to make Nasser 'disgorge'. His attitude was that Egypt had broken, if not a treaty, then at any rate an international understanding, and that this represented a threat to navigation which was not acceptable. America was as keen on getting the canal internationalized as were the British and French. Yet there seemed a hope that it might be possible to separate them from their partners, so Nasser repeated several times that nationalization of the canal had long been contemplated and was not intended as a rebuff to America or to Dulles personally.

What Egypt wanted from the London conference was that it should go on talking as long as possible and that at the end it should come up with no unanimous conclusions. Nasser wanted to gain time. So did the British — but for very different reasons. Eden needed to complete his military preparations; Nasser was working on world public opinion.

As soon as the conference opened the Russians and Indians raised the question of Selwyn Lloyd's position. It was assumed that he would be chosen as conference chairman, because Britain was the host country, but they objected on the grounds that Britain was a party to the dispute. It was known that his nomination would go through, but this was a valid procedural point. Moreover, when the question of voting came up, and Lloyd wanted to have United Nations procedure, with majority voting, adopted, he was obliged, following objections by Krishna Menon for India and Shepilov for Russia, to surrender the point if he was to keep the chairmanship. It was further agreed at the first session that the conference proceedings would be kept confidential, that there would be no official spokesman, but that each delegation could give separate briefings, if it so wished. Minutes of each meeting were handed to the Russians and Indians, among others, who in turn handed copies to Ali Sabri.

Krishna Menon, who, for all his great talents, was always something of a prima donna on an occasion such as this, was responsible for one awkward moment for Egypt. He prepared a resolution to be put to the conference which, while confirming that the canal was an integral part of Egypt, recommended that one third of the directors on the board of the new agency to run it should be drawn from those countries which were major users of the canal. When it was pointed out to him that this would be unacceptable to Egypt he took umbrage and refused to discuss the matter with anyone for three days. Finally, the Russians obliged by tabling a resolution which exactly represented the Egyptian point of view, for which India was obliged to vote.

The conference ended by endorsing, by eighteen votes to five, a set of proposals for the future of the canal which were largely the work of Dulles. It was further agreed that a committee should be appointed to carry these draft proposals to Cairo, explain them to Nasser and, if possible, persuade him to negotiate a new convention for the canal on that basis.

The committee of five consisted of Robert Menzies of Australia (Chairman); Loy Henderson deputizing for Dulles; Osten Unden, Foreign Minister of Sweden; Dr Ardalan, Foreign Minister of Iran, and Ato Aklolou Hapte-Wold, Foreign Minister of Ethiopia. The mission arrived in Cairo on the evening of Sunday 2 September and saw Nasser the next day.

*   *   *

The reports that had reached Cairo spoke of Menzies as being an extremely tough character who was bringing with him an ultimatum which would amount to a knockout blow for Nasser. Accordingly Nasser had settled that he would receive the members of the mission in his office in Kubba Palace, not in a conference hall, to avoid giving the impression that these were going to be negotiations.[1]

At their first meeting Menzies surprised Nasser by his affability.[2] 'I know you,' he said. Somewhat taken aback, Nasser asked how — had they met before? 'No,' said Menzies. 'But before I left London I went to the BBC and asked them for all the film footage they had on you. So, Mr President, I sat down and watched you for hours, and in particular your Alexandria speech about the canal. So I know you well.' 'I'm glad you do,' said Nasser.

After the preliminaries they got down to business. Nasser said he wanted to reach an understanding, but he was unhappy about the atmosphere in London when the mission had left, the continuing threats of military action and obvious preparations for it, and the barrage of propaganda against Egypt in the world's press. Menzies explained the procedure he hoped would be followed. The mission would present its proposals, together with an explanatory memorandum, that morning, giving the Egyptians time to study them so that they could give their reply the next day. He thought that neither side should say anything to the press except what was jointly approved. Nasser agreed, but said that he knew the facts of life, and that there would have to be some contact with the press and that therefore some things were bound to leak out. So it would be better for each side to have its own spokesman rather than hope to have one spokesman who could act for both. Menzies said he would like to have two meetings each day, one in the morning and one in the afternoon. Nasser said that, apart from this first day, there could only be one meeting daily, in the evening. 'Mr Menzies, it looks as if I may have a war on my hands,' he said, 'and in the morning I must be preparing for it.'

Loy Henderson had asked if he and Byroade, now in his last days as ambassador, could see Nasser privately, and a meeting was arranged for the evening of the mission's arrival. Nasser complained to them that the mission was apparently the bearer of a resolution which he was obliged either to accept or reject. 'That is nonsense,' he said. 'I don't work in that way. I want to reach an agreement. Instead you send this Australian mule to threaten me.' Henderson said, 'Mr President, you mustn't be afraid of Mr Menzies.' Nasser said he was not afraid of anybody. Henderson assured him that every member of the mission came in a very friendly frame of mind:

> They want to do a job. Menzies is a blunt man, and he is not here to dictate terms. He is a man you can talk to. Don't be misled by his bluntness. If he felt he was simply being used as a messenger boy he would go straight back to Australia. His mission can amount to very nearly the same thing as negotiations, and he wants to make a success of it. He is not here to act as spokesman for the British empire.

They begged Nasser not to break off the talks after the first meeting, as they feared, remembering the Allen mission, he might do. But he assured them that he had no intention of doing that.

In fact, Menzies, the elder statesman of empire, represented a breed of politicians with which Nasser had had no previous experience, but at a dinner the same day, Monday, at which Nasser was host, they tried to take each other's measure. It was held in the Manyel Palace, which had belonged to Prince Mohamed Ali, the uncle of King Farouk, a beautiful building in the Islamic style which still contained many mementoes of royalty. Menzies recalled that he had been inside the palace twice before, during the war, but had never seen the room used for dinner. Looking round he noticed a bust of Khedive Ismail and said to Nasser: 'Mr President, may I be permitted to go and salute the great man who sold his shares in the canal to Britain?' 'Go ahead,' said Nasser. 'You can kiss him if you want to.' Menzies walked across and patted the bust. Then he saw various signed photographs of British royalty which had been presented to Prince Mohamed Ali. 'I know this crowd,' he said.

Nasser had not been looking forward to the dinner, but Menzies, who of course was sitting next to him, set out to be entertaining. He talked about Churchill, 'that great man', and hinted at the pressures Eden was under in trying to follow in his footsteps. He said that the last time he had met Churchill he was not only very deaf, 'but going gaga, completely gaga'. He said he could mimic Churchill so perfectly that when on one occasion during the war the Australian broadcasting service had failed to pick up part of one of Churchill's broadcast speeches he had been asked to complete it, and had done so without being detected. 'You remember that famous speech about fighting on the beaches,' said Menzies, and began to quote it. 'Don't you think that is very like his voice?' he said, turning to Nasser. 'I never heard Churchill speak,' said Nasser. Nothing daunted, Menzies said that he could also do a very good imitation of Bernard Shaw and began to quote from *Major Barbara*. Most of his audience had not the slightest idea what it was all about, but there was a lot of applause and polite laughter. Loy Henderson did not join in because he had an upset stomach and asked for yoghurt.

Nasser learned that after Monday's evening session Menzies had been driven round to the American embassy, and stayed there an hour. 'He must have been going to get his orders,' Nasser commented. This confirmed him in his conviction that the resolution brought by the mission was inspired by Dulles, that Eden would have to do what Dulles wanted, and that therefore the real political duel was between Egypt and Dulles, with Dulles determined to get the canal internationalized. 'He wants to get by diplomatic means,' Nasser said, 'what Eden hasn't been able to get by military means.'

The next day, Tuesday, produced a crisis. Nasser said he would take up some of the points which had been raised by Menzies and try to explain the Egyptian attitude. Dulles had said that the canal must be insulated from the politics of any one nation (that was included in the resolution of the eighteen). 'But how can this be done?' asked Nasser. 'It is a part of Egypt. Dulles is misusing words. Was the London conference a technical one? Are the proposals you have brought me technical proposals? No; both the conference and proposals are political.' Nasser referred to all the threats of economic sanctions and military action. What were those, he asked, if not political?

Nasser said Menzies had talked about international cooperation, and he agreed about cooperation but rejected domination.

You talk about the need for trust, but trust is a two-way traffic. I have read a statement by Sir Anthony Eden, or it may have been by Mr Dulles, that he didn't trust Gamal Abdel Nasser. I must confess that I don't trust them either — I am also prepared to say that I don't trust the proposed users' committee. They didn't trust me to run the canal, and I don't trust them to run it. At the beginning of this meeting you said that nationalization of the canal had created a major change in the situation. What did you mean by that? It has never been possible that there should be a solution which did not reflect the will of the Egyptian people, because the canal is an integral part of Egypt. If there is an attempt to impose a solution, it will mean trouble.

This was the spark which touched off the crisis. Menzies said: 'Ah! If you think a solution involving a new board to run the canal is going to cause trouble, we are going to have to face trouble whatever happens. If there is an agreement to create a users' committee you say there will be trouble, but if there is no such agreement I can assure you that there will be trouble.' Menzies leaned across the table towards Nasser to make the point more emphatic, and this annoyed Nasser. 'All right,' he said, 'so there is going to be trouble either way. If I accept your proposals the trouble will come from my people, and if I don't accept the trouble will come from you. So there is nothing more to be said.' Menzies replaced his papers in their folder as a gesture of finality.

Loy Henderson stepped in to try to save the situation. 'Mr President,' he said, 'I don't think Mr Menzies meant what he said as a threat.' Dr Ardalan hastened to add that he wished to dissociate himself from any threat. 'I must explain that my being represented on this committee does not mean that Iran has any intention of imposing any solution on Egypt. Iran will not agree to anything which detracts from Egyptian sovereignty.' Then it was the turn of the Ethiopian delegate: 'My government only took part in the London conference,' he said, 'because it wanted to help in finding a solution to the crisis. All we want to do is to find a way of reconciling freedom of navigation in the canal with Egyptian sovereignty. My personal aim in coming to Cairo has been to learn the Egyptian point of view.' 'And that,' said Nasser, 'is why I was willing to receive you.'

Then it was Loy Henderson's turn:

I want to explain that the United States is not a colonial power. Our policy has been against colonization since independence. We could never agree to join any colonialist arrangement, and if the American government had thought that the purpose of this committee was to impose a solution on Egypt we would not have taken part in it. Our only wish is to reach a solution that is compatible with Egypt's full exercise of its sovereignty.

The Swedish delegate spoke in similar terms, so Menzies was left isolated.

The last meeting took place in the evening of Wednesday, 6 September. Menzies began by insisting that his remarks at the previous meeting had never been intended as a threat. He said he wanted to clarify two points. The first concerned what he had called 'the insulation of the canal from politics'. His interpretation of this was that there should be some international body to which matters affecting the canal could be referred — something on the lines of the International Court of Justice. And Menzies reminded Nasser, as an example of that court's impartiality, that when the question of Iran's oil had been referred to it the British judge on the court had given judgement against his own government. He said the proposed users' committee would be concerned not with political questions but only with the technical running of the canal. It would be wrong for Egypt to regard this as a foreign body, because its members would be appointed only with the consent of the Egyptian government.

What they were afraid of, Menzies went on, was that either there might be obstacles to freedom and navigation in the canal — some countries forbidden to use it for political reasons (he was obviously thinking of Israel, but didn't mention the name) — or that it might be milked for other purposes. 'If one day your minister of finance wanted to raise money for something like the High Dam, and decided that the best way to do it was to increase the canal tolls, that is what we would describe as political.' The second point he wanted to clarify, said Menzies, was about the users' committee. Nasser had said Egypt was ready to cooperate but refused to be dominated. But how could that committee dominate Egypt? How could twenty or twenty-five men dominate a country? What armies had they got? Nasser said: 'I want to ask you, Mr Menzies, what you mean by politics. We seem to have different interpretations of the word. Is nationalism a part of politics?' (He was really just spinning out a dialogue which he could see was destined to come to its negative end very shortly.) Nasser said he thought the real point at issue was freedom of navigation in the canal, but there was already an agreement about this.

The Swedish Foreign Minister raised a fresh point. 'Suppose,' he said, 'a country wanted to complain because its ships had been denied passage through the canal, and proposed taking its complaint to the International Court. Would Egypt agree to that?' Nasser said, 'Yes, why not?' The Ethiopian delegate said, 'All right, let's do it,' but Menzies stepped in to say that this was outside their brief. They had been sent to explain the principles adopted by the eighteen nations and were not authorized to discuss anything else. He could see that the mission's solidarity was crumbling, so he felt the time had come to bring the meeting to a close. 'Do you think there is any need for another meeting?' he asked Nasser. Nasser said he thought probably not: 'But if you have nothing better to do, come and have lunch with me over the weekend.' So the meeting broke up at 8.45 p.m., and Menzies and his colleagues went back to London to prepare their report.[3]

While the conference was in session there had been a great deal of argument over the role of the canal pilots. There were more than two hundred of these, mostly French and British, though Egypt had for years been pressing the company to employ more Egyptians and at the time of nationalization their number had risen to forty. Knowing that British and French pilots were being encouraged by their governments to resign, as one way of proving Egypt's incompetence to run the canal, the new Canal Authority was trying to recruit suitable pilots in many European countries. The pay offered was excellent, and many applications were received at Egyptian embassies, among the applicants being three admirals, one each from Spain, Portugal and Italy. But on August 27 the new authority was able to publish a glowing report on the results of its first month of operations. Not only was traffic in the canal working smoothly, but its volume was up by fifteen per cent over the previous month. Mahmoud Younis was the hero of the hour.

¹ Nasser came back to Cairo from Alexandria to meet the mission, but as his house was in the hands of the builders he went to stay at the former headquarters of the Revolutionary Command Council at the northern tip of Gezira Island. One of the many plots to assassinate Nasser involved a French commando team going in rubber boats from the French embassy, a short distance away on the west bank of the Nile, and destroying the Revolutionary Command Council building. This was scheduled for 15 September, the original date for Musketeer I, but was not implemented.

² The following passages are based on the unpublished minutes of the Menzies Mission's meetings in Cairo.

³ Shortly before the Menzies Mission arrived a spy-net organized by Britain, headed by James Swinburn, business manager of the British-owned Arab News Agency, was discovered, and two British diplomats who had been in contact with student elements of a religious inclination were expelled. In both cases the idea seems to have been to encourage rioting in the main cities which, on the analogy of what happened in 1882, might provide an excuse for foreign military intervention.

14

REASSURING THE
SAUDIS

ALTHOUGH SUPPORT for Egypt throughout the Arab world all this time remained at its highest pitch and, on the surface, virtually unanimous, there were some who were hesitant or doubtful. One such was King Saud. He was offended because he had not been consulted over a major decision taken by someone who was supposed to be an ally — a decision which could well have involved his country in war. He, and all leading members of the royal family, felt neglected, and this prompted uneasy (but unspoken) suspicions that perhaps this neglect reflected their true stature on the international stage. They wanted reassurance. This is something that the royal family and Saudi Arabia are always seeking — to be kept informed, to be asked for advice, to be flattered. But, alas, such reassurance is something which not all the money in the world can buy.

True, King Saud was prompt with a message to Nasser conveying his unequivocal backing for nationalization, and he followed this up with a letter (which, like almost all communications from the same source, bears no date) informing Nasser that the Saudi Foreign Minister had been instructed to summon the American ambassador and draw his attention to the dangers of the situation in which Britain and France were striving to mobilize world public opinion against Egypt. The ambassador was told how important it was that Dulles should not join forces with Britain and France or encourage them. America should behave in a constructive way. 'Brother Feisal sent me the following report,' the letter went on:

> Sheikh Yusuf Yassin [Deputy Foreign Minister: Prince Feisal was Prime Minister] met the American ambassador who showed him a letter from Dulles which reads: 'Your Majesty knows that the United States has agreed with Britain and France to call a conference in London on 16 August about the canal. I want your Majesty to

know that the United States has pressed on the convening governments to name Saudi Arabia as one of those countries which should
be invited to attend, but unfortunately they have said that Saudi
Arabia does not meet the criteria they have laid down for attendance.' The American ambassador told Feisal that he would like to
know the wishes of your Majesty's government. Does he still wish
to take part in the conference? If he does, the United States will insist
on his being sent an invitation.

Feisal's report went on to say that he had told the ambassador
that the struggle over nationalization was a matter of vital importance to the kingdom.

Your Majesty has heard all that was being said about the possible use
of force, and believes it would lead to horrible and unpredictable
consequences, because the Soviet Union would be sure to intervene
if Britain and France did. So it is now up to you, the Americans, to
exercise moderation and not to go along with the ambitions and
greed of the British and French. Your Majesty knows that what
really interests the world is freedom of navigation in the canal, and
that your Majesty is prepared to use your good offices with our
brothers, the Egyptians. We conveyed to the ambassador, on behalf
of your Majesty, two points. First, that if force was used the Soviet
Union would intervene directly in the area. Second, that if force was
not used, the Soviet Union would emerge as Egypt's main backer,
and this would give the Russians enormous moral influence. For
these reasons the situation is an extremely dangerous one. We must
be prepared to compete with the Russians in maintaining a friendly
influence in Egypt.

Feisal reported that the ambassador had given Sheikh Yusuf
Yassin a great deal of important information. He said that the
Americans wished to uphold Egypt's sovereign rights in the canal,
but hoped to see some international system established there. The
ambassador did not think that the British would use force and
confirmed that Eisenhower was using all his influence to prevent
Eden from doing anything rash. But the fear was that Egypt might
take some provocative step, like interfering with British shipping in
the canal, or somehow subjecting Eden to insults or humiliation.
'We think,' said Feisal, 'that you should write to your brother,
President Gamal, to tell him that.' Concluding this long letter,
King Saud wrote: 'My dear friend, this is what I have learned from

my brother Feisal. I want you to know that your cause is our cause. We are sure that you will act with your customary wisdom. But there is one thing I must ask you. Do you think we should insist on the Americans' arranging a place for us at the London conference? Would this be in the interest of Egypt? Please reply urgently.' Nasser was not keen on the idea, so Saudi Arabia did not attend. So the matter ended, without America's generous sponsorship being put to the test.

In another letter, also undated, King Saud instructed his ambassador to inform Nasser 'immediately' that the position being taken up by Britain and France was so disturbing that it had deprived him of sleep for four days and nights. The letter continued:

> We have decided to postpone our official visit to Indonesia so that we can remain near our dear brother, and so that we can consult together and cooperate in this crisis, which is not simply a crisis for Egypt but one which affects us equally. We have again been in touch with the Americans, and are pressing our views on them. We beg of you, my dear brother, to let us know what your plans are, so that we may understand the situation. We are standing shoulder to shoulder with you, so tell us what you intend.

Under this almost daily barrage of demands to be consulted Nasser felt that a personal contact was necessary. So he decided to go to Saudi Arabia on 23 September. The Saudis suggested that he and the King should meet at Dahran rather than Riyadh; the choice of the oil capital as venue would have a symbolic significance. Nasser welcomed the idea. For the Saudis the presence in the kingdom of Nasser, now the principal figure on the international stage, would enhance their prestige. At Nasser's suggestion they were to be joined by President Quwatli.

In Dahran Nasser was greeted by tumultuous scenes. It was more than a hero's welcome, proving that even in this American-dominated outpost on the Gulf, Arab nationalism had as deep roots as anywhere else. At one stage the crowds became so pressing that Feisal and some of the other princes had to link hands to act as a bodyguard. It was embarrassing for Nasser, because everyone knew that the people were there to cheer him, not their King, so he made a point of grasping Saud's hand demonstratively.

The serious talks took place after they had moved from Dahran to Riyadh. Nasser had to listen to a string of complaints. Apart from the perennial matter of not being consulted, the Saudis expressed considerable annoyance at the huge sums of money they were paying out without getting any dividends. Jordan, they said, never seemed satisfied, and the Syrians ought, after all, to be self-supporting. And now America had sent McCloy of the Chase Manhattan Bank with the message that Britain had asked Washington to put pressure on the oil companies to suspend royalty payments to the Saudis for six months, so that they would have less money to spend on the various activities they were sponsoring in the Arab world.

Coming back to the question of consultation, the Saudis stressed that the canal was a part of the broader Middle East oil complex, and that nationalization had raised a general principle which had far-reaching implications for Saudi Arabia. Already some irresponsible elements were talking about nationalizing the entire Middle East oil industry, and there was talk in Syria, and even in Egypt, in favour of cutting the oil pipelines from Saudi Arabia, should there be a military attack. If that was done, how were the Saudis expected to go on paying all their clamorous clients? The Saudis were also worried because the growing hostility to the Hashemites threatened to bring the whole institution of monarchy into disrepute.

In Riyadh, as in Dahran, it was no use pretending that it was not Nasser who was the man the crowds wanted to see, rather than his hosts. Feisal felt he had to give a warning. 'You must beware of stirring up the mob,' he said to Nasser. 'Brother Gamal, the mob is a fickle and unprincipled force. They are like a wild beast. If you let them out of their cage you will never be able to get them back in again. We could all become hostages to the mob.'

By this time Dulles's pet scheme for a Canal Users' Association (SCUA) had been launched, and the Saudis had been asked to use their influence with Nasser to get him to accept it, though obviously this was something he could not do. The Saudis warned Nasser about the danger of alienating the Americans. Egypt, they said, might find itself threatened with an attack by Israel as well as by Britain and France.

It was not easy to decide how much significance should be attached to such warnings. The Saudis have always preferred hints and nuances to direct statements and an *abba* (a cloak) is draped over their every utterance. The relationship between the two brothers, Saud, the King, and Feisal, the Prime Minister, could also be deceptive. In the presence of visitors, Feisal sat at his brother's feet, apparently hanging on his every word and awaiting his orders. But this performance was no more than make-believe.

Nasser got the impression that Saud was bewildered by his visit. It had produced scenes the like of which he had never witnessed before. Here was the symbol of the new forces in the Arab world being received everywhere with rapture. It represented a change in the established order of things which Saud did not like at all, and which he felt boded ill for the future.

Saud was not the only monarch to hasten to Egypt's aid with noble words. A letter from King Hussein of Jordan dated 29 September to Nasser read:

> We wish to assure our brother that Jordan, even though subject to aggression, will stand up to the barbarism of the Jews and to the reactionary design of those who are plotting mischief against us. Jordan will do everything in its power to hasten the day when the Arabs can rid themselves of the evil thing that has been planted by imperialism in the heart of our lands. We have prepared ourselves for a long battle between the Arabs and our common enemy. This is a battle that will demand patience.

The Hashemites are great spinners of words.

Light relief, much needed at this time, was provided by a letter from the Prime Minister of Libya, Mustapha Ben Halim. He said he had been talking to the Under-Secretary at the Italian Ministry of Foreign Affairs and had told him that Italy must support the Egyptian case. 'We have used our influence,' he wrote, 'and so are surprised to learn that you are not happy about the attitude that has been adopted by Italy at the London conference. This shocks us, because we thought we had done much to mobilize Italian opinion. So we beg you, Mr President, to take action regarding this diplomat who ignores our activities.'

15

OVER TO THE
UNITED NATIONS

'AFTER NASSER HAD AGREED to meet the Menzies Mission in Cairo in September,' Selwyn Lloyd wrote in his book *Suez 1956: A Personal Account*, 'I told Dulles that I felt strongly that if Nasser rejected our proposals we ought to go to the Security Council straight away.' Those proposals had now been rejected, but Dulles came up with a device which, though this was not admitted at the time, was designed as a delaying action rather than a serious blueprint for action. This was the Suez Canal Users' Association (SCUA), by which those nations which used the canal should combine to manage it themselves, hiring the pilots and collecting the tolls. Although almost immediately after selling this device to the British and French governments Dulles emasculated it, in their eyes, by announcing on 13 September that there was no intention 'to shoot our way through the canal', it led to a second London conference, attended by representatives of the eighteen nations which had sponsored the proposals put to Nasser by the Menzies Mission.

This opened on 19 September. It was therefore not until 23 September that Britain and France asked for a meeting of the council to be called for 26 September to consider 'the situation created by the unilateral action of the Egyptian government in bringing to an end the system of international cooperation on the Suez Canal which was confirmed and completed by the Suez Canal Convention of 1888.' The following day the Egyptian government tabled a countercomplaint to take into consideration 'actions against Egypt by some powers, particularly France and the United Kingdom, which constitute a danger to international peace and security and are serious violations of the Charter of the United Nations.'

Egypt's ambassador to the United Nations at that time was Omar Lutfi, an able and experienced diplomat of the old school. In a telegram sent on 24 September he reported that he had heard that

Selwyn Lloyd and Pineau were expected in New York the following week. It would have to be taken into account that the council
chairman during October would be France. He had not been able to
contact Hammarskjöld, who was away from New York, but he
had spoken to Sobolev, the Russian ambassador to the United
Nations, who thought that Egypt ought to register its own
complaint. Two days later he reported:

> I met Sobolev, who told me that he would object to the discussion of
> the Anglo-French resolution because it dealt with matters outside the
> jurisdiction of the Security Council, this being a purely internal
> Egyptian affair and there being no connexion between nationaliza-
> tion of the Suez Canal Company and the 1888 Convention. I also
> met Cabot Lodge [American ambassador to the United Nations]
> who told me that everything to do with the Suez Canal crisis was in
> the hands of Dulles.

Lloyd arrived in New York on Tuesday 2 October, and the
Security Council began consideration of the two resolutions before
it on the Friday afternoon. In his book, Lloyd reports a meeting he
had with Popovic, the Yugoslav Foreign Minister, on Thursday.
'As usual he was full of charm but I knew that he would be under
orders to help Egypt as much as he could. He did, however, go so
far as to say that Yugoslavia disapproved of the way in which
Nasser had nationalized the canal.' Dr Fawzi, who had now come
to New York to lead the Egyptian delegation, reported back to
Cairo his own meeting with Popovic on the same day: 'We agreed
to coordinate our attitudes both in content and in manner of
presentation. Popovic told me that Tito hopes Egypt will not lose
control of the situation in the United Nations, and become a
football between Moscow and Washington. He said we might find
ourselves in agreement with Russia for the time being, but we
should remain careful.'

In the same telegram Dr Fawzi described a meeting he had had
with Hammarskjöld, who said that, as a result of his recent contacts
with Ben-Gurion, he hoped he might be able to restrain him. Some
days earlier he feared Ben-Gurion was quite out of control, and
there was still a danger that the extremists in Israel would gain the
upper hand. Hammarskjöld said he thought that to begin with
Egypt had come out well from the Suez crisis, but that latterly it

had been losing ground because the Egyptian government was not making any positive suggestions. He was not putting forward any definite suggestions himself as to what should be done, and he thought it would be a mistake to propose a repeat of the Menzies Mission. But one way forward might be to hand the problem over to either the whole Security Council or a part of it, with Egypt added, acting as a committee. But in that case Israel would want to join in because of its interest in the Gulf of Aqaba.

Fawzi had asked Hammarskjöld if he thought Britain and France really wanted to reach an agreement, because if they did not there was no point in their going on wasting their time. Hammarskjöld said he had known Selwyn Lloyd for a long time, and had discussed the situation with him on many occasions. He felt sure that, in spite of all appearances to the contrary, Lloyd genuinely wanted to reach a peaceful solution. He thought it was safe to rule out the possibility of Britain's using force. As for the French, he felt they had enough internal problems to keep them busy.

Fawzi had also met with the Russian Foreign Minister, Shepilov, and had gathered from him that the Soviets were opposed to the idea of the Security Council forming a special sub-committee to consider the Suez crisis. Given the composition of the Council, Shepilov pointed out, the majority on any such committee would inevitably be opposed to Egypt. Shepilov then went on to ask Fawzi's opinion about a rumour that a body called the 'Committee of the Nile' was about to be set up. Fawzi replied that he knew little more than the Russians about this idea, which was but one of many rumours — mostly originated by Egypt's enemies in the hope of spreading confusion — then circulating within the UN. (In the event, the Committee of the Nile never materialized and the rumour was quickly forgotten.)

As for the debate in the Security Council, Shepilov told Fawzi, the Russians thought that it would end in a resolution endorsed by a majority. For this reason, he suggested, it might be better for the Egyptians to try to reach an agreement outside the Council. Since Shepilov was also quite clear that Egypt could not accept any compromise on sovereignty or the ownership of the canal, Fawzi understood him to be hinting that the Soviets might be prepared, if it came to the point, to use their veto to defeat a majority resolution in the Council.

Shepilov asked what Dr Bedawi was doing in Washington. (Dr

Hilmi Bahjat Bedawi, a former minister, a leading authority on international law, now a banker, and highly respected, had been chosen by Nasser as chairman of the board of the new nationalized Suez Canal Authority, and as officials of the old company were still busily lobbying in Washington and other capitals it had seemed appropriate that Dr Bedawi should keep in touch with shipping companies, banks and other interested parties. His movements had been widely reported in the American press.) Fawzi explained his function. Shepilov gave a warning that if the Americans got involved in anything it was not going to be easy to get them out. They wanted to replace Britain and France. Fawzi said Dr Bedawi's mission was essentially to create a favourable climate of opinion, and Shepilov agreed that if it was a matter of tactics it was all right. He thought the Americans disagreed with the British and French only about means, not about ends. They all agreed that the Suez Canal ought to be internationalized. So, without conceding any matters of principle, Egypt's aim should be to persuade the Western states that they were somehow involved in the running of the canal, while ensuring that it really remained under Egyptian control.

Shepilov asked if Egypt would accept the idea of a consultative body, and Fawzi said he thought it could be matter for discussion. Shepilov mentioned the importance of timing in the eyes of Britain, France and America. They did not want Egypt to have sufficient time to prove that it was capable of running the canal efficiently. If this was proved it would make them look extremely foolish in the eyes of world opinion. Shepilov thought that the West was not concerned solely with questions affecting the canal; he could not help asking himself whether Western leaders did not see in this crisis a golden opportunity to get rid of certain people they disliked and cripple certain unwelcome political tendencies.

Ali Sabri was by now also established in New York, where he was running an intelligence outpost. On 5 October he reported that he had contacted Kermit Roosevelt and talked over relations between their two countries since the arms deal. He had told Roosevelt of his belief that Dulles wanted to brand the Egyptians as Russian puppets, and showed him examples of the leaflets being distributed in the Security Council by the Egyptian journalists hostile to Nasser now living in France. Roosevelt said that Egypt ought to be looking for a compromise way out and suggested that Ali Sabri should go to Washington after the meeting of the Security Council to contact people like Allen Dulles.

That same day, Fawzi reported to Nasser on a meeting with Galal Abdu, the Iranian representative. France, being a party to the dispute, had handed over the chairmanship of the Council to Iran, and Abdu was feeling acutely embarrassed at having to preside over these crucial meetings. He was hoping that Entezam, his Foreign Minister, would soon arrive to take over from him. Fawzi told him they did not want him to show any favouritism towards Egypt, but simply to act as a neutral chairman. Abdu put forward the idea of a High Commissioner for the Suez Canal, to represent the maritime nations using the canal, but Fawzi reported that he had talked him out of this.

The next day Fawzi had a meeting with Dulles, who began by saying that he was trying to limit the scope of the debate as much as possible. He had been obliged to accept the British resolution. He told Fawzi (who quoted his exact words in English) 'my credit is almost exhausted'. He could not manage the British and French in the Suez affair as he had been able to over Formosa and Korea. Dulles said he thought the Security Council debate would end on Monday (8 October) and that private informal talks would then start after an interval of two or three days. Fawzi reiterated that Egypt would never accept internationalization of the canal or the participation of any outside elements in its running. Dulles mentioned other problems in the area, such as Palestine and Algeria, and said that it would be impossible for any of them to be tackled as long as the Suez Canal question remained unresolved.

Fawzi reported his impression from the outset of their meeting that Dulles was wanting to discuss the High Dam, and, sure enough, this was what he spoke of next. He said that when he announced his government's refusal to participate in building the dam he had never meant to insult Egypt or to cast doubts on its economy, but quite honestly he had come to the conclusion that this was such a costly undertaking that it would exhaust the Egyptian economy for a long time, and so bring the Americans into odium if they were associated with it, and the Egyptian people were suffering by having to tighten their belts. Dulles said he did not mind if the Russians were prepared to participate in it (which was strange, because nobody had mentioned the Russians, the current idea being simply that Egypt should finance the project through the canal revenues). Dulles agreed that it would be better for Egypt itself to build the dam, because then, if this did lead to any popular resentment, it would be a purely Egyptian affair.

Dulles told Fawzi that he thought some responsible people in Britain and France did not want to see a peaceful solution to the dispute. He thought that negotiations should now be directly among Britain, France, and Egypt, with perhaps some other parties acceptable to all three joining in. He said it was most important, if they were going to move on to real negotiations, to establish certain agreed guidelines and principles. Fawzi noted that Dulles did not insist that his brain-child, the resolution adopted by the eighteen nations at the London conference, should be the basis for negotiations. Dulles suggested that Fawzi and Dr Bedawi might find it helpful to have meetings with the leading legal counsellor at the State Department. Fawzi concluded his telegram by saying he wished to emphasize what Dulles had had to say about Palestine and Algeria, because he felt that when the canal crisis was out of the way the Americans would be ready to discuss these problems with Egypt, and Dulles had hinted at the possibility of meetings for this purpose in Washington.

On 7 October Nasser sent Fawzi a telegram reporting a talk he had had with Krishna Menon, who reported that Britain had accepted an Indian proposal for the canal, but wanted arbitration if differences arose over tolls or discrimination. Nasser said he could accept that. Menon would be putting forward his proposals as an Indian initiative on which other interested parties could build, but in fact they would reflect the Egyptian point of view. Nasser said he didn't know what their final shape would be, as Menon was going to do the drafting on his flight between Cairo and New York. Fawzi should send this back to Cairo as soon as he was given it.

That same day Fawzi met Shepilov and told him that America was going to take a different line from that of Britain and France. Shepilov said it was important to wait and see what the British would do: 'If they allow us to reach a settlement here in New York, it will be all right. But if they do not allow us to do so it will mean they are mobilizing for war.'

On 9 October Fawzi reported that Dulles had asked to see

Popovic the next day and that the latter feared an attempt would be made to pressurize him. The Security Council had by now agreed to continue its debate in secret session, and Fawzi had talked to Hammarskjöld who said that he was uncertain how these meetings, which were to take place in his office, should be arranged. 'I said I left all that entirely to him, but we were willing to attend.' Hammarskjöld said he was worried because Krishna Menon was due to reach New York that night, after calling in at Cairo to see Nasser, and he would probably produce what Hammarskjöld called 'Indian lines'. (In fact Krishna Menon did appear at the Security Council meeting the next day. He was wearing a Kashmiri headdress, round his shoulders, and seemed to expect everyone to applaud his entrance.) Fawzi said he felt that Hammarskjöld was neither optimistic nor pessimistic. They discussed the possible use of Article 51 of the Charter, to insist that Britain should declare outright that it renounced the use of force unless sanctioned by the United Nations. Fawzi reported that Dulles was circulating members of the Security Council with a document justifying his action in withdrawing American backing for the High Dam.

On 10 October Fawzi reported to Nasser on the first secret session of the Security Council. He had had a talk with Lloyd before the meeting opened and had agreed to postpone a statement that he was due to make to the council. When the proceedings started, Lloyd had asked for a forty-eight-hour delay so that he, Pineau and Fawzi could meet and try to formulate a basis for negotiations. Lloyd had also said that he wanted the declaration of principles by the eighteen nations to be tabled, and suggested that Egypt should also table any counterproposals it wished. Fawzi had told the council that Egypt had never received any invitation to real negotiations, only threats. He had then distributed copies of the Suez Canal Authority's first report to the delegates. The representative of France had commented on what he saw as the essential difference between an international administration of the canal and an Egyptian administration; the first would include Egypt, but the second would be purely Egyptian, and this was something to which the eighteen nations could never agree, from both a political and a technical point of view.

Pineau had suggested that he, Lloyd and Fawzi should see Hammarskjöld together after the meeting broke up, which they did, 'and I think we had a good discussion'. The most significant thing was that Lloyd and Pineau had seemed to concede that there was no point in reiterating the declaration of the eighteen nations. When the 1888 Convention was mentioned Fawzi emphasized that Egypt wanted to give even more guarantees over the canal than had been contained in that convention. He was asked what he meant when he talked about cooperation between the Egyptian Canal Authority and the users, and he explained that Egypt had no objection if the users wanted to organize themselves in some way, but it would not negotiate with any group claiming to represent the users. He was asked if Egypt would object if the users collected canal tolls, to which he answered that this would be very strange; they would be taking money from one pocket and putting it into another, and he warned that from now on only ships which had paid their tolls to the new Egyptian Authority would be allowed to pass through the canal. He was next asked if Egypt would object if its users placed their own pilots on their ships. He said there would be no objection as long as it was recognized that it was the Egyptian pilot who was responsible for the ship. Fawzi said that Egypt had gone to great lengths to meet some of the objections that had been raised since nationalization. He was asked what sort of cooperation Egypt had in mind, and Hammarskjöld asked how he thought the Egyptian Authority and the Users' Association could be amalgamated. 'Yes,' said Pineau, 'that is what we want, an omelette.' Fawzi said that the attitude of the two bodies towards the canal was completely different. Lloyd asked whether it could be agreed that there should always be a certain percentage of foreign nationals involved in the running of the canal, and Fawzi said that could probably be arranged.

Pineau said it would be very difficult to have to tell the Israelis that a solution had been found to the Suez Canal problem but nothing done about their problems. Why would not Egypt agree to submit its case to the International Court of Justice or to arbitration? Fawzi said things were complicated enough without dragging in Israel. He commented in his telegram that he had not wished to go into more detail without referring back to Cairo for guidance. He felt it was important, if only from the public relations point of view, that Egypt should present itself in as reasonable and constructive a light as possible.

Later the same day the chairman of Aramco, Terry Duce, who, like many other interested parties, had been haunting the corridors of the United Nations, approached Fawzi and asked whether he would be interested in hearing his company's point of view. He said that he came with the blessing of Dulles, and was speaking on behalf of other major oil companies as well as some of the large banks. He did not know whether this was the right time and place to raise the matter, but he said that they would be happy to enter on negotiations about the canal, leaving the politicians on one side. He emphasized the growing importance of tankers in the industry, even small ones being more reliable than pipelines, which were not suitable over long distances because they were so vulnerable.

Fawzi had met Shepilov before the secret meeting of the Security Council. As usual, his main theme had been that every sort of evil was to be expected from the West. If it had been left to the Russians they would have simply told the West to go to hell, but they had refrained from doing so to avoid making things more difficult for Egypt. They had, however, been obliged to swallow a lot of insults, and at times the Russians felt themselves torn between their responsibilities as a superpower and their friendship towards Egypt. As a superpower they would have liked to use their fists, but as a friend they did not want to make anyone angry. Fawzi had commented that he thought this a very wise approach.

That same afternoon Fawzi had met Krishna Menon, who told him that he had invited Hammarskjöld to dinner with him. Fawzi begged him to stop saying that Egypt had accepted the resolution he was proposing and that this represented Nasser's final word. It was agreed that instead Menon should say that India had reason to believe that if the West accepted the Indian proposal Egypt would follow suit. 'I notice,' reported Fawzi, 'that everyone is fed up with Krishna Menon. Hammarskjöld, Lloyd, Pineau, and Shepilov have all separately told me so. "Why don't we get rid of this man?" Pineau had asked.'

Still on the same day, Fawzi had a talk with William Rountree, the Assistant Secretary of State, and said to him: 'Let's face it, you want to get rid of the present regime in Egypt. That is made quite clear from a reading of your press. And starting with the replacement of Byroade, and the withdrawal of the High Dam offer, all your government's actions have been unfriendly.' When they had moved on to discuss the current crisis Rountree had said the real problem was that Britain and France were desperately afraid for their prestige. They felt that if they failed to pass the present test they would be reduced to the status of second-class powers. 'I hope,' Rountree added, 'that one day you will understand how grateful you should be for the role that is being played by the American President. If you had been on your own you would by now have been involved in a war.'

The next day, Thursday 11 October, saw more repercussions from Krishna Menon's activities. Nasser told Fawzi that the Russian ambassador had been to see him, with the information that Menon had shown Shepilov a proposal which, he said, both Nasser and Selwyn Lloyd had accepted, though Lloyd had asked Menon not to publish it immediately because this would only give the Egyptians the excuse to be more intransigent. Nasser had told the ambassador that he was not aware of having agreed anything. He had discussed general principles with Menon, and had not seen the text of his proposal. Fawzi and Shepilov should keep in touch with each other.

This they were doing, for that day Fawzi reported a surprisingly impractical suggestion from Shepilov, that all member states of the United Nations should be treated as canal users and invited to contribute to the discussions. But Hammarskjöld had already given warning that Israel and the other Arab states were applying to join in the debate, and these proposals for expanding it threatened to turn the Security Council into a circus.

A further telegram from Nasser to Fawzi on 11 October told him to concentrate on one point above all others — weakening SCUA. It was out of the question that there could be any discussion of tolls being paid to SCUA, or of Egypt's accepting technical advice from it, or of giving SCUA the right to insist on the allocation of a fixed proportion of tolls for development.

Replying, Fawzi said he got the impression that Pineau was in a hurry to bring their discussions to an end. He complained of having a lot of parliamentary duties waiting for him back in Paris and said he couldn't stay in New York much longer. Shepilov, on the other hand, said that in spite of all the manoeuvres being resorted to by the Western powers he was ready to talk with them in the Secretary-General's office. But he added that he was fed up with the behaviour of Krishna Menon, who did not seem to realize that the situation was very different from what it had been in London in August. There, with Egypt absent, Menon had tried to perform as spokesman for Egypt and for the Third World as a whole. But now in New York Egypt could speak for itself. Shepilov felt that some of Menon's ideas were dangerous — for example, letting representatives from user countries sit on the board of the new authority would risk giving it an imperialist majority. Fawzi said he thought some of Menon's ideas might prove to be not unacceptable. Shepilov ended by saying that he thought any possibility of military intervention could now be ruled out, as, indeed, could an economic blockade.

At the meeting of the three foreign ministers that day in Hammarskjöld's office Fawzi suggested that they should put on record the points that had been discussed, and that Hammarskjöld should draw up minutes of the meeting, to be submitted to each of them for emendation if necessary. This was agreed to. Lloyd said the main requirement was how to find some substitute for the declaration of the eighteen, but warned that this would have to be found within the next twenty-four hours. There must either be agreement on the original declaration, or some modification to it, or they must announce their disagreement. Lloyd wanted to preserve the 1888 Convention, but accepted the opinion of legal experts that Article 8 could be dropped.[1] Fawzi agreed that the article had always been a dead letter and ought not to be there.

Lloyd and Pineau asked Fawzi if Egypt intended to cooperate with SCUA. Fawzi said he was not aware that that body had ever been born. Lloyd said angrily that it most certainly had been born. Fawzi said, 'You never told me whether it was a boy or a girl.' Lloyd was not amused. 'It was born to live,' he said crossly. 'I changed the subject,' said Fawzi, 'because I felt that a sense of humour was not Lloyd's strong point.' So they went on to discuss the percentage of canal revenues that should be devoted to improvements.

After the meeting Hammarskjöld told Fawzi he thought that Lloyd was trying to understand the situation and to show flexibility, but that Pineau was doing his best to complicate matters. He suggested Fawzi should concentrate his efforts on Pineau, instead of trying to drive a wedge between Lloyd and Pineau, which could prove dangerous. Fawzi met Dulles that afternoon, who said he thought they had reached a critical stage at which something positive might be achieved. The French, he said, were spoiling for a fight and trying hard to round up allies, but the British knew that if they were pushed into a showdown the sole burden would be on them. 'It seems to me,' concluded Fawzi, 'that Dulles may know more than he is prepared to tell me.'

The next day, Friday 12 October, Fawzi reported a meeting with Eugene Black, who had suggested that the World Bank had still a role to play. It could, he said, collect the canal tolls, add some loans of its own, and in this way finance the High Dam. At the morning meeting in the Secretary-General's office there was no agreement on the minutes of the previous meeting prepared by Hammarskjöld, and it was accepted that each of them had better make his own minutes. It was obvious, said Fawzi, that Lloyd and Pineau were now regretting having weakened on the resolution of the eighteen, for they said that this was still their government's policy. Fawzi said that if this was so they would find themselves back where they had started from. Lloyd and Pineau said they were willing to discuss other proposals with him, but gave a warning that by so doing they would be in no way committing their governments. Fawzi said he could see a look of disgust on Pineau's face.

After the meeting Hammarskjöld told Fawzi he thought that every time Lloyd made a tentative step forward towards a reasonable solution, Pineau hauled him back, telling him to stand firm. At the afternoon session Pineau said he had instructions from his government to stick to the resolution of the eighteen, but that if Egypt had any alternative proposals to make he would take them back with him to Paris. If his government found them useful they would consider them; if not they would abide by the resolution of the eighteen. Pineau added that France and Britain might decide to submit written questions to the Egyptian government, requiring written answers. Lloyd said that if no agreement was reached now they would be submitting their resolution to the Security Council to be voted on.

In reply Fawzi reminded Lloyd that he had agreed earlier that Egypt could never be expected to accept the resolution of the eighteen. And what, he asked, was this talk about written questions? It was a new and quite impossible suggestion. Egypt was not going to sit for an examination, waiting to be told by the examiners if it had passed or failed. He said Egypt had never dodged any of the questions that had been put to it. After the meeting Hammarskjöld spoke very critically of Pineau. He said he had at one point noticed that Fawzi was becoming extremely impatient with Pineau, as indeed he himself was, but he thought it was always a mistake — almost an admission of defeat — to display anger. Finally, Hammarskjöld complained of the way Krishna Menon was complicating things.

The British and French then acted on Lloyd's threat and put the issue to the vote in the Security Council. In fact two resolutions were put before the Council and there were two votes. The first resolution was based on the so-called 'six principles' which had been adopted by the London conference. The principles were all very general and, despite some misgivings, the Egyptians found them unexceptionable; this resolution was, therefore, passed by the Council. But the British and the French had then pressed on and insisted that a vote also be taken on the resolution of the eighteen: this the Soviets duly vetoed.

This was followed by another secret session of the Security Council at which Pineau had been in the chair (France had replaced Iran following the Soviet veto). Pineau reported that the meetings in the Secretary-General's office had taken place in a cordial atmosphere. He said the talks had been exploratory in character, aimed at trying to find some points of contact between the parties. Hammarskjöld had drawn up a memorandum in two columns, headed 'Requirements' and 'Arrangements', the first listing the demands put forward by all parties concerned, and the second ways by which these might be attained. Hammarskjöld asked the council not to pay too close attention to the exact wording of the memorandum, because it had been written in considerable haste.

Fawzi approved Hammarskjöld's summary. Lloyd agreed that the atmosphere in which their talks had been held could be described as cordial, but insisted that difficulties still remained. Much the most important thing now was to define the items in the Requirements column. For the British government the most promising formula was still the resolution of the eighteen, but they were open to other suggestions and hoped that in the coming days Egypt would be able to state in writing how it thought the desired agreement could be reached. Pineau said he agreed with Lloyd that it was better at that point not to get involved in detail, for example, whether the tolls could be collected by the users. Fawzi intervened to say that Egypt could only accept SCUA as a customer, paying tolls to Egypt, not collecting them for itself. Dulles said he thought reaching an agreement would take a long time, and Shepilov said he thought a good first step had been taken by the three foreign ministers. Lloyd said he hoped Egypt would make acceptable interim arrangements for running the canal. Spaak, the Belgian delegate, wanted all parties to give a pledge not to take any steps that could prejudice negotiations.

Lloyd came up to Fawzi after the council meeting and said he thought things were moving in the right direction. He said he would do his best to keep things under control. Shepilov, whom Fawzi also saw after the meeting, warned him to be on his guard because there were some people who were unhappy about the way events were developing. Pineau, he said, was still trying to throw a spanner in the works, and Krishna Menon was annoyed because the sort of complicated situation had not yet arisen which he would be called upon to sort out. 'We will stand by you,' said Shepilov, 'and do what you want us to do, even if you don't want us to table a resolution.' He asked what Egypt was getting financially out of the canal, and Fawzi told him the answer was that Egypt was getting nothing at all. Shepilov congratulated Fawzi on Egypt's performance. 'You have been patient,' he said. 'Time is on your side. We have surmounted many difficulties, and Egypt has won the battle.'

The following day, Saturday 13 October, Krishna Menon's anger reached boiling point. He met Ali Sabri in the Waldorf Astoria and complained that he was being deliberately excluded from the meetings in the Secretary-General's office, and said he held Fawzi and Hammarskjöld responsible for this outrage. 'Who are Fawzi and Hammarskjöld?' he exploded. 'Hammarskjöld is just a Swedish edition of Fawzi, and Fawzi is just an Egyptian edition of Hammarskjöld. Both of them are extremely dim and second-rate.' He then rushed off to the Security Council, where he installed himself in the Indian delegate's seat. He scribbled something on a piece of paper and passed it across to Fawzi, saying, 'Kindly send this to your President in cipher.' The message was that he asked Nasser's permission to leave New York because negotiations were now confined to three or four people meeting in the Secretary-General's office. 'Everybody tells me that Dr Fawzi is behind my exclusion,' the message ended. Fawzi duly had the message encoded and sent off, but without any priority.

Popovic reported a message from Tito, recommending the new Canal Authority to come up with new plans for enlarging and improving the canal, even if this meant adapting some of the former company's plans. Popovic said Dulles had told him he felt it was time for Egypt to make a great effort to be constructive, so that nobody could accuse it of not having been helpful. 'If Egypt has anything to contribute this should be done now; otherwise it will be too late,' had been Dulles's advice.

Hammarskjöld the same day asked for a private meeting with Fawzi, to whom he showed a list of topics he wanted to raise on his own responsibility at their meeting that day. He said he wanted to escape from the atmosphere of crisis which had marred their meeting the day before. Fawzi said he had no objection, but commented that, although not all the points raised by Hammarskjöld were in line with the Egyptian point of view, he thought it best to keep in with Hammarskjöld, especially as events seemed to be moving towards a new crisis. Hammarskjöld told Fawzi he had on the previous day pointed out to Dulles that the situation had deteriorated owing to Pineau's obstinacy, and asked if some pressure could not be put on him. Fawzi assured Hammarskjöld that it would be pointless for the resolution of the eighteen to be tabled; if it was, this would only lead to recriminations. Hammarskjöld said he had Krishna Menon coming to lunch with him. 'How can we explain politely to him that we are quite prepared to survive his threat to go back to India?' Fawzi said that at the foreign ministers' meeting that day Lloyd and Pineau had interrupted the meeting because they wanted a private consultation. They went over to a window and whispered together, but Fawzi had not heard what they were talking about. He described Pineau's mood that morning as 'very louche — less arrogant but more mysterious.'

On the 14th Hammarskjöld said he had talked with Pineau and Lloyd and they had agreed to leave it to him to make a summary of their discussions, setting out the points of agreement and disagreement, and on that basis drawing up an agenda for their next meeting. He felt their discussions had made a good start, and he had never expected agreement to be reached as a result of one session. He was accordingly thinking in terms of a second round of talks to be held at United Nations headquarters in Geneva in about a fortnight's time. By then he would hope to have the British and French comments on his memorandum. Their next meeting could therefore be expected some time between 28 and 31 October.

It was during the Security Council's debate that Harry Kearn of

Newsweek told Fawzi that the Supreme Commander had been appointed for the Anglo-French forces being assembled in the Mediterranean and that his name was Keightley. This was the first time we had heard that name.

Before leaving for Cairo on 19 October Fawzi was handed a memorandum by Hammarskjöld in which he said that the forthcoming meeting in Geneva was intended to prepare the basis for formal negotiations. He showed Fawzi the draft of a memorandum he was proposing to send to Lloyd and Pineau, both of whom had now left New York, in which he said that he felt that the Egyptian point of view had been sufficiently clarified, and Egypt had shown sufficient goodwill, for there to be adequate grounds for serious negotiations. He added that Krishna Menon's intervention had been confused and confusing. Hammarskjöld was very annoyed by the stories being put out in London and Paris to the effect that Egypt had not come up with any fresh proposals, and by reports in American newspapers about warlike preparations in Britain. Hammarskjöld had lunch with Fawzi just before he left and brought a message from Dulles denouncing all the 'rubbish' that had appeared in *The New York Times* and other papers that there were plans to 'put teeth into SCUA' as part of a preparation to invade Egypt. Dulles said he had asked one of his assistants to assure Ahmed Hussein in Washington that there was no truth in reports that the American government was unhappy at the way the debate in the Security Council had gone.

As October entered its final week Nasser had every reason to suppose that events were moving very much as he had forecast when he sat down to write his appreciation of the situation before committing himself to the nationalization of the canal. Despite the fact that British and French forces were continuing to mass in the eastern Mediterranean, it seemed ever more unlikely that they would be used. Dulles had recovered from his initial outrage and was now uttering words of reassurance rather than threats. The Soviet Union had given unequivocal support and the debates at the UN had provided ample evidence that Egypt had been successful in mobilizing world opinion.

If it ever crossed Nasser's mind that he had been over-hasty in devoting only two lines of his appreciation to Ben-Gurion, he could have looked for reassurance to a memorandum which the intelligence department had drawn up at the beginning of October. After expressing the belief that 'following Egypt's initial successes (failure of the Menzies Mission, etc.) the West will try to concentrate on trying to isolate Egypt from the rest of the Arab world,' the memorandum went on to consider the attitude of Israel:

a) Criticism by Israel of actions by Egypt since nationalization has been very restrained. Many recent broadcasts have emphasized that Israel should not allow itself to be used as a catspaw by the imperialist powers.

b) In spite of pressure from Britain and France to take part in projected military measures against Egypt Israel has up till now adopted a position of neutrality, and has kept its borders more or less quiet.

c) This restraint may be the result of pressure from America, which does not wish to see a war between Israel and the Arabs, which could only benefit Britain and France.

d) According to our reports public opinion in Israel is against getting involved in the present conflict, its only interest in this being to try to secure freedom for Israeli shipping to pass through the canal. It should be noted that the Israeli authorities revealed a British plan to use Israel as a weapon with which to frighten the Arabs, and there is consequently a campaign in the press against Britain. It should also be noted that for the first time a statement by the Israeli communist party was allowed to be broadcast over the government radio. This demanded that Israel should keep out of all conflicts among Egypt, Britain, and France.

Three weeks later there were no grounds for believing that any of these assumptions had changed. Indeed, it seemed as if Nasser and his colleagues could now look forward to a breathing space of a week or so before negotiations were resumed in Geneva. But before that week was out it was to become apparent just how drastically Nasser had underestimated his opponents' capacity for folly.

---

[1] This article gives 'the agents of the signatory powers in Egypt "the right to" proceed to the necessary verifications' in the event of any threat to freedom of navigation in the canal.

16

THE CAMPAIGN THAT
NEVER WAS

ON MONDAY 28 OCTOBER I was due to dine with the newly appointed Greek ambassador at the Mena House Hotel, near the Pyramids. I had recently returned from New York, where I had been watching events, and the Greeks, both at the London conference and at the United Nations, had adopted a sympathetic line towards Egypt. We arrived early, at about 6 p.m., so that I could get back to deal with the day's news. But hardly had we reached the hotel when I was summoned to the telephone; a call from Nasser had been transferred to me there from my office. 'Something very strange is happening,' he said. 'The Israelis are in Sinai and they seem to be fighting the sands, because they are occupying one empty position after another. We have been monitoring closely what's going on, and it looks to us as if all they want to do is to start up sandstorms in the desert. We can't make out what's happening. I suggest you come over.'

I went back and apologized to the ambassador, telling him that I would have to leave. Nasser was in his office with Field Marshal Amer, and he, like all those present, was in a state of bewilderment. Reports were now coming in that Israeli troops were in action near the Suez Canal (this referred to the parachute drop at the Mitla Pass), but this was just another illogical factor in the equation. If this was a war the Israelis would be making use of their air force — no command in its senses pushes its élite troops a hundred miles ahead without air cover — but so far there had been no news of activity in the air, only of tanks and armoured cars operating on the ground. Nor had there been any attack on the Egyptian air force.

It was impossible to make out what was the Israeli objective. There was some idea that the attack in Sinai might be a feint, and that the real thrust would be against Jordan, but this seemed most improbable in view of the British presence there. Another theory was that the parachute drop at Mitla might be to divert attention from a bigger assault in the north of the peninsula, aimed at occupying the Gaza Strip. But the only plausible explanation offered was that Israel now believed Britain and France to be on the point of reaching a settlement with Egypt, so the crisis was over, and a frustrated Israel was trying to settle its own private scores with Egypt in a hurry. It was assumed that Egypt was now facing a clash with Israel alone. This was confirmed by Eisenhower's message to Nasser that the Western powers would keep out of the conflict, and by the knowledge that fresh talks were due to start in Geneva that day which gave good prospects of reaching an agreement. Accordingly before the meeting broke up two orders were given: first, the Second Infantry Brigade, less a battalion, was ordered to cross the canal at Suez and destroy the Israeli parachutists at first light; second, the Fourth Armoured Division was to cross the canal the next morning and prepare for battle in the region of Bir Rod Salem.

On Tuesday morning the Israeli air force made its first appearance in support of the troops who were still in action around Mitla — it later transpired, however, that most of these planes were French Super Mystères, of which sixty, together with their pilots, had been handed over to the Israeli command. But for the first twenty-four hours the plan behind the Israeli attack continued to be mystifying. What had been launched was, it seemed, as much a propaganda war as a shooting one. Much play was made over Israeli radio of the alleged discovery of 100,000 blankets in some of the Egyptian positions that had been overrun. These, and certain other items of equipment, were, it was claimed, of no possible use for the Egyptian army and so must have been installed in preparation for a Russian army which was due to appear on the scene. This canard was eagerly taken up by the media in Britain and America, where the accusation that Egypt was nothing but a Soviet puppet remained the main propaganda theme, as it had been ever since the arms deal.

Later, of course, it would be possible to discern the method behind the apparent Israeli madness. If the threat to the canal, which was to provide the rationale for Anglo-French intervention, was to appear realistic, Israeli forces had to at least make a feint in that direction. This was the true explanation for the assault at Mitla — though it should be added that the Israeli command was dismayed by the zeal of the officer in charge there, Colonel Sharon, who disobeyed orders by pressing the attack on the pass itself and, as a result, lost thirty-eight men killed and one hundred and fifty wounded.

In Cairo, the first indication that some larger design was unfolding also came on Tuesday morning. By 11 o'clock reports had begun to come in of Canberra aircraft carrying out reconnaissance missions over Lake Bardawil in Sinai, Suez and Port Said. These were obviously British planes.[1]

Nasser asked me to go and see Raymond Hare, the American ambassador, to tell him of our observations. Hare suggested that perhaps the British were worried about the fate of their civilian experts in the canal zone, should the fighting spread. When I told Nasser this, he said, 'It's not convincing.' Then at 6 o'clock (4 p.m. London time) came the Anglo-French ultimatum.[2]

News of the ultimatum was received with astonishment bordering on disbelief. Britain and France's collusion with Israel was now staring us in the face, but this was a possibility which had been discounted, because it was assumed that, however determined on a war Eden might be, he would have had some consideration for his friends in Iraq and other Baghdad Pact countries, and for British prestige and interests in the Middle East, all of which would be irreparably damaged if he committed the one unforgivable sin — combining with Israel to attack an Arab country. Nasser found the whole situation made no sense at all — it was, in fact, quite mad.

The ultimatum was due to expire at 6 p.m. on Wednesday 31 October. At that moment Nasser was in his house in Heliopolis receiving the Indonesian ambassador. He heard the sound of bombs dropping and rushed up to the roof. British Canberras and Valiants could be seen in action. Their target was supposed to be Al-Maza, the military aerodrome, but in fact the bombs fell on the nearby international airport. The Israeli assault could at last be explained as part of a concerted plan, aimed at luring Egyptian forces into Sinai, thereby leaving the canal area unprotected, allowing it to be occupied by the Anglo-French forces and so opening the way for an advance on Cairo.

Nasser left his house and went to the office of the Commander-in-Chief, where he found a confusion of men and ideas, everyone talking at the same time as in a *dowar*. He called the meeting to order. Salah Salem, one of the original Free Officers group, took the floor. 'Gamal', he said, 'you have made many sacrifices for your country. Now is the time for you to make one more — one last sacrifice. It is you the British want. What you should do is go to the British embassy and surrender yourself to Trevelyan before he leaves.' 'Is it me they want?' asked Nasser.'Yes,' said Salah Salem, 'that is what Eden has said.' 'Is this supposed to be a private vendetta between Eden and me?' said Nasser. 'If it was only that, I would certainly go and give myself up. But isn't it something bigger than that?'

This cleared the atmosphere, and several more spoke. Dr Fawzi said he was in no position to assess the state of preparedness of the Egyptian armed forces, but if they were having to face Britain and France as well as Israel the best course might well be not to offer any resistance but to seek a political solution. Should that course be chosen he was prepared to do battle at the United Nations. Egypt had just successfully fought one battle there, and he thought they could probably arrange for a ceasefire to be followed by a second equally successful political struggle. Fawzi spoke like the experienced diplomat he was, but his proposal annoyed Nasser. He ordered everyone out of the room except for those directly concerned with military matters.

Nasser came back to the house late at night. By that time he had taken two fundamental decisions. The first was that Egypt must resist force with force. To do otherwise would mean abject surrender as well as the betrayal of the other Arab nations who had given Egypt virtually unanimous support. Moreover, world opinion, already strongly favourable to Egypt, would become even more so when it saw one small country fighting three of the greatest military powers in the world. This could be Egypt's finest hour. So Egypt would fight, and fight to the end. If the army was defeated and Cairo occupied he would organize and lead a guerrilla resistance movement, and he asked me if I was ready to look after the information side of this, broadcasts, leaflets, and so on. That same evening he ordered a small group to reconnoitre a suitable spot in the Delta near Tanta, where he could establish his headquarters, and as soon as this had been done a mobile transmitter was despatched there in preparation.

The second decision was to withdraw from Sinai. The trap into which he had so nearly fallen was now obvious, and he gave the order that the Fourth Armoured Division should be pulled back across the canal. Amer protested that the Egyptian army would never retreat.

'It's not a matter of dying heroically,' said Nasser. 'It's a matter of fighting heroically.' 'But Gamal,' said Amer, 'some months ago when I went to the Military Academy I found the officers were being lectured on how to conduct a withdrawal. I stood up in front of the class and told them that from now on there will be no instruction in any military institution about withdrawal.'

Amer had unfortunately lost his nerve. He went on arguing with Nasser, telling him that in any case even if the order to withdraw was given it would not be obeyed. Nasser made Amer sit down in front of him. 'I am going to be Dayan and you Amer. Let us try to work out what each of us is likely to do.' But Amer remained unconvinced, and Nasser was sorely tempted to dismiss him on the spot. Instead, he went into the operations room, took the telephone and had himself put through to all the senior officers in the Fourth Division, down to battalion level, telling them who he was and explaining to them the absolute necessity of an immediate with-drawal if they were not to be caught in the trap prepared for them. They were not to wait till morning but to start the withdrawal that instant. Mahmoud Younis was instructed to open all the bridges over the canal for them to cross by. It was now about 11 o'clock. Nasser was exhausted, but there was going to be no sleep for him that night. So after taking a shower he went back to command headquarters.

Several other measures had to be taken that day. The assets of British and French subjects were sequestrated and restrictions placed on the movement of some of them. There was no wish to behave harshly to them, many of them having lived in Egypt for a long time. Also it was decided that there would be no declaration of war against Britain and France. This would have meant putting them in the same category as Israel and denying their shipping the use of the canal, which was too big an undertaking at that time. But all measures short of a state of war were to be taken, even though this involved some legal complications. This was a decision that required not only foresight but also much courage.

* * *

On Thursday morning I received a telephone call from Raymond Hare. I naturally assumed it was some political or military aspect of the crisis that he wanted to discuss, but instead he began rather hesitantly: 'Mohamed, there is an embarrassing business I have to talk to you about. You know Professor Cresswell [now seventy-seven years old and the world's leading authority on Islamic architecture, domiciled in Egypt since the end of the First World War, a man of immense dignity as well as learning]? Well, he has an invaluable collection of books and papers, but because he is a British subject these are now under sequestration. If this unique record of Middle East civilization were to be lost it would be a tragedy. The professor has agreed to move all his collection to the American embassy and to sell it to us at a nominal price. Can you help?' I said I would do what I could, knowing how important it was to keep in with the Americans in every possible way, now that they seemed to be distancing themselves further and further from Britain and France. So I told Hare that I would take the matter up with the President. Hare said: 'I know that this is an inconvenient moment, but can I send Cresswell to you? He is here with me now.' I said I could not see him just then, because I was going out.

I went over to Command Headquarters to find out what was going on, and when I got back I remembered that I had done nothing about Cresswell. I was told that the professor was waiting outside my office, and I asked him to come in. As he sat down we could hear the noise of bombs falling. 'I never thought this could happen,' he said. Then the telephone rang; it was Nasser, who asked what I was doing, so I told him about Cresswell and what Hare had asked me to do. He said he would agree to anything I decided, and I should tell Kaissouni about it. Then we went on to talk about other matters. When I put down the telephone I said to Cresswell, 'Professor, your papers are safe.' 'Are you sure you have been given permission?' he asked. 'I was talking to President Nasser,' I said. Cresswell was a good Arabic speaker and so he understood what I had been saying, but still could not believe it. 'Do you mean to say that at a time like this the President was prepared to worry about my papers? Mr Heikal, I am ashamed for my country, but I congratulate you on yours. At a moment of supreme crisis you have shown that you understand what civilization is and what culture means.' When Cresswell had gone I telephoned to Hare to tell him what had happened. Almost all the embassy staff were pressed into service, transporting Cresswell's collection from his house in Gamaliyeh to the embassy, where a lot of it remains to this day, though some parts of it have been transferred to institutions in America, contrary to the undertaking that this rescue operation was performed for the benefit of Egypt. So, in yet another way, America was stepping into the shoes left empty by Britain.

Much has been written about the so-called 'Sinai campaign' of 1956, and it became the basis for the carefully fostered legend of the Israeli command's brilliance and the Israeli army's invincibility. But in fact there was no such thing as a 'Sinai campaign'. The Egyptian forces in Sinai in October 1956 consisted of the Third Infantry Division, divided into three brigade groups, one in Rafah, one in Abu Aweigla, and one in El-Arish, which also contained divisional headquarters. There was one infantry battalion at Sharm el-Sheikh and a light car battalion on the frontier between Kosseima and Ras el-Naqb to act as a warning screen. In the Egyptian-administered Gaza Strip there were two Palestinian battalions and some national guards, but all poorly equipped and detailed for local security. The Third Division's role was purely defensive, to hold any Israeli attack until the main Egyptian force could cross the canal and engage the enemy.

Israel's principal object, once the advance into Sinai had begun, was to keep casualties to a minimum, and the order was therefore given that there was to be no serious engagement with the enemy for the first forty-eight hours. Ben-Gurion and Dayan knew that after that Egypt would be facing its real enemies — Britain and France — though Dayan admits that doubts about Eden's resolution persisted to the last moment, and if the invasion had been called off Israel would have pretended that the Sinai operation was no more than a long-range raid and would have withdrawn all its forces. Nothing was to be done to provoke the Egyptian air force into action because it was feared that it might retaliate with bombing raids on Tel Aviv and other Israeli cities. Ben-Gurion was particularly worried about the threat posed by the Ilyushin 28s. Hence the lack of any air activity in the opening stages of the assault, which had so puzzled the command in Cairo. But of course the Israeli authorities knew that destruction of the Egyptian air force was the task allotted to the RAF. Israel's role in Sinai, in fact, was purely that of a decoy.

The Israelis knew that once the bombardment of Cairo had begun the Fourth Division would have to be pulled back from its move into Sinai. They thought this would take between thirty-six and forty-eight hours to effect, though in the event it was completed in thirty hours. The Israelis therefore faced six Egyptian battalions, divided into three separate locations, unsupported by any air cover, whereas they had the backing not only of their own air force but also of French aircraft flown by French pilots. French units also bombarded Egyptian positions from the sea, though this was intensive rather than accurate, causing only ten casualties. Back in October, General Burns had told Hammarskjöld he was amazed at how thin Egyptian defensive positions in Sinai were, and said he feared this might be a temptation the Israelis would be unable to resist. In fact six brigades which had been in Sinai had been withdrawn earlier in the year so that they could train on their new Russian arms.

The original Israeli operational plan, code-named Kadesh, which Ben-Gurion had ordered Dayan to prepare a year before, had been aimed at clearing Egypt out of Sinai and the Gaza Strip and so securing freedom of navigation for Israeli shipping in the Gulf of Aqaba. But this was never put into operation because, as a result of the collusion with Britain and France and their revised planning, Israeli troops had to be present near the canal to provide the excuse for the ultimatum to 'separate the combatants'; hence the parachute drop at Mitla, and hence the uncharacteristically piecemeal nature of the Israeli attack.

Even so there were at least two major engagements in Sinai in which, in spite of its great superiority in men and weapons, Israel was by no means an easy victor. The Israeli army has always allowed considerable freedom of action to its junior commanders, but there is a point at which initiative becomes insubordination. This point was reached on several occasions in Sinai, notably in the case of the Seventh Armoured Brigade. Its commander, General Samhouni, like the others, knew about Operation Kadesh, but not that this had now been superseded by the collusion and the Anglo-French ultimatum.

In complete disregard of Dayan's orders [to stay put for twenty-four hours and avoid unnecessary casualties], the local commander committed the Seventh Armoured Brigade into the battle twenty-four hours earlier than had been planned. This gross disobedience, involving the formation which contained most of Israel's tanks, put at risk the plan for deceiving the Egyptians as to the scale of the operation. The Egyptians checked this attack, and only after forty-eight hours of hard fighting did resistance in this central area collapse with the capture of Abu Aweigla. Here the Egyptians fought with determination and even managed to mount an armoured counterattack.'[3]

As this account by a historian of the campaign makes clear, the troops of the Egyptian Third Division amply fulfilled their function of performing a delaying action. Their job done, they were ordered to make their way back as best they could, if necessary disguising themselves as bedouin.

But Dayan took Samhouni's insubordination so seriously that he flew to the Seventh Brigade's headquarters and, having publicly upbraided its commander for wasting valuable lives in attacking targets that would have fallen to Israel without bloodshed in a few hours' time, dismissed him from his command. This was, in fact, only one instance of the confusion that was caused by the change of plans. Some units stuck to their orders, others pressed ahead, and there were several occasions when Israeli forces fired on each other and when Israeli planes bombed their own positions on the ground. There were many other examples of confusion. For example, the troops dropped at Mitla were supposed to have been followed by five first-aid trucks, but only one arrived. The battalion which was sent to occupy Sharm el-Sheikh only had just enough fuel to get it there; none to spare if it had been obliged to fight or withdraw. As the American Military Attaché wrote in his report, major errors committed by Israel in Sinai could be attributed to poor planning and poor direction by its high command.

All the same, when the fighting was over, Dayan and his military associates set about creating the myth of the great 'Sinai campaign'. They believed, as did Ben-Gurion, that in the final analysis the army was the only guarantor of Israel's continued survival as a state — that it was a vital ingredient in the structure of the state. Therefore the army had to be glamorized and its failures suppressed. Not only would this propaganda help to keep the nation together, but it would also, so it was hoped, act as a powerful deterrent with the Arabs. The invincibility of the Israeli army, a myth to enhance which even the bungled Sinai operation was pressed into service, became Israel's secret weapon.[4]

Anglo-French plans for the invasion of Egypt, code-named Musketeer I and Musketeer II, were a hotchpotch of political and military contradictions. Almost all of those involved with them were thinking in terms of the war that had ended just over a decade ago. How else can be explained the bombardment of Port Said by the big guns of the British fleet? This undefended city was not Hitler's Atlantic Wall. Or the estimate that it would take up to a week to knock out the Egyptian air force? This was not Goering's Luftwaffe.

In fact, one of the most significant of the decisions taken by Nasser immediately after the bombs started to drop on Cairo was not to engage in any battles in the air. He realized that for Egypt pilots were more important than planes. As he told those who questioned this decision, 'We have 120 pilots fully trained for combat, and another 250 to 260 still in training. If I sent these to fight against the combined air forces of Britain and France I would be mad. At some stage the British and French are going to withdraw — probably after a month or two. But we are going to be in a state of war with Israel for years, and we shall need all the pilots we can get. Planes can be replaced overnight, but it takes years to train a pilot.' This meant that many planes were destroyed on the ground, but others were flown to safety in the Sudan and Saudi Arabia. Pilots whose planes had been lost were ordered to keep out of the danger zone.

Many British and French in key positions expected Nasser to accept the ultimatum. They thought that when the bombs began to drop there would be panic in the streets of Cairo and the other main cities, and they assumed that this would be Nasser's calculation too, and even if he wanted to resist they believed that he would be overruled by others more realistic around him. With their memories of 'Black Saturday' in January 1952, they had visions of mobs looting and burning, of a complete collapse of order. Later Trefor Evans, oriental counsellor at the British embassy, a man who knew Egypt well and who wished the Egyptian people well, confessed to me that he and the ambassador had been astonished by what they considered the totally 'un-Egyptian' behaviour of the people in

Cairo. Everyone kept their nerve; there was no panic and no disorder. The world was treated to the spectacle of a small country faced by infinitely superior strength refusing to lie down in terror as it was supposed to do. The message Nasser received that day from Nehru was typical of world reaction.[5]

In Syria, meanwhile, it will be recollected that the CIA-backed coup had been supposed to take place on Tuesday 29 October, the day of President Quwatli's departure for Moscow. But Colonel Sarraj had got wind of what was afoot and most of those involved were arrested on the Sunday. Michel Ilyan managed to escape across the frontier to Beirut. He arranged to meet his CIA contact on Tuesday morning, just when news of the coordinated attack on Egypt by Britain, France, and Israel was coming in. Ilyan was in a towering rage; he felt tricked and humiliated. He had been prepared to engage in a local conspiracy to topple a president of whom he disapproved and thwart young nationalist officers whom he and his associates feared, but to find that this was apparently part of a much wider plot which would have involved them all in collusion with Israel was more than he could stand. He would happily have murdered the CIA man.

Quwatli called Nasser on the telephone on Tuesday morning, asking for the latest news and offering Syria's help for Egypt in every possible way. Nasser told him that it was still impossible to make out what the enemy were up to. Quwatli said he was going to cancel his visit, but Nasser insisted that he should go. It would be useful for the head of a sister country to be on the spot in Moscow, and if there was anything particular they needed him for they could always get in touch with him, through the Egyptian ambassador. So Quwatli set off, though reluctantly.

The question of what should be done about the Russians had, of course, been very much on Nasser's mind. Many of his aides started asking what the Russians were up to — why were not Egypt's supposed friends rushing to its side? Nasser had to point out to them that though the Russians had sold Egypt arms they were not allies; there was no treaty of mutual defence between the two countries. If he called for active Russian support at that — juncture it would mean bringing in the Red Army; this was not the moment for volunteers. And if the Red Army came in it would require the use of aerodromes and bases.[6] Defence of Egypt would pass out of Egyptian hands, and he himself would no longer have any control over the situation. It would mean a war between Russia and Britain and France, and that would inevitably swing America back to support of the two Western powers instead of taking a stand against them, as it was then doing.

Nor were the Russians the only uncertain quantity in the equation that was taking shape. There was much discussion in Cairo about what game, exactly, the Americans were playing. Their hostility to the tripartite aggression was being made increasingly open and uncompromising, yet it was difficult to understand why Eisenhower had not simply picked up the telephone and ordered Eden to stop. The Americans seemed prepared to let the attack go ahead, presumably knowing that it was bound to fail. When its failure was clear, Britain and France would be left morally bankrupt — and perhaps financially so too — and America would have to bail them out. America would have to rescue Israel from near disaster as well. The United States would be left dominating the world stage, having taken a stand against its friends on grounds of principle. It would be America's supreme moment, and an opportunity which could be taken full advantage of. That, at any rate, was the political pattern which we seemed to see unfolding.

One matter of immediate concern to the Americans was, of course, the security of the pipelines which carried oil from Iraq to the Mediterranean. Kermit Roosevelt managed to get a message to Ali Sabri in Cairo in which he urged the Syrians, through whose territory the pipelines passed, to take especial care that no harm came to them. This message was passed on to Damascus, arriving on the afternoon of 30 October at the office of General Hafez Ismail, then head of the joint Egyptian-Syrian command and later Chief of Staff of the Egyptian army.

As it happened, just half an hour before he received Roosevelt's message, Ismail had been given another message concerning the pipelines with the request that he pass it on to Nasser in Cairo. For the Americans were naturally not the only ones to be aware that all the European countries, not least Britain and France, were desperately vulnerable to an interruption in their oil supplies. Indeed, as has been already mentioned, Eden had warned Khrushchev and Bulganin earlier that year that any such interruption would in itself be a *casus belli*. But in the event it was not Soviet machinations, nor even what Eden saw as Nasser's all-pervading influence, which brought about the disaster which was to cause Britain to endure many months of petrol rationing.

What happened was that elements of the Syrian army, acting on their own initiative, blew up, not the pipeline, which would have been bad enough, but the pumping stations, a far more serious matter.

The Syrian army had undergone great changes in recent years. In the days of the French the officers had been recruited from the traditional feudal families, and those who had risen to the top in the immediate postwar coups d'état, men like Husni Zaim, Sami Hinnawi, and even Adib Shishekli, were eminently corruptible. But now a new type of officer had come into prominence, better educated, from the middle and professional classes, and most of them ardent nationalists and supporters of the idea of a union with Egypt.

These younger officers, led by Abdel Hamid Sarraj, head of the *Deuxième Bureau* and as such the most powerful man in Syria, with plenty of material at his disposal to keep a check on every politician in the country, now saw their ally attacked and their own country unable — or unwilling — to do anything to help. In the days leading up to the invasion Sarraj had been able to pass on valuable intelligence to Cairo, particularly about the French pilots in uniform in Cyprus waiting with their planes to be sent to Israel. But that was not enough; some more positive assistance was now demanded.

So on the morning of 30 October, when news of Israel's incursion into Sinai came through, Sarraj went to the headquarters of the *Troisième Bureau*, responsible for movements, to discuss possible action. He was told that nothing could be done unless there had been a declaration of a state of emergency or of war. Some of the senior officers he spoke to were worried about what could happen if they became involved in an unauthorized conflict — it might jeopardize their pension rights or, if they were so unfortunate as to get killed, their widows' claims to compensation. They recommended Sarraj to go to see the acting President, Nazim el-Qudsi.

Sarraj and his party went to the office of the army Chief of Staff, General Tewfiq Nizamuddin, and asked him where they could find the acting President. They were told he was in a suite at the Orient Palace Hotel, so that became their next port of call. Qudsi received them in his dressing-gown. They put it to him that Syria was Egypt's military ally, and Egypt was now under attack. What steps were being taken to honour their alliance? Qudsi said that before he left for Moscow Quwatli had spoken on the telephone to Nasser who had told him that he didn't require any specific action on the part of Syria. That did not satisfy the officers. 'How can we leave it at that?' they asked. 'If the army does nothing in a situation like this there is a strong likelihood of a coup against the government.' Their temper was not improved on learning that a senior officer, Colonel Killani, Director of Operations, had written to the Iraqi ambassador in Damascus asking for £S20,000 for purposes that could easily be guessed at.

Sarraj said afterwards that he felt as if he and those who thought like him were inhabiting one valley, while all the old-style politicians and officers, who had been left in charge by Quwatli when he went to Moscow, were cut off in a completely different valley. He decided that something would have to be done without waiting for authorization, and that the most useful thing they could do would be to sabotage the West's oil supplies. But to make a real impact this would have to be done on a massive scale. The sort of attacks on the pipelines which were from time to time carried out by bedu raiders were only a minor irritant; the damage could be repaired in a few days. But the pumping-stations were a different matter. With them out of service the West would be in real trouble.

Sarraj did, however, feel that General Ismail should be made aware of what was planned. He found him in a restaurant discussing the military situation with some of his subordinates. When Sarraj explained what he intended to do and asked that Nasser be informed that the pumping stations would soon be destroyed, Ismail recommended that he wait for a reaction from Cairo. But this Sarraj was unwilling to do. He left, and he and his group loaded three tons of explosives onto trucks belonging to army intelligence. By the time Roosevelt's message reached Ismail, he could not, even had he so wished, have done anything about it. Sarraj's men were already on their way out into the desert, maintaining radio silence and beyond any means of recall. At 5 p.m. on 2 November all three pumping stations were destroyed. No oil was to flow between Kirkuk and Tripoli for another six months.

After seeing the sabotage team on its way, Sarraj had returned to Damascus where he received word that the Prime Minister wanted to see him, so he went round to Sabri el-Asali's office where he found several cabinet ministers assembled. However, he was more than a match for them. The Minister of Public Works, Majdeddin Jabiri, said the American ambassador had been to see him to complain that there had apparently been an interruption to the oil supplies. The Prime Minister expressed considerable anxiety that the British might be planning to invade Syria as well as Egypt. He had heard that there was a special brigade which had been detailed for that operation. And though diplomatic relations with Britain had been broken off and the ambassador expelled, the Americans were looking after British interests. There were several American naval vessels lying off Latakia, in constant radio contact with the embassy. It all looked very threatening. The first necessity was for Sarraj to go and see what had happened to the oil pipelines. Sarraj said it was nothing to do with the pipelines. 'According to our information the three pumping-stations have flown away.' 'What do you mean, flown away?' exclaimed Asali. 'They no longer exist,' said Sarraj. 'No longer exist!' shouted Asali. 'I shall resign!' Sarraj said he could do nothing about that.

Hafez Ismail had to report back to Nasser that it was too late to protect the oil supplies. The information had to be passed on to Kermit Roosevelt, and in some ways this was unfortunate, because the Americans still tended to think that Nasser controlled everything that went on in the Arab world, and found it hard to believe that a major step like this could have been taken without his sanction. But in fact in those days everybody in the Arab world was acting on his own initiative; any attempt to coordinate strategy or tactics would have been impossible.

The fact that the British and French forces did not land immediately the ultimatum expired, but instead delayed for a further four days, lost them the chance — and it was only a chance, for the outcome was by no means a foregone conclusion — of occupying the entire length of the canal and so presenting the world with a *fait accompli*. As it was, by the time the landings began, the world had seen the appalling devastation caused in Port Said by the naval bombardment. There were no war correspondents at the front — and indeed no front — at that time, but pictures of the houses and shops reduced to rubble, and of civilians killed, including some particularly striking ones taken by a Swedish photographer, were sent to Beirut and taken to London by the prominent Lebanese businessman, Emile Bustani, who had many friends in Britain. These were shown in the House of Commons and had a considerable impact. Other copies were flown to New York and shown at the United Nations.

The delay also allowed Egypt's most powerful friend, the Soviet Union, a chance to consider what role it should play. The Russians are always reluctant to take up a firm position in support of another country until they have weighed up three factors: is the other party going to stand firm? Is world opinion behind it? And is it likely, if they do intervene, that the opposition will give way? By the time that the Anglo-French forces had actually landed in Suez it had become clear in Moscow that the answer to all three questions was 'yes'.

Initially, of course, the Soviets had been taken by surprise just like everyone else. When President Quwatli arrived in Moscow he had naturally been asked what he knew about the Israeli attack which had been launched the previous day. All he could tell his hosts was that he had spoken to Nasser before leaving but had heard nothing from Cairo or Damascus since. There was to be a meeting between Quwatli and the Soviet leaders in the Kremlin on 31 October, the day on which the ultimatum expired and bombs began to drop on Cairo. Quwatli asked for Marshal Zhukov to be present and was clearly in a state of great agitation when the meeting started. 'They are trying to destroy Egypt!' he shouted. 'It's a conspiracy!' Khrushchev tried to calm him down, and asked him what fresh news he had. But all Quwatli could tell them was that he had tried without much success to listen to Damascus radio.

Khrushchev asked Quwatli what he wanted them to do. 'You ask me what I want!' Quwatli exclaimed, jumping up. 'It's for you to tell me what you are going to do!' Khrushchev tried again to calm him. 'I am asking you what you think is the best way we can help you.' 'Go to the help of Egypt!' said Quwatli. 'But how?' asked Khrushchev. 'With the great Red Army which defeated Hitler,' said Quwatli. Zhukov interposed. He produced a map, and pointed out to Quwatli that if the Red Army was to intervene it would have to go through Iran, Iraq, and Israel, as well as Syria. He asked for more practical suggestions, but Quwatli was at a loss. He went to consult the Egyptian ambassador.

The ambassador, Mohamed el-Kouni[7] exchanged a few words with Khrushchev at a reception on the evening of Friday 2 November. Khrushchev told him that, while the Soviet Union was full of admiration for the heroic resistance Egypt was putting up to aggression, there was unfortunately no way in which it could be helped militarily. 'We are going to mobilize world public opinion,' was the best comfort Khrushchev could offer. Kouni tried to look more pleased than he felt. He and Quwatli reported their impressions of the Russian attitude back to Cairo, and a meeting was held, at which Nasser presided, to consider what line to take. The Russians, it seemed, were open to suggestion, but what could he suggest? It was agreed that a message should be sent to Moscow explaining the whole diplomatic and military situation, the contacts that had been established with other governments, and so on, and leave it to the Russians to decide for themselves on the best course of action.

Four days later, in the early afternoon on Tuesday 6 November, Kouni was summoned to the Ministry of Foreign Affairs to see Shepilov. He was handed the text of the ultimatums that had just been sent to Britain, France, and Israel. 'We have taken a very firm position, Mr Ambassador,' he was told, 'and we shall stand beside you to defeat aggression.'

By then the Red Army had crushed the Hungarian uprising,[8] and the Russians were in a better position to concentrate their attention on the Middle East. They could see that the Suez expedition was a military failure, that the British and French were divided and both angrily disowned by the Americans. World opinion was solidly against them. So it was that the previous night, Monday 5 November, ultimatums in the form of messages emanating from Bulganin were sent to Eden, Mollet, and Ben-Gurion. Those to Eden and Mollet hinted at the use of nuclear weapons against the aggressors, while that to Ben-Gurion was even more menacing: 'Fulfilling the will of others, acting on instructions from abroad, the Israeli government is criminally and irresponsibly playing with the fate of peace, with the fate of its own people. It is sowing hatred for the state of Israel among the peoples of the East such as cannot but make itself felt with regard to the future of Israel and which puts in jeopardy the very existence of Israel as a state.'

There has been a tendency to discount the impact of those Russian warnings. Certainly in Britain the clinching argument which persuaded the Cabinet to accept the idea of a ceasefire for the next day, 6 November, was the drain on sterling, and the American refusal to shore up sterling unless there was a ceasefire. But in Israel Bulganin's message was decisive. According to Golda Meir, Foreign Minister in 1956, Ben-Gurion's speech agreeing to a conditional withdrawal from Sinai was 'definitely made in response to the Soviet threat'. Other Israeli leaders, including Peres and Eban, concurred. As Navon[9] said: 'The Russian threat we took as deadly — physically, militarily. We had information that it was real.'[10]

With the benefit of hindsight it is easy enough to see that the aggression was doomed to failure almost before it began. But at the time Nasser had no means of knowing that the two super-powers were, in their very different ways, about to call a halt to the venture. On Friday 2 November he had gone to Al-Azhar, Cairo's old Islamic university, and broadcast an address to the nation. Egypt, he told them, had always been the graveyard of invaders.[11] The previous day the Egyptian people had been told not only that they were to resist but that they were to be provided with the wherewithal for resistance. In five days a million small arms were distributed. Most of these were antiquated and would not have served much useful purpose, but a tenth of them could have been effective.

Much of the news now coming from the rest of the world was a comfort to Nasser. On Thursday there had been such stormy scenes in the House of Commons, the opposition 'knowing that something very dirty was going on but unable to prove it', that MPs almost came to blows and the Speaker had to suspend the session for half an hour.

The 'something very dirty' was what came to be called *collusion* — the secret arrangement whereby the governments of Britain and France were to coordinate their attacks on Egypt with an attack by Israel. This plan was brought to Eden by General Challe, deputy to General Ely, the French Chief of Staff, on 14 October. The idea was that Israel would be encouraged to attack across Sinai, whereupon Britain and France would 'call on both sides' to withdraw from the canal, the pretext for this being the need to contain the fighting and prevent damage to the canal. This would provide the two governments with the excuse to send in their troops. Eden accepted the idea enthusiastically, but the French and Israelis still had doubts about his resolution, so insisted that the deal should be signed and sealed at a clandestine meeting in a private villa at Sèvres near Paris. This took place in the evening of 22 October and was attended by Ben-Gurion, Dayan, and Peres for Israel; Pineau, Bourges-Maunoury (Minister of Defence), and Abel Thomas (a leading intermediary at the Ministry of Interior for negotiations with Israel) for France; Selwyn Lloyd and Patrick Dean of the Foreign Office for Britain. It was at this meeting that the terms of the ultimatums to be delivered to the two sides were drawn up.

Anthony Nutting, Minister of State at the Foreign Office and so Selwyn Lloyd's deputy, was appalled at the proposal. It would mean, as he was to write later, 'Our traditional friendships with the Arab world were to be discarded; the policy of keeping a balance in arms deliveries as between Israel and the Arab states was to be abandoned; indeed, our whole peace-keeping role in the Middle East was to be changed and we were to take part in a cynical act of aggression, dressing ourselves for the part as firemen or policemen, while making sure that our fire-hoses spouted petrol and not water and that we belaboured with our truncheons the assaulted and not the assaulter.'[12] Nutting resigned his post on 25 October, though his decision was not made public until a week later. Another minister, Sir Edward Boyle of the Treasury, also resigned.

On Sunday there was a mass demonstration in Trafalgar Square, addressed by three former Labour ministers, Aneurin Bevan, Anthony Greenwood, and Edith Summerskill. 'We are stronger than Egypt, but there are other countries stronger than us. Are we prepared to accept for ourselves the logic we are applying to Egypt?' asked Bevan. After the meeting the demonstrators tried to force their way down Whitehall to Downing Street, but were turned back by the police. Eight police were injured and there were many arrests. Nasser watched with fascination films of the Trafalgar Square meeting with the speech of his friend Bevan, and the visible evidence of the strength of opposition to Eden. So by Monday, when the landings actually took place, Nasser could see that their failure was inevitable. All plans for the Egyptian leadership to go underground and preparations for guerrilla war were cancelled. The mobile radio which had been sent to the Delta was transferred to the canal area where it broadcast encouragement to the people most immediately threatened by invasion.

Inevitably in the light of the Natanson affair, once Israel had invaded Sinai the government had to take precautionary measures against the remaining Jews in Egypt, many of whom were stateless. Some of these were interned, others encouraged to leave or had their property sequestrated. Immediately world opinion was mobilized on their behalf. Nahum Goldmann, President of the World Jewish Congress, tried to get a message passed to Nasser about them, as did Nehru and Eisenhower. Nehru's letter was an appeal on behalf of British and French subjects as well as Jews (see Appendix 4).

All this time United Nations headquarters in New York was naturally the scene of intense activity. On 30 October, when the Egyptian representative, Omar Lutfi, told Hammarskjöld of the Israeli attack in Sinai, he was advised to keep his eye on London and Paris. It was there that he might expect to see surprises. There was an emergency meeting of the Security Council the same day, with a six-hour debate on a resolution sponsored by the United States which called on Israel to withdraw its forces behind the armistice lines immediately, and on all member states to refrain from the use of force or the threat of force in the area. This brought a British and French veto, the first in the organization's history.

Two days later, on Thursday 1 November, after the Anglo-French ultimatum had expired and been rejected by Egypt, Lutfi sent a telegram to Nasser reporting a talk he had had with Sobolev. The Russian delegate had received instructions to table as strong a resolution as possible condemning the British and French action. 'We face an emergency,' he said, 'and it should be Egypt's aim to mobilize all friendly African and Asian governments and prepare for action under Article 377 of the Charter ['uniting for peace']', even if that meant a conflict with Hammarskjöld. But in the same telegram Lutfi reported that Hammarskjöld had said he was determined to submit his immediate resignation as Secretary-General. He found it quite unbelievable that two permanent members of the Security Council, both signatories of the 1950 tripartite declaration aimed at guaranteeing peace in the Middle East, should plan and execute such an act of aggression. He wanted me, said Lutfi, to inform you of his intention. When Nasser read this telegram he immediately sent one to Hammarskjöld begging him not to carry out his threat.

Hammarskjöld did not resign. In fact, the following day Lutfi is found reporting Hammarskjöld's deep concern about rumours that Egypt intended to withdraw from the United Nations. (There had been a number of agency messages to this effect.) He said it would be madness if Egypt's sense of frustration led it to take such a course. Lutfi told Hammarskjöld that these rumours were baseless, but he wanted confirmation from Cairo. Hammarskjöld also wanted Cairo to reply to the letter he had sent earlier summarizing the common ground that had emerged after his series of discussions with the British, French, and Egyptian Foreign Ministers. He felt that a quick reply to this letter would be a great help in this crisis. Hammarskjöld followed this up with a written note: 'I have given further thought to what I said to you. I feel it is vitally important to get answers to my questions through quickly. I am also convinced of the enormous impact that a positive reaction by Egypt would have.' Later there was to be another scare — Hammarskjöld complaining that Egypt had not paid its UN dues, and this was giving rise to fresh rumours about an Egyptian withdrawal. Lutfi explained that as America had frozen all Egyptian assets they had not the funds available.

The next day, 3 November, Lutfi reported an approach by the Indian ambassador to the United Nations about a proposal for a UN force to be sent to the canal area to be made up of contingents from the United States (who would provide the air transport), Czechoslovakia, and an Asian country. Hammarskjöld approved the plan. This was the first that Cairo heard of the idea which the Canadian Foreign Minister, Lester Pearson, had been working on, and which emerged as the United Nations Emergency Force (UNEF).

On 4 November it was time for the Security Council to turn its attention to events in Hungary. A vigorously worded resolution was tabled condemning Russia's invasion and the Red Army's crushing of the Nagy government (or 'the reactionary conspiracy against the Hungarian people' as that day's TASS message called it). The Russians felt strongly that, in return for the support they had given Egypt throughout the Suez crisis, Egypt should vote with them at the United Nations. Omar Lutfi reported that the Hungarian question was complicating matters, and asked for instructions. He was told to abstain when it came to a vote. This he did, to the great indignation of the Russians. (When it was all over Cabot

Lodge was to complain bitterly to Fawzi that Egypt had only abstained. Why, he asked, had it not voted against Russia, in the same way that the United States had voted against its allies, Britain and France, when they committed aggression? Britain and France had at least withdrawn from Egypt, which was more than Russia had done from Hungary. When he reported this conversation back to Cairo, in December, Fawzi commented that he had the feeling from talks with his American and Russian colleagues that both super-powers felt they deserved a reward for backing Egypt.)

As negotiations over the composition of UNEF went ahead, Krishna Menon was reported telling Hammarskjöld that Egypt would refuse to accept contingents from any Baghdad Pact country (an obvious reference to Pakistan). Lutfi expressed concern at Menon's fondness for claiming to speak in the name of Egypt. 'Krishna Menon,' he said, 'is a pain in the neck.' A day later Lutfi was able to pass on news of a lunch that Dr Bunche had had with Raphael Gadaon of the Israeli delegation. Gadaon said that Israel's policy was now based on the assumption that Britain and France would refuse to withdraw from the canal on the ground that the UN force was inadequate, in which case Israel would also refuse to withdraw. Fighting would then be resumed. Volunteers from Eastern bloc countries would appear on the scene, and this would completely change attitudes at the United Nations, forcing America back into alliance with Britain, France and Israel. But, by this stage, if the Israelis seriously entertained any such scenario, they were simply whistling in the dark.

---

[1] In these early hours the British were so anxious to preserve the fiction that there was no collusion with Israel that, when one of their small reconnaissance planes crashed in Sinai and Israeli troops went to the rescue, they were warned off.

[2] On the afternoon of 30 October Eden made a statement to the House of Commons: 'As a result of consultations in London today, the United Kingdom and French governments have addressed urgent communications to Egypt and Israel. In these we have called on both sides to stop all warlike action by land, sea, and air forthwith and to withdraw their military forces a distance of ten miles from the canal. Further, in order to separate the belligerents and to guarantee freedom of transit through the canal by the ships of all nations, we have asked the Egyptian government to agree that Anglo-French forces should move temporarily — I repeat temporarily — into key positions at Port Said, Ismailia, and Suez. The governments of Egypt and Israel have been asked to answer this communication within twelve hours. It has been made clear to them that if at the expiration of that

time one or both have not undertaken to comply with those requirements, British and French forces will intervene in whatever strength may be necessary to secure compliance.'

Pineau summoned the Egyptian ambassador to the Quai d'Orsay and tried to oblige him to remain standing while the ultimatum was handed over, but the ambassador pulled up a chair and sat down. The Egyptian ambassador in London was not treated with the same discourtesy, but both ambassadors left the room without accepting the ultimatum.

[3] *Suez: The Double War* by Roy Fullick and Geoffrey Powell (London, 1979) p. 94.

[4] See, for example, Dayan's summing-up: 'The military victory in Sinai brought Israel not only direct gains — freedom of navigation, cessation of terrorism — but, more important, a heightened prestige among friends and enemies. Israel emerged as a state that would be welcomed as a valued friend and ally, and her army was regarded as the strongest in the Middle East. . . . The main change in the situation achieved by Israel, however, was manifested among her Arab neighbours, Israel's readiness to take to the sword to secure her rights at sea and her safety on land, and the capacity of her army to defeat the Egyptian forces, deterred the Arab rulers in the years that followed from renewing their acts of hostility.' Major-General Moshe Dayan, *The Diary of the Sinai Campaign* (London, 1966) p. 206.

[5] 'I need not tell you how deeply shocked we have been at recent developments. The Israeli aggression was bad enough and had to be condemned but much worse has been the ultimatum to Egypt by the UK and France and the subsequent action they are taking. All our sympathies are with you and I am sure that the countries of Asia and Africa and many of the countries even of Europe and America will realize that naked aggression is taking place against Egypt and that the freedom of a country which has recently been liberated from colonialism is in peril. This is a reversal of history which none of us can tolerate.

'The future of the United Nations itself also is at stake. The countries that were associated at Bandung have a special responsibility in this matter.

'I have conveyed my views in firm language to Eden. Also to President Eisenhower and President Tito and asked them to use their influence. I am also communicating with Moscow, Rangoon, Djakarta, Colombo and Karachi.

'In the grave crisis and responsibility that you are facing we send you all our good wishes — Jawaharlal Nehru.'

[6] Later, after the ultimatums to Britain, France, and Israel, Russia did offer volunteers to fight in Egypt, but by now there was no urgent need for them. Not only were volunteers unnecessary, but any suggestion of Russians coming would have antagonized America. Naturally there were many would-be volunteers in Arab countries, and even the President of Lebanon forwarded on to Nasser a letter received from many men of Lebanese origin in South America offering their services.

[7] Mohamed el-Kouni was an experienced diplomat, very able, cultured and hard-working. He had particularly good relations with the American and British ambassadors, Charles Bohlen and Sir William Hayter (who strongly disapproved of the Suez operation and resigned from the diplomatic service not long afterwards). He and his wife were a superb host and hostess. Ever since the arms deal Egypt had been Russia's most favoured foreign nation. (The Russians always have a foreign favourite; after Nasser it was the turn of Castro and then Lumumba, and

more recently Ortega.) As favourites, Egyptians serving at the embassy in Moscow found themselves recipients of many privileges — tickets for the Bolshoi, the best caviar, free furniture, and even antiques. One Egyptian diplomat was able to take back home with him furniture for five rooms.

[8] In the last week of October a popular uprising against the hated communist regime broke out in Budapest and other Hungarian cities. There was heavy fighting during the night of 23 October, and at dawn next day Imre Nagy, formerly imprisoned during the days of Stalinist repression as a 'traitor' and 'Trotskyist', became Prime Minister. He headed an all-party government and promised free elections, and asked for talks to be initiated to arrange for the withdrawal of Soviet troops from Hungary. The Soviet government agreed to talks, but meanwhile built up its forces in the country, and at dawn on 4 November attacked in Budapest and elsewhere, crushing all popular resistance after a few days. Nagy was murdered. On 4 November an emergency session of the Security Council voted on a resolution calling on the Soviet Union to cease all military action immediately and withdraw its troops. This was supported by nine members of the council, but nullified by a Soviet veto. Yugoslavia abstained. In the General Assembly a similar resolution was supported by all except the communist bloc, which voted against, and India and the Arab countries, which abstained.

[9] Yitzhak Navon, Political Secretary to the Prime Minister 1952–63, and later President of Israel 1978–83.

[10] See interviews conducted by Michael Brecher and recorded in his *Decisions in Israel's Foreign Policy* (London, 1974) p. 290.

[11] 'The Nile, graveyard of all invaders' was the title of one of the many popular songs which were sung everywhere at this time. Several were addressed to Nasser, like one which began: 'O Gamal, opener of the door of freedom.' A well-known singer, Abdel-Halim Hafiz, wrote a song which told the whole story of the High Dam. There has probably never been a time when there has been such a spontaneous crop of political and religious songs. They were popular in all Arab countries, though naturally not heard on the radios of Baghdad and Amman. Some of them were actually banned in Saudi Arabia.

[12] Anthony Nutting. *No End of a Lesson: The Story of Suez* (London 1967) p. 94.

17

AMERICA THE ARBITER

SUEZ HAD MANY LOSERS, and two clear victors — President Nasser and the Americans. Britain's attempt to re-establish itself in the area it regarded as peculiarly its own had resulted in disaster, as had France's attempt to sneak in by the back door. So the Americans could see no rivals. Or rather, they had only one rival competing with them for influence, and that was Nasser. Obviously there was now no question of getting rid of him;[1] he was a person who would have to be worked with. But there would be no harm in clipping his wings, and the Americans saw three ways in which this might be done. Egypt might be prevented from returning to Gaza, which would mean that the war had brought Egypt a net loss of territory — a sobering consideration. Secondly, a wedge might be driven between Egypt and Saudi Arabia; and thirdly, the stationing of UN troops in Sinai might result in the opening up of the Gulf of Aqaba to Israeli shipping, if necessary accompanied by additional American guarantees. In their first aim the Americans had to accept failure, but in the other two they were successful, and in achieving the last they sowed the seeds for the war of 1967.

The first UNEF contingents, from Norway and Colombia, arrived in Egypt on 16 November. With them came Hammarskjöld who was eager to settle with the Egyptian government various points in connexion with their future role. Egypt wished from the outset that work should not start on clearing the canal (which had been blocked in several places once the fighting began) until the British and French forces had been completely withdrawn. As there was considerable pressure from the countries which were the canal's main users to get it cleared, this was a very strong bargaining counter for Egypt.

As long as foreign troops remained on Egyptian soil there was always the danger of fighting breaking out again. A telegram from Fawzi in New York reported a meeting with Shepilov on

28 November who had said that, though he thought this was unlikely, it could not be ruled out. But he was understandably
cautious, adding that he did not want 'to sin again', as he had done
in October when he told Fawzi he thought that Britain and France
would definitely not attack. Interestingly, Popovic at the same time
asked Fawzi what he called a personal question — did he think
Russian warnings about a possible resumption of the fighting were
part of a deliberate campaign to frighten Egypt? Fawzi said that, on
the contrary, he thought they were meant as an encouragement.

It was not only Cairo that was receiving warnings from Moscow. At the end of November the Syrians were extremely worried
about reports of troop concentrations in northern Israel, and asked
the Russians if they could check. This they did, and confirmed large
concentrations, especially opposite Nasava and Tabariya, uncom-
fortably close in the light of modern conditions of warfare.
Moscow added that it thought the atmosphere in both the United
States and Israel was favourable for an attack on Syria.
Hammarskjöld's view was that the Russian scare over Syria was
mainly intended to divert attention from the repression that was
still going on in Hungary.[2]

Nasser continued to study the climate of opinion in Britain
closely. On 29 November he recommended Fawzi to take a careful
look at Aneurin Bevan's speech in the House of Commons the day
before, in which he had said that Egypt could not be expected to
negotiate on the future of the canal as long as any occupying troops
were left. In fact Nasser picked up quite a lot of ideas from the
British press. On 1 December he told Fawzi to notice the remarks
of Opposition spokesmen, quoted in the press, to the effect that the
most Britain could expect after the Suez fiasco was a guarantee of
freedom of navigation in the canal. 'Even British public opinion,'
commented Nasser, 'is beginning to realize that concessions which
Egypt might have been prepared to make before the aggression
could not be expected to be made now.' There was a lot of
speculation in the British press about what Nasser was going to do
next, and the *Daily Express* one day published what it claimed to be
an exclusive account of 'Nasser's secret plan' for operations in
southern Arabia. This was a complete invention, but Nasser
thought it interesting. 'Well,' he commented, 'they are now even
supplying us with good ideas!'

The *Daily Express* was not the only one to attribute malevolent new designs to Nasser. On 14 December Fawzi had a meeting in the State Department with Hoover, Murphy, and Rountree, at which Hoover said that his government had reports about Egyptian activities in other Arab countries which might not be known to him or to the Egyptian ambassador, but which no doubt Nasser himself was aware of. These concerned saboteurs in Kuwait, Lebanon, and Israel. 'If your fanatical agents are not stopped,' said Hoover, 'this will end all chances of restoring understanding or stability.' He added that as America could no longer count on getting oil from Arab countries it was now embarking on the biggest programme of exploration for oil the world had ever known and the biggest ever programme for the construction of giant tankers. The sabotage groups he referred to were not Egyptian-inspired, but one consequence of the aggression was that in almost all Arab countries people started to take action on their own initiative, and many of them who did so liked to call themselves 'Nasserites'. Not for the first time the West assumed that all hostile acts were controlled by a lot of buttons on Nasser's desk.

Although the British and French made strenuous efforts to delay their departure from Egypt the odds were heavily stacked against them and the last of their troops left on 22 December. The French took with them a mass of looted hardware, including private cars. They showed a particular fondness for Fords, Mercedes and Plymouths. Getting Israel out of Sinai was to prove a much more difficult task — Hammarskjöld told Fawzi on more than one occasion in December that he thought it would be five times more difficult, particularly to extract them from Gaza.

In a victory address to the Knesset on 7 November Ben-Gurion claimed that 'together with the armistice agreement, the armistice lines between us and Egypt are vanished and dead.' In other words, Sinai and Gaza were now a part of Israel, and to mark the change of ownership went a change of names, the Gulf of Suez becoming the Gulf of Suleiman, Sharm el-Sheikh becoming Ophira, and so on. There was a great deal of officially inspired propaganda aimed at proving that Sinai had never really been part of Egypt. It was claimed that Sinai had always been a part of the Ottoman Empire, not of the Egypt of Mohamed Ali, and that Israel was the heir to the

Ottomans. But Egypt insisted that the United Nations resolution called for a withdrawal by Israel to the frontiers it had before it invaded on 29 October, and refused to be drawn into wasteful quibbles.

As a result of world pressure, exerted through the United Nations and led by America, Israeli troops were compelled to withdraw gradually from most of Sinai, but as late as 16 February 1957 Ben-Gurion told Eisenhower that unless Israel was allowed to keep the civil administration and police authority in the Gaza Strip, and had a guarantee that Israeli shipping could navigate freely in the Gulf of Aqaba, there would be no final withdrawal. This angered Dulles, who told Eisenhower that giving in to Israel 'would almost surely jeopardize the entire Western influence in the Middle East and make it almost certain that virtually all the Middle Eastern countries would feel that the United States policy toward the area was in the last analysis controlled by Jewish influence.' Eisenhower was prepared to go to the extent of stopping not only government grants to Israel but even private gifts as well, estimated at that time to be running at about $40 million a year, with another $60 million from the purchase by Americans of Israeli bonds. He broadcast an explanation of why he was prepared to take this unprecedentedly firm stand against Israel, and on 1 March Golda Meir, the Israeli Foreign Minister, told the General Assembly in New York that Israel was arranging for a 'full and complete withdrawal from the Sharm el-Sheikh and the Gaza Strip'.

Getting Israel out of Gaza was one thing, getting Egypt back into Gaza was quite another. As soon as UNEF was constituted Nasser had told Fawzi to expedite the despatch of UN units to the Gaza Strip because reports were coming in of Israeli atrocities there. Sinai and El-Arish, he said, were a secondary consideration compared with Gaza. A little later Hammarskjöld told Fawzi that the information he was getting indicated that the people of Gaza might not want to go back to an Egyptian administration but would prefer to be under the United Nations.

UNEF headquarters were established at Abu Suweir about twenty kilometres west of Ismailia, where there was a usable airfield. Liaison officers were appointed by the Egyptian government as well as by the British, French, and Israeli commands, who passed on information from their units in the field. By this means it was possible to arrange for Egyptian troops to move in immediately after a position had been vacated by the force that had been occupying it.

After Hammarskjöld had gone back to New York it seemed that a lot of latitude had been left to General Burns who, Nasser complained, more often behaved as if he was General Gruenther, the Commander-in-Chief of NATO. Burns' high opinion of his own importance even extended to designing a splendid uniform for himself. When Israeli troops had withdrawn from Sinai, Burns had moved his headquarters from Abu Suweir to Rafah, right on the border of the Gaza Strip, where, in spite of his protests, an Egyptian liaison officer was already installed. A resolution was introduced by Lester Pearson at the General Assembly calling for the Gaza Strip to be placed under UN control, and this of course was in accordance with the wishes of the American government. Burns himself flew into Gaza with some UNEF troops to be greeted by pro-Egyptian demonstrations. A shot was fired, probably by someone in one of the Scandinavian contingents, and the whole population of Gaza erupted. Diplomatically, Burns withdrew the Scandinavians, replacing them by the Yugoslavs, but they objected that the mission with which they were charged — to keep order in the town — exceeded their instructions. When Burns went to the Governor's office in Gaza, which he intended to make his own, he found an Egyptian General, Hassan Abdel Latif, already there and preparing to take over the civil administration. This provoked a tremendous international outcry, Ben-Gurion threatening to send Israeli troops back into the Strip, Eisenhower making vigorous protests, and so on. But the supporting demonstrations for the Egyptian action left no doubt that any attempt to impose a UN presence in Gaza would lead to certain bloodshed and unpredictable consequences, so wisely the Egyptian *fait accompli* was not interfered with.

To have given up Egypt's position in Gaza — or worse, far worse, to have left Israel in possession of its gains — would have made the sweets of victory elsewhere taste extremely bitter. But, crucial though it was, the issue of Gaza was by no means the only problem which had to be sorted out between Egypt and the UN. Hammarskjöld had wanted to spend Christmas with the newly installed UNEF in order to see how it was settling in. But he came first to Cairo, bringing with him a long agenda of matters to be discussed with Nasser. He felt obliged to raise the question of where the true frontiers of Egypt lay, though he had no sympathy for Israeli pretensions, but a stop was quickly put to that. Much more complicated were points connected with the composition and status of the UN forces. Originally Hammarskjöld had wanted contingents from the Scandinavian countries, and from Canada, partly because the main architect of UNEF had been the Canadian Foreign Minister, Lester Pearson, and partly because the force commander was the Canadian General Burns, who was on the spot as Chairman of the UN Truce Commission. But Egypt had insisted on contingents from India, Yugoslavia, and Indonesia, and had vetoed any contingents from Baghdad Pact countries. Nor was Egypt happy about the Canadians. Trying to put as bold a face as possible on Britain's withdrawal, Eden had told the House of Commons that while one lot of Her Majesty's troops were moving out, another lot (Canadians) were moving in. Also during the general election campaign in Canada the position of the Canadian contingent had become one of the issues, the Prime Minister, St Laurent, maintaining that their presence in Eygpt did not depend on the will of the Egyptian government.

General Burns wanted a special Canadian reconnaissance unit to be part of his command, and got verbal approval for this from Hammarskjöld. He then made the mistake of making arrangements for its inclusion direct with the Canadian Minister of Defence, without informing Cairo. Consequently, when the ship bringing the unit from Naples reached Alexandria it had to be sent back. But after the dispute had been satisfactorily settled they were allowed in.

Hammarskjöld wanted all UN forces to be granted diplomatic immunity, but Nasser told him that this was impossible. They could be given certain guarantees about movement and so on, but as long as they remained on Egyptian soil they would have to be subject to Egyptian law. Another contentious point, which led to quite a heated argument, was the circumstances in which the UN forces could be withdrawn. Hammarskjöld wanted this to be only after a vote in the Security Council, but Nasser insisted that they were where they were on sufferance from Egypt.[3]

The point which led to the most prolonged discussion concerned Israel's demand that its shipping should be allowed through the canal. Hammarskjöld had come to the conclusion that Israel's case was a good one, and was prepared to argue it energetically.

Fortunately he and Nasser and Fawzi got on exceptionally well together. Hammarskjöld and Fawzi were, in fact, in many ways very similar. Both were highly cultivated men, never happier than when discussing literature or music.[4] Both men liked talking round a subject, using allusions and analogies, testing out the ground of each other's thoughts. Nasser enjoyed listening to exchanges between the two and from time to time shocking them with blunt, down to earth interjections. An example of this was when they were discussing the privileges Hammarskjöld wanted to secure for UNEF forces. There was a long exchange between Hammarskjöld and Fawzi, each quoting different legal precedents. Nasser eventually intervened: 'I can't give an opinion on your legal arguments,' he said. 'I've read the memorandum that's been prepared for me, and the only comment I have to make is that what you are asking is, quite frankly, impossible.' That 'impossible' ended the discussion.

It was the same story over Israel and the canal. Once again there was a long exchange of legal arguments, till finally Hammarskjöld said: 'But suppose the Israelis take their case to the International Court of Justice?' Nasser replied: 'Dr Hammarskjöld, I am going to speak to you completely frankly. As long as I am in this country no Israeli ship is going to pass through the canal. The idea is totally unacceptable.' Hammarskjöld produced a copy of the *Jerusalem Post* where it was stated that if he failed to persuade Nasser to let Israeli vessels through the canal he would have to resign. Nasser said: 'And if they do go through the canal *I* shall have to resign.' Hammarskjöld brought up the question of the canal's being isolated from politics. Nasser said: 'It is exactly what I was afraid would happen. That principle is being used, as I knew it would be, on behalf of Israel. But I tell you that Israel is not going to be allowed to use the canal. I appreciate your position. I know the tremendous pressure you are under from Ben-Gurion and others. But I am not concerned with the niceties of international law. Whatever the legal position may be, Israeli ships are not going to go through the canal.'

There was a pause, then Hammarskjöld laughed. He said, 'Mr President, I can see that you have a very charming garden outside. Why don't we go and have a bit of a walk there, and cool off. Then we can come back and resume our discussion.' Nasser said, 'All right, let's go out. We can talk about poetry if you like — poems about the spring.' And they went out laughing.

When they returned, Hammarskjöld reverted to the 'six princi-ples', one of which was that the operation of the canal should be insulated from the politics of any country.[5] 'Are you bringing them up for discussion,' asked Nasser, 'or as a matter of history?' Hammarskjöld said he was afraid the Israelis would not yield. Nasser said, 'Dr Hammarskjöld, I know that you are a superb negotiator, but does negotiation mean that one side dictates and the other side accepts? If this is what it means I don't want to go on negotiating. I am not a person you can scare, as Menzies found out, though he came backed by all the big guns of the eighteen nations. So please, Dr Hammarskjöld, don't talk in the way that Pineau used to talk.' 'Ah no,' said Hammarskjöld, 'not Pineau! Compare me with anyone, but not with Pineau!'

America had not been able to keep the Egyptians out of Gaza, where events had moved too rapidly for the rival international authority to establish itself. Weaning Saudi Arabia away from Egypt required a more considered strategy, though in the end the desired results were achieved.

Although, as has been seen, King Saud and his brothers were gratified by the visit Nasser had paid to them at the height of the crisis, they had used the occasion to air a number of grievances. These were not altogether removed as a result of the discussions held at Dahran and Riyadh, and the Americans were still using the Saudis as a channel by which pressure could be brought to bear on Egypt. Nasser's visit began on 23 September and two days later King Saud had sent a report on it to Washington. This produced a letter to the King from President Eisenhower in Arabic dated 8 October.

Your Majesty,
I have read with delight your Majesty's letter of September 25, in which you once again manifested your interest in preserving peace in the Near East and in trying to find a solution to the dangerous situation which has been created by Egyptian action over the Suez Canal. I am glad to hear your account of the talks which took place between you and President Nasser.
As far as the general relations between the United States and Egypt are concerned, it is my wish, and the wish of my administra-tion, to try to strengthen those relations on a basis of mutual

understanding and trust. As far as the problem of the Suez Canal is concerned my hope is that the talks now going on at the United Nations will create a better climate between Egypt and the countries using the canal and that, with sincerity on both sides, a successful outcome may be reached. . . . I am sure that I can count on your Majesty to help in convincing your friends of the need to show this sincerity. I pray to God to envelop your Majesty with his protection. Your sincere friend, Dwight Eisenhower.

The King was able to give an optimistic answer:

It was a good omen that I received this letter at a moment when it appears that mutual trust and wisdom are helping all parties concerned to reach a satisfactory solution to the Suez Canal problem . . . I have always been convinced that your aims and our aims coincide, and I will devote all my attention to this matter, exactly as you are doing. God will ensure that we all do what is right.

Relations between Saudi Arabia and Egypt at this point were still sufficiently cordial for both letters to be sent on to Cairo.

A month later, on 19 November, in the immediate aftermath of the Suez fiasco, Nasser sent King Saud a copy of an appreciation of the international situation which he had drafted for circulation to the heads of state of those countries whose support throughout the crisis had been of particular importance. In this, special attention was devoted to the repercussions the crisis might be expected to have on the Baghdad Pact. 'The pact,' he wrote, 'is now frozen. Britain and her allies are thinking of trying to convert it into an Islamic pact which will attract all Islamic countries not already members of the pact.' Pakistan was seen as being given a key role in this change and charged with mobilizing the Islamic world against the alleged infiltration of communism into the area. Attention was drawn to the statement made by the Prime Minister of Pakistan on 10 November in which he claimed that Anglo-French intervention had been beneficial, because if Israel had succeeded in penetrating deep into Egypt the whole Middle East would have been engulfed in war. He accused Egypt of aiming at the conquest of Israel, and cited the quantities of arms alleged to have been captured in Sinai as proof of this. Nasser also referred to a statement made by the Foreign Minister of Pakistan in London, in which he said that Pakistan planned to recognize Israel as a country which was there to stay. He concluded that the real aim of this new development was to separate Egypt from Saudi Arabia, Syria and Jordan and so liquidate Arab solidarity.

A few days later, on 24 November, a letter came from King Saud to Nasser which, though not a direct answer to the above, touched on the same theme:

Last week we had an unexpected visit from His Excellency Iskander Mirza, President of the Islamic Republic of Pakistan. He stayed with us two days and then, to our surprise, went on to Baghdad. We pray that God may grant you what you wish, and send you a résumé of what the President told us. . . .

He said that his purpose in coming here was to make a personal apology for the attacks which had been made on Saudi Arabia by some Pakistani newspapers at the time of the visit paid here by Pandit Jawaharlal Nehru. He took the opportunity to have many discussions about relations between our two countries and the general international situation. The President of Pakistan spoke of the communist threat to the Middle East and of the infiltration into Egypt and Syria by communists disguised as experts and technicians allegedly there to train the armed forces in the use of Russian weapons. I assured his Highness [sic] that both Egypt and Syria are combatting communism, and will not allow its destructive influence to spread into them, nor will they cooperate in any way with Soviet Russia. The only use they have for Russia is as a necessary supplier of arms for their defence, and that only after all other sources of supply had failed. I insisted that I personally, and my country, had nothing whatever to do with communism.

The President referred to the Baghdad Pact. I told him frankly that we could not accept a pact about whose formation we had not been consulted and which included among its members Turkey, a country which has recognized Israel, and Britain, a country which was the leading aggressor against Egypt, and an aggressor also against ourselves [a reference to Buraimi]. The President said that he was not acting as spokesman for the Baghdad Pact, but was speaking as representative of one Islamic country and proposing to sound out heads of other Islamic states, starting with us in Riyadh, in the hope of finding a means for reconciliation and cooperation between Moslems for their common benefit.

I told the president that, as far as Turkey was concerned, we were prepared to improve relations on condition that she breaks with Israel. As for general reconciliation and cooperation, I said that we did not feel the present time was ripe, but that when the situation was clearer, and the invading forces had withdrawn from Egypt, we might then be prepared to discuss the next phase.

In a further letter King Saud reported that Iskander Mirza had shown considerable irritation at what he alleged was Nasser's refusal to meet his Prime Minister, who had expressed a wish to visit Egypt. 'He told me,' the King continued, 'that in spite of this there would be no weakening in Pakistan's support for Egypt, but he trusted that even in these difficult moments I might be able to put in a word on their behalf. I hope therefore that you may be able to receive the Prime Minister soon. I know that you are very busy; I am aware of the many burdens on your shoulders, for which I pray that God will help you; but it would be an excellent move if you could summon the Pakistani ambassador and tell him that there has been a misunderstanding — that you did not refuse to meet the Prime Minister of Pakistan, but that you were distracted by other preoccupations, and that now you are prepared to welcome him. If this can be done it will find a warm response in my heart.'

Nasser promptly sent King Saud an explanation of what had really happened:

> Our ambassador in Karachi saw a news item in one of the Pakistani papers which said that the Prime Minister told him it was true that he would like to visit Egypt if he received an invitation. We felt this was a strange way to arrange a visit, and said so, adding that though this was not an appropriate moment, as Hammarskjöld was shortly due in Cairo with no date fixed for his departure, we would welcome such a visit at a later date. I feel I should warn your Majesty that imperialist propagandists and those who are trying to revive the Baghdad Pact are exploiting this incident in an attempt to create misunderstandings between Moslem countries and to present Egypt as a country which prefers cooperating with the communists to cooperating with other Moslems.

This brought a relieved response from Saud: 'I agree with your Excellency, that hostile propaganda is hard at work to separate us from our peoples, but God in heaven appreciates our good intentions.' But he hoped that Nasser would be able to fix a date for the visit of the Pakistani Prime Minister 'as that would be the best answer to this hostile propaganda'.

As the next stage in the exchange between the two heads of state, the Egyptian ambassador in Riyadh was instructed to deliver a personal message from Nasser to Saud. He was summoned to the royal palace at dawn, where he found the King and Prince Feisal. The King told him to read Nasser's letter aloud, so that they could both hear it. After he had done this Saud said: 'Tell my brother that if ever Egypt's head is lowered, all our heads will be lowered.' He then returned to the question of the Pakistani Prime Minister's proposed visit to Egypt. 'I do not understand why President Nasser is reluctant to see him,' he said. 'This gives hostile newspapers an excuse to attack Egypt. My friend, such a meeting would protect you from many evils. Why are you hesitating?' The ambassador reported that at this point Feisal intervened to say, 'It is very easy to gain enemies, but very difficult to win friends.'

Moving on, Saud said: 'I have good news for President Nasser. I was told today that America will never join the Baghdad Pact. But what I have to tell you must be kept strictly between ourselves. I have been pressed to let Saudi oil pass to the refinery at Bahrain, but I have refused. I said that not one drop of oil should go there until all the invading armies have withdrawn from Egypt. I swear by God that I am now losing a million dollars a day as a result of having broken our relations with Britain and France, but that counts as nothing compared with the maintenance of brotherly relations between ourselves and President Nasser.'

Feisal asked the ambassador if he had heard that the Russians had agreed to send oil to France. The ambassador said that he had not. Feisal assured him it was true. Saud exclaimed: 'The curse of Allah on them! The Russians are the worst of all. But I want to urge his Excellency, President Gamal Abdel Nasser, to show moderation. We must all pursue moderate policies now that the British have said they will be out of Egypt by Christmas.'

The ambassador said King Saud then rang a bell and summoned Sheikh Yusuf Yassin, the Deputy Foreign Minister (Prince Feisal was the Foreign Minister), and handed Nasser's letter to him. The King stood up, put his hand on the ambassador's shoulder, and said, 'Will you lunch with us today?' He then went out, and Sheikh Yusuf Yassin took the ambassador into his office. 'We must find a way,' he said, 'whereby President Nasser and the Prime Minister of Pakistan can scotch the intrigues going on against them.' Then he in his turn asked, 'Did you know that the Russians are selling oil to

France? This will give you some idea of the intentions of these dogs. And wasn't Russia the first country to recognize the state of Israel? Russia has now got an interest in Egypt, but tomorrow it will be the turn of Israel. The policies of some countries are like the tracks a car makes in the sand; you cannot tell whether it is going or coming.' The ambassador explained that Egypt was opposed to communism, but that if it had not been for Russian arms Egyptian resistance to the invaders would have collapsed and the country been occupied. 'Did Britain become a communist country because it was allied to Russia during the war?' asked the ambassador.

Saud followed up this interview with a handwritten letter to Nasser dated 5 December, in which he congratulated Nasser on the impending withdrawal of British and French forces. 'But,' he went on, 'it must be clear to his Highness [as he still sometimes insisted on calling Nasser] that this is not the end of the story between us and our enemies. We must show wisdom in what we broadcast and what is written in our newspapers. We must try not to increase hatred, otherwise Britain and France will try to exact retribution before they leave. There is an Arabic proverb that when the wise man has achieved victory he does not let his enemy feel that he is defeated. This proverb is in line with the wisdom of his Excellency the President, and I therefore hope that the President will ask the Egyptian newspapers and broadcasting services to be moderate in what they publish and avoid spiteful and provocative remarks about the West.'

In other letters to Nasser the King suggested that the ambassadors of Arab countries in Amman should collectively congratulate King Hussein on abrogating the Anglo-Jordanian Treaty, reported an invitation to meet the Shah (this was the second string in the Baghdad Pact's bow, following up the Pakistani initiative), which he felt unable to accept — 'we are not very happy with the Iranians' — and two other invitations, to meet the Sultan of Morocco in Spain and by the King of Libya who wanted to visit Saudi Arabia, both of which he was prepared to agree to.

More significant was a letter dated 24 December 1956 which showed that Eisenhower had been trying out on Saud some of the ideas which were contained in his special message delivered in person to Congress on 5 January and to be known as the 'Eisenhower Doctrine'. 'I want to consult you,' the King wrote, about how we can achieve benefits and avoid fresh dangers after Israel's withdrawal. President Eisenhower has sent us some very interesting ideas, but we have told him that these cannot be discussed until after the Israelis have withdrawn. I would be glad of an opportunity to meet your Excellency and to know your views on the extent to which you think we should cooperate with America, if they are prepared to help us and to give unconditional support to our interests and our army. What is your feeling? You know my own view has always been in favour of friendship with the United States, providing this does not require us to sacrifice our sovereignty or our independence.

The countries willing to cooperate with America were being brought into line. Next came a letter reporting the imminent arrival of President Camille Chamoun of Lebanon, immediately after Christmas. But there was a disturbing postscript in a letter from the King to the Saudi ambassador in Cairo:

> Please tell President Nasser we have heard that an officer from the Syrian *Deuxième Bureau* is to arrive in Riyadh and to join some Egyptians in a plot to assassinate Chamoun while he is our guest. We cannot believe this to be true. We cannot believe there is a single Arab with the character or morals capable of such a deed, more particularly to someone who is enjoying our hospitality. We have told those who reported this to us that we do not believe it, but we open the door of caution to inform you, convinced that you will be as disturbed by it as we have been. If, which God forbid, it turned out to be true, we should be obliged to take appropriate steps.

On receipt of this letter Nasser got in touch with Colonel Sarraj, and was able to reassure the King that the story of the plot was a pure fabrication, but it was ominous that this sort of canard, involving Egypt and Syria in an action so calculated to damage the Saudis, should be circulating.

King Saud came to Egypt for the talks he so much wanted in the middle of January. He had been convinced that at Suez Egypt had lost most of its army and its entire air force, but in fact the Russians had been most cooperative, and all the planes destroyed on the ground had been replaced. All the same for months hardly an aeroplane had been seen in the skies over Cairo and the other main cities, but when the King came the air force demonstrated in strength for his benefit. On 29 January the King visited the United

States, having first made it a condition that he was to be greeted at the airport by the President. Although this was not customary, and set what might become an awkward precedent, Eisenhower agreed.

---

[1] The abortive attempt by the French to assassinate Nasser in the RCC building has already been mentioned. The British intelligence people, who had so shocked their CIA colleagues by the bluntness of their language, had not been behindhand. Soon after the nationalization of the Suez Canal Company a German mercenary was hired to do the job. He arrived in Cairo, but the authorities received a tip off about him. Then a strange thing happened — he simply disappeared. One day he was identified in his hotel; the next day he had vanished without trace. He never checked out from the hotel, and there was no sign of him at the airport. For several days the search for him went on, but without success. The only assumption that could be made was that somehow he had been smuggled out of the country under diplomatic cover. The Egyptian authorities also had information about three British subjects who were sent to Cairo to assassinate Nasser, but not until they had got cold feet and left.

More serious was an Israeli assassination attempt. They recruited a Greek waiter working in Groppi's, the firm responsible for presidential catering, who was given poison to put in a cup of coffee with which he would have the opportunity of serving Nasser. But his hand shook so much when it came to the point that he gave up and confessed.

[2] These warnings curiously foreshadow those which came from Moscow in the days leading up to the 1967 war.

[3] A decision which was to have far-reaching consequences in 1967.

[4] Fawzi's first post had been in Rome in 1923, where he had seen the rise of fascism, and this, and the deteriorating scene in Europe, as he said had 'opened his eyes and ears and mind'. He once told me he was fortunate in that fate had destined him for a profession which allowed him to enjoy the vision of a voyager.

[5] The six principles had been formulated at the first London conference and later endorsed by the Security Council. The other five were: freedom of navigation in the canal without discrimination; respect for Egyptian sovereignty; tolls to be fixed by agreement between Egypt and the canal users; a fair proportion of tolls to go to development; disputes to be settled by arbitration.

[6] Canal clearance was, not surprisingly, one of the areas in which the Americans moved in decisively. The task was entrusted to General A. Wheeler, commander of the US Engineering Corps and a consultant to the World Bank. His deputy was another American, Jack Connors.

❊18❊

OBSEQUIES FOR
A PACT

IN THE IMMEDIATE AFTERMATH of Suez, Britain's erstwhile friends
in the Middle East faced an unenviable dilemma. In private, they
were, if anything, even more determined to oppose Nasser who
seemed more threatening than ever now that he had emerged from
the crisis a clear victor. But in public it was still more urgent that
they should be seen to distance themselves from their ally, Britain,
who had committed two unforgiveable sins — losing, and collud-
ing with Israel in an attack on an Arab neighbour. But without the
sponsorship of a great power the Baghdad Pact was a hollow
pretence: Britain had to go, but a replacement must be found.

There was, of course, only one possible candidate — the United
States. And the Americans needed no wooing. The Eisenhower
Doctrine, embodied in a message the President sent to Congress on
5 January 1957, was, in effect, a declaration of America's intention
to step into the shoes which Britain was, willy-nilly, vacating.
Eisenhower proposed to offer up to $200 million a year to help
build up the economies and independence of Middle Eastern states,
and he also suggested that the services of the American armed
forces might be available to protect cooperating states 'against overt
aggression from any nation controlled by international communism.'

The business of easing Britain out of the Middle East and easing
America in as a substitute was conducted with almost indecent
haste. Its progress can be followed clearly in the records of the
deliberations of the Baghdad Pact members.

On 6 November, before the ceasefire was announced, there was a
meeting of the Pact Council in Baghdad at which Britain was not
represented, though it had before it a communication sent to it by
the Foreign Office in London:

Her Majesty's Government fully understand the concern of its

Baghdad Pact allies regarding the very grave situation which has arisen in the Middle East. It is their firm conviction that the action which has been taken to separate the Egyptian and Israeli forces was the only way to prevent a general conflagration in the area. Her Majesty's Government are most appreciative of the initiative of the governments of Iraq, Iran, Pakistan and Turkey. The views offered both individually and collectively by those governments have weighed heavily in the decison to bring to an end military action in Egypt. We have listened with close attention to the friendly and constructive advice offered by the four governments on the proposals formulated by the Middle Eastern members of the Baghdad Pact, which are in general consonant with Her Majesty's Government's own wishes. As regards a settlement of the Palestine problem, Her Majesty's Government's views are well known and were stated by the Prime Minister at the Guildhall on 9 November 1955. Her Majesty's Government believes that the opportunity is now ripe for a general settlement of the Middle Eastern problems which have defied solution for so long, and in this settlement all members of the Baghdad Pact would be able to play a valuable and constructive role. They further believe that by true cooperation in this task the Baghdad Pact would be greatly fortified.

This was followed up the next day by a letter from the British ambassador in Baghdad, Sir Michael Wright, to the Iraqi Foreign Minister and acting Prime Minister, Ahmed Mukhtar Baban:

Your Excellency,
   The Iraqi government will no doubt have heard the announcement made by the British Prime Minister, which included the ordering of a conditional ceasefire in the Suez area from midnight GMT. [In fact no conditions were attached.] My government would have liked to have been able to give the Iraqi government prior notice of this decision, and has asked me to assure your Excellency that the counsel of the Iraqi government weighed very heavily with the British government in arriving at it. My government are confident that the Iraqi government will welcome the step which they have now taken. I am to add that the government will continue to spare no effort to ensure the withdrawal of Israeli forces from Egyptian territory through the channel of the United Nations or by any other appropriate means.

The last phrase, 'any other appropriate means', was no doubt deliberately enigmatic. But though it had not been possible to give the Iraqis advance notice of the ceasefire there is no question that consultations between the two governments had been extremely close, ever since that momentous dinner party at 10 Downing Street on 26 July when Nuri had given his advice: 'Hit Nasser now, and hit him hard.' In fact it was more than likely that the Iraqis had been told in advance about the Anglo-French landings, though probably not of the role Israel was to play in the attack. It is significant that on the day that the pumping stations were blown up Nazim el-Qudsi, the Peoples' Party leader and former Prime Minister, a good friend of the Hashemites, asked Sarraj if he could not have waited another two days. Almost certainly the Iraqis passed on the information they had received from London to their friends in Syria and Saudi Arabia, telling them that the Arab world had better start immediately trying to reorganize itself without Egypt and without Nasser.

But the afternoon of that day saw a more significant meeting, in the Marmar Palace in Tehran. Here the Shah was host to the President of Pakistan, Iskander Mirza, and his Prime Minister H.S. Suhrawady, Adnan Menderes, Prime Minister of Turkey, and Nuri Said, Prime Minister of Iraq. Minutes of the meeting were taken by Ahmed Mukhtar Baban, the Iraqi Foreign Minister, who, with his colleague Burhanuddin Bashayan, on this occasion acted as secretaries.

The Shah began by referring to reports that Britain was going to agree to a ceasefire, which prompted Iskander Mirza to exclaim, 'Ah! That would be a good chance for us to bring more Moslem countries into the pact.' His Prime Minister said he had spoken to Eden and demanded that the other pact members should be free to act as they thought best. The Shah said: 'I asked the British to leave Egypt to the international forces. I said we wanted to save the pact and to save Britain. We shall always need Britain, but the British should realize that it would be better for them to keep out of the pact, at least for the time being. We who remain in the pact can continue their friends and allies.'

Suhrawady suggested that there was another solution, which would be to create a completely new pact, made up solely of Islamic countries. 'Even if Britain makes things easier for us by withdrawing from the pact it would be easier for other Islamic countries if the pact they were asked to join was a new one.' The Shah commented: 'Yes, after that America could come in, and then, maybe later, Britain.'

Nuri Said thought it might be better to freeze the pact. 'We can't accept the United States openly as a member of a pact,' he said, 'until the Palestine problem has been solved. When earlier America wanted to join the pact the Jews in America insisted that to compensate there would have to be a separate defence agreement with Israel, so the Americans dropped the idea.' The Shah expressed himself uncertain whether Britain would agree to withdraw from the pact, and Nuri thought they would certainly not agree easily. Iskander Mirza suggested that perhaps they should first agree among themselves on a course of action and then ask the British what they were going to do about it.

'I told the British ambassador,' said the Shah, 'that I could control public opinion, and that I would do this to save the pact. I would explain that I was rallying the Moslem countries.' Suhrawady said he wondered if the British intended to stay in Suez. 'Would it be a bad idea if they did?' asked the Shah. Iskander Mirza thought it would be better if the arrival of the international forces was delayed for a while 'as this would give us a chance to overthrow Nasser'. 'But in that case, what would be the position of Russia?' asked the Shah. 'The Russians might send troops to Syria. I think we should study the statement put out by Bulganin.' Iskander Mirza said that with his own eyes he had seen instructions, in the handwriting of Gamal Abdel Nasser, sent to Egyptian ambassadors instructing them to cooperate with Indian embassies 'just as if they were Egyptian embassies'. On that note the afternoon session was wound up.

When the next morning's session began, confirmation of Britain's acceptance of a ceasefire had come through. The Shah began the proceedings by saying he thought Britain should be allowed to benefit from its action: 'I think we must now try to prevent the situation from gradually collapsing.' Iskander Mirza: 'It is important that we don't waste time discussing the past. Unless we do something positive, we shall become the laughing stock of the world.' Nuri: 'We should wind up our talks today, so that it might be made to appear that the ceasefire came about as a result of pressure from us meeting here.' The Shah said he had seen the British ambassador that morning and told him he thought it was going to be difficult to save the Baghdad Pact with Britain in it. 'I asked for a Cabinet minister to be sent from London to Tehran immediately to discuss the situation with me. We four must act together. Britain should withdraw from the pact, temporarily if necessary, and the United States should come in. That is the only way by which the pact can be preserved.' Suhrawady agreed that, if Britain stayed in, it would be impossible for new countries to join the pact, 'but this would mean another slap in the face for an already humiliated friend.'

Nuri Said returned to his favourite theme. 'Britain,' he said, 'always fails to do anything about Palestine. The British were responsible for the Balfour Declaration.' Hussein Ala, the Iranian Minister of Court, said it had to be recognized that the Suez affair had been a serious reverse for the pact, particularly with regard to its military credibility. 'Yes,' said the Shah, 'Hussein Ala is right. We must avoid giving the impression that the pact is an aggressive one, but unfortunately Britain's action at Suez lends colour to that accusation.' Hussein Ala said he thought they ought to study the statement by Voroshilov calling for a freeze on all pacts. It might be the opening they were looking for. It would make it easier to get Britain out of the pact and America and other countries into it.

The Shah said the British ambassador had told him his government wanted to remain a member of the pact, and he had replied that the aim must now be to save the pact and to repair the damage Britain had inflicted by failing to invade Egypt properly. 'We can't leave the pact to be used as a toy in the hands of a power which still dreams in colonialist terms.' The most important thing now, he said, was to strengthen relations between the four countries there represented. Events in Egypt and Hungary had shown that the United Nations was powerless to prevent aggression. The Shah then called on the President of Pakistan to say something about the soundings he had been making in Arab countries.

Iskander Mirza obliged. 'The Arab League,' he said, 'is useless. It is a collection of zeros. The Baghdad Pact does not weaken the Arab League; rather the contrary. All this talk about neutralism is nonsense. I told the Arabs I have been meeting that if Britain failed to retire from the pact we would kick it out. They all said they would be happy to see Britain go, and when that was done they would be ready to collaborate with us, more especially since they could now expect the imminent collapse of Nasser, who had been weakened economically, politically and militarily. We have always said that the pact needed the support of a major power, but that cannot be Britain after it has attacked an Arab country.'

Nuri intervened, 'Menderes knows that following our meetings in Baghdad and Tehran I spoke strongly to the British and Americans about the importance of the Palestine issue, because this is going to be exploited by Russia. The refugees are the natural raw material for communism. But they never listen to me. We have a right to discuss our affairs without Britain because we are all Middle Eastern countries and the Middle East is more important to us than it is to them.'

Menderes said, 'I think it is only fair to point out that the accusation that the Baghdad Pact was imperialist was being made by Russia and Egypt even before Britain joined it. They wanted to force us onto the defensive. But now we must stand up for ourselves. Egypt is going to be less of a threat because it will be preoccupied with all the damage that has been done to it. We must be quite clear what we want. Do we really want other Arab states to join the pact? Do we want the United States in? Let us discuss all this logically, and to hell with emotion. Let us start by considering Egypt. Egypt is an Arab country and an Islamic country. We love it, and we wish it well, but we cannot forget that Egypt is owned and ruled by a man who is working against the interests of all of us.'

'We are here,' Menderes went on, 'because we think Russia is our enemy, but Nuri says that Israel is the danger. I am prepared to agree, but Russia presents a much bigger danger to Turkey. And Cyprus is more important to us than Israel — and we have seen that Egypt backs Greece. To return to the case of Britain. Britain has been acting on her own behalf, not on ours. Britain does not face the same problems as we do, because we are all in an Arab sea or a Moslem sea. Look at Syria. It is now in the arms of the Soviet Union. We have been told that Quwatli has agreed to make Syria a Russian satellite state and that is clearly a threat to Turkey. All of us see the problem from a different angle, but after Hungary how can anyone say that Russia is not our enemy? Russia is our enemy number one, but Britain is our friend. We don't want Britain to leave NATO. We want to keep Britain's friendship in Europe, but it's going to be difficult to keep it in the Middle East. I am sorry for the British. They have accepted a ceasefire, but would the Russians accept a ceasefire in Hungary?'

The Shah said: 'We are all determined to save the pact, and agree that this cannot be done with Britain in it. We must make a break. I myself have always been in favour of the British alliance, and have made many sacrifices for that friendship. Unless it is strengthened the pact is just a piece of paper. Britain should release us from the dilemma it has placed us in by withdrawing from the pact, so that the door is opened for the United States to come in. That is the only way.'

Nuri: 'My friend Menderes has misunderstood my thinking about the communist danger. Our concern over Palestine is because a just solution of the Palestinian problem could destroy the position of Russia, and Nasser would be its first victim.'

Menderes: 'I only said that Nuri put the communist danger in second place.'

Suhrawady: 'Let us be clear on this — the enemies of the pact are Russia and Egypt.'

Shah: 'What about Israel?'

Suhrawady: 'Israel is certainly opposed to the pact. There is no doubt that a majority at the United Nations are opposed to it too. The trouble is that Britain has done something which has played into the hands of the pact's enemies, so it can't remain with us in the pact.'

There was a final meeting on 8 November at which Menderes said he thought an open invitation ought to be sent to America to join the pact. The Shah agreed. 'While we are all happy about what the British tried to do to Nasser, if they stay in the pact it will create problems for Iraq, Iran, and Pakistan. Britain can be no more help to us, but there must be an American presence. I am prepared to state categorically that the absence of the United States from the pact has been one of the main causes of confusion in the Middle East. You will recall that at our meeting in Istanbul we warned the Americans that by treating their enemies better than their friends they were encouraging people to threaten them. Have you noticed that Tito is being given twice as much American aid as goes to the entire Middle East?'

Menderes said he thought Nasser's prestige had been destroyed, and thereby any danger from Egypt had been removed. Suhrawady feared this might mean that Egypt would be left a prey to communism. After which it was agreed that someone should go to see King Saud, because it was most important that he should join the Baghdad Pact or some variant of it. A memorandum in the handwriting of Bashayan, presumably written during one of the meetings, suggested that Nasser could be isolated by a combination of the Baghdad Pact, Saudi Arabia and Lebanon, and, with American backing, Libya and Morocco.

With hindsight it seems extraordinary that an organization which set its face so resolutely against the tide of history and the spirit of the times should have played so large a part on the international stage.[1] Yet, as has been seen, it was the main cause of division between Arab countries, the main bone of contention between Britain and Egypt, and the symbol by which Britain and America judged who were their friends and who were their enemies. No doubt these divisions would have existed without the pact; it was, after all, simply the latest of many attempts by the West to organize the defence of the Middle East against the threat of communism; but there was always an air of make-believe about the whole undertaking. Like the film-set of a palace, the pact could present a façade of noble proportions, with impressive porticoes, windows, balustrades, and pediments, but behind this there was nothing except the wooden props holding it all up.

The archives of the pact were seized by the revolutionaries after Brigadier Qasim's coup in July 1958[2], and — this being in the days before he quarrelled with Nasser — sent by him to Cairo. But already much of what went on in the pact's councils had been leaked to Cairo by friendly figures who took part in its deliberations.

An example of the unreality which characterized all the pact's activities is a planning paper prepared in June 1955 called 'Assumptions for Global War'. This foresaw a surprise attack by the Soviet Union, aimed at achieving global conquest. It was assumed that in this event Israel would make no military contribution towards helping the allies, but would maintain benevolent neutrality towards them and act in its own defence. The Arab countries, while preferring that the allies did not cooperate militarily with Israel or make use of its bases and communications, would not object if this could be shown to be necessary for an allied victory. Lebanon and Saudi Arabia would be expected to allow the allies use of bases and transit facilities. Jordan would maintain benevolent neutrality but not allow the use of bases. Egypt and Syria would remain neutral. The lines by which an advance against the Soviet Union could be mounted through Kurdistan and the Caucasus were listed, as were the targets for aerial bombardment by Turkey, Iran, and Iraq. It is difficult not to feel that the politicians and generals from these countries were being fobbed off with the illusion of taking part in great strategic decisions which the British and Americans knew were only paper games.

In the military and economic committees Britain and America in effect decided policy and the others listened and obeyed. But there was one committee in which their opinions were genuinely sought, and this was the security committee. On this, too, the Americans were represented, though their presence was not made public, as it was on the economic committee. This was in fact the pact's most important committee, for though it was unlikely, to say the least, that armies from the pact countries were ever going to march through the Caucasus and liberate Tiflis, there were quite a lot of practical things they could do in the field of countersubversion. But although the pact was supposed to be thinking globally, the concerns of its member states remained obstinately localized. Thus at the first meeting of the committee the Turkish delegate concentrated on the threat his government felt came from Syria, though he hastened to add that the report which had been prepared for the committee might give a misleading impression; his government was not recommending the use of force but only peaceful pressure. The Iranian delegate asked that any steps the Pact Council might take with regard to Syria should be extended to cover Afghanistan. The Pakistani delegate referred to India.

The British delegate, Philip Adams, read a report on propaganda. The aim of the Soviet Union, he said, is to divide the pact members and attack weak links in them, particularly groups which were articulate and influential. Special attention should therefore be paid to these groups and they should be provided with material demonstrating that the Soviet Union was opposed to their real interests. Committee members were warned that the Soviet Union was adept at making use of 'front' organizations — the World Federation of Trade Unions and the General Federation of Arab Labour were given as examples. Professional syndicates in Arab countries —

doctors, lawyers, engineers and so on — were said to have been contaminated.

At a meeting of the intelligence committee in March 1956 the chairman said that, whereas each member country must of course take its own measures against communism, there were certain external problems which affected them all. Syria was a case in point. This strategically important country had become the centre for the distribution of communist propaganda in the Middle East, and the legalized Communist Party there was collaborating with others. The Syrian army had been penetrated, many of the officers in most sensitive positions being communist sympathisers. If this process continued unchecked, and there was a war with the Soviet Union, Turkey would find at its back door three divisions threatening Alexandretta and its communications with Iraq and Iran.

Members of the pact, said the Turkish chairman, must be prepared to fight communism not only in their own countries but in the whole area. He described the measures which had already been taken against communism in Turkey: the Communist Party was outlawed; anyone distributing communist propaganda faced twenty years in gaol, while if organized in groups of two or more the penalty was death. On the positive side the Turkish government was paying special attention to the press and theatre, anticommunist newspapers and playwrights being officially encouraged. All the same he could not regard the results so far achieved as satisfactory. Even if ninety-five per cent of Turks repudiated communism because it was Russian and irreligious, a hundred active communists could still pose a real threat.

The British delegate, Philip Adams, said it was important that there should be closer liaison with the noncommunist press in the area, with trade unions, student groups and religious organizations. In the course of the discussion it was suggested that if funds from Saudi Arabia could be prevented from reaching Syria this would be very helpful; it was rumoured that recently gold worth £20,000 had been transferred in this way.

There was talk of setting up a new organization to disseminate propaganda against subversion, material for which might be distributed through diplomatic missions. While it was not possible for diplomats to work openly against a country to which they were accredited they could contact its citizens, whose help in this matter would be essential. But clandestine methods of distribution would also be necessary. The Pakistani delegate said that the pact's propaganda was too defensive. They should not be content with refuting communist charges, but should emphasize what was happening to Moslems behind the Iron Curtain.

One of the pact's propaganda exercises involved the production of forged travel brochures purporting to emanate from the Egyptian Ministry of Tourism. These were in Arabic, but probably printed in London. They included details of a tour of Cairo in which many attractions were offered:

> Visit to palace of ex-King Farouk, now a home for revolutionary soldiers. Visit to villas confiscated from the rich and now homes for revolutionary officers. Visit cemetery to lay wreaths on the graves of Salah Salem and members of the Moslem Brotherhood. Attend meeting in Liberation Square and listen to speech by a man of the people describing how the colonialists were expelled from Syria by the popular will backed by Soviet arms. Visit to factory where forged travel documents and other papers are prepared, and where alleged conspiracies can be manufactured as required.

Another important operation funded by the pact was sending pilgrims on the *haj* to act as anticommunist propagandists. 'Our aim,' the council report stated, 'should be to select educated and nationalist-minded people, able to nail communist lies and expose the dangers of communism. They should use every opportunity to protect *hajis* from their own country from becoming involved in subversive plots. Special attention should be paid to pilgrims from Egypt, Syria, and Lebanon, who should be befriended and warned that it is a sin to cooperate with godless communism, which aims at the overthrow of all existing regimes.' These propagandists were told it was most important that they should not disclose the fact that their pilgrimage was being paid for, and that they should refrain from any activities which might draw the attention of the local authorities to them. They were told to destroy any written instructions after these had been read and understood, and to practise economy. In 1955 some 3,600 pilgrims were despatched from pact countries, and they continued to be sent in considerable numbers each year as long as the pact lasted.

The pact financed other travellers, youth and sporting groups and people attending specialist conferences, but all taking part had to be carefully screened beforehand to ensure their suitability. The pact's headquarters also contained long lists of people in all member countries who could be considered reliable 'in the event of an emergency'.

Some other Baghdad Pact documents are worth recording, as illustrating the attitude which prevailed in that organization even after Suez. Thus, in April 1957 the Iraqi Military Attaché in Beirut is found reporting back that he had been told 'by a very close and trusted friend of Abdel Nasser' that Nasser intends to attack Iraq and Kuwait in order to get control of their oil revenues. He is not interested in controlling Lebanon or Jordan. 'Gamal wants to make the West believe that he is the person around whom everything in the Middle East revolves.' Not to be outdone, the Iraqi Military Attaché in Cairo uses the occasion of the visit to Cairo by Archbishop Makarios to assert that this has been designed as another opportunity for Nasser to demonstrate that everybody backs him, and that therefore the West must come to terms with his predominant position.

A little later, in July 1957, there is a rather pathetic report by one of the pact's agents on a tour he had made on its behalf. His name was Mohamed Amin Bokhara, and he claimed to be the leader of the Moslems in Turkestan. He had visited five Arab countries, including a visit to el-Azhar, over a period of forty-five days, but everywhere had found great enmity towards the West and the Baghdad Pact, and correspondingly strong sympathy for the Arab liberation movement. 'This means,' he writes, 'that any project directed against communism must expect to come up against powerful opposition, either open or covert.' In the pact's archives were report after report, page after page, about alleged 'communist activities'. It is scarcely surprising that there should have been so much material when it is realized that even the Baath parties, and of course Nasser and the Egyptian government, were filed away under this heading. A great deal of this material undoubtedly came from American sources.

At the beginning of 1958 there is a paper foreshadowing what was to happen in a few months' time. The Iraqi Director of Military Intelligence submitted a report to Nuri Said, still Prime Minister, in which he warned him that the officer class was in a state of crisis. They were complaining that they heard much too much about

America and communism, and much too little about Palestine and Arabism. They asked what was the point of Iraq's remaining a member of the Baghdad Pact.

An illustration of this smouldering resentment can be seen in a report written after a meeting of the pact's Security Committee on 11 February 1958. The Iraqi officer responsible for internal security states that at this meeting he had raised the problem of Zionism, only to be told by the American representative that this was a subject they had no authority to discuss. 'I told my American colleague,' the officer wrote, 'that if our aim is to strengthen the Baghdad Pact and persuade others to join it, then we would have to discuss Israel. When we left the meeting he was extremely rude, though he later tried to apologize. He informed me that the American and Iraqi governments had agreed that there should be no discussion of Israel.' These words, written almost on the eve of the pact's demise, could well serve as its epitaph, for they neatly summarize the fatal contradiction that had been built into it from the outset.

---

[1] The first stage in the pact's history was the agreement for friendly cooperation signed by Turkey and Pakistan, with American encouragement, on 2 April 1954. Iraq signed an agreement with Turkey on 24 February 1955, and the Baghdad Pact thereby got its name. Britain joined on 5 April, Pakistan on 23 September, and Iran on 3 November. France, always concerned above all with maintaining some influence in Syria and Lebanon, never joined, nor did America, though it sent observers to the first meeting of the economic committee, and in 1957 took part in the military committee. America had already, before Suez, been an unpublicized member of one of the pact's most influential committees, that dealing with security.

[2] The Iraqi revolution which overthrew the Hashemite monarchy in that country was, effectively, the end of the Baghdad Pact. It also resulted in the death of the pact's most ardent supporter, Nuri Said, who was killed in the course of the fighting.

EPILOGUE

THE POLITICAL AND MILITARY war which was fought out at Suez is not over, though some of the battle-lines have changed. Of the three principal forces which interacted on one another thirty years ago, one, Britain, has ceased to have any major role to play. But the other two, America and Arab nationalism, are left confronting each other, and they seem today to be as far apart as ever Britain and the Arabs, and particularly Britain and the Egyptians, were in the 1950s.

After the 1967 war most Americans felt that they had won and that the Middle East was at last controlable. Egypt's military defeat had been enormous. Nasser's influence had surely been checked in a manner that Eden and Mollet would have thoroughly approved of. But in fact America in 1967 made precisely the same mistake that Britain and France had made in 1956 — they used Israel as the instrument with which they tried to shape events in the Middle East. True, America had learned one lesson from the Suez fiasco; collusion was less blatant, but it was for that very reason more lasting in effect and so more damaging. America and Israel were now committed to a partnership, and the price America had to pay was to allow Israel a veto over policy. America became Israel's hostage, obliged to give open-ended guarantees to territorial ambitions which have never been formulated because no boundary has ever been set to them.

For a time the implications of this new collusion could be hidden by the flood of new riches which oil brought to the area, and by the absolute confidence in American omnipotence which was fostered by men like the Shah and President Sadat. But illusions have in the end to give way to realities.

A second mistake which the Americans made was to suppose that history can ever stop at a particular moment in time. They have never appreciated the capacity of a people to absorb shocks, even

apparently most devastating shocks, especially if they are people
like those in the Arab world whose story has been that of a whole
series of shocks to be suffered but eventually, however long the
process may take, recovered from.

Yet America has had many warnings. The Iranian revolution was
traumatic for them, though the inexperience and narrow vision of
its authors have obscured its real significance. The assassination of
Sadat was another warning, but again the meaning of the persisting
malaise in Egypt has not been understood. A third warning was the
humiliating failure of the American attempt to control events in
Lebanon. When the last marines left Beirut the lesson was one no
friend of America could ignore.

For the withdrawal from Lebanon was an admission of defeat
that confirmed what Arabs had always believed and the Americans
had always denied: that the Israeli tail wagged the American dog. It
was now plain that, when it came to the crunch, the influence of
America's Arab friends, most notably King Fahd and the Saudis,
counted for nothing when put in the balance against Israel and the
need to placate public opinion back home. The same lesson was
brutally brought home to President Mubarak when the Americans
hijacked an Egyptian aeroplane to Malta. When an apology was
demanded by Egypt, it was refused; President Reagan's sights were
set on his popularity ratings in the polls, not on the feelings of
foreign friends.

The Tehran hostages, Camp David, the murdered marines — all
these failures have of course been the subject of endless departmen-
tal and academic analysis in the United States. But all this effort
more resembles an audience watching an exciting Hollywood film
— the tension is high, the sense of involvement sometimes almost
unbearable, but at the end of the film each member of the audience
goes home to forget about the drama on the screen and to sleep
peacefully. But what is happening in the Middle East is no film, and
the Americans can have no cause for peaceful sleep.

APPENDIX 1

THE SECRETARY OF STATE
WASHINGTON

Cairo, May 13, 1953

My dear Mr Prime Minister:

I wish to extend to you and to your colleagues my sincere thanks for the many courtesies which you have shown to me during my visit to your country. Mr Stassen and I appreciate deeply all the assistance which we have received, and we particularly enjoyed the pleasant dinner party that you gave for us during our stay.

My discussions and observations here have been of material assistance in giving me a fuller understanding of Egypt's point of view on many problems. With respect to the Suez base problem, I firmly believe, as I said to you during our conversations, that a fair and equitable solution is of paramount importance not only to Egypt and the United Kingdom but to the rest of the free world.

As a result of my meetings with you and your colleagues I shall be able to carry back with me to President Eisenhower vivid impressions of your new and active leadership, revitalizing and giving fresh hope to the Egyptian people. In parting, please accept my best wishes to you and to your colleagues.

Yours sincerely,

His Excellency,
Mohammed Naguib,
President of the Council of Ministers and
Commander-in-Chief of the Egyptian Armed Forces,
Cairo, Egypt

H **H**

APPENDIX 2

Text of proposed message from Egyptian President Nasser to President Eisenhower, 22 January 1956.

My dear President,

Knowing and sharing the worldwide anxiety for the preservation of peace, I wish to address myself to you, whose many declarations on behalf of peace and justice are well known to my countrymen. The people of Egypt have no desire other than to grow in the peaceful fruition of our national inheritance. Having so recently acquired the pure — that is to say sovereign — possession of our lands, it could not now be our wish to desert their enjoyment for the purpose of military conquest or adventure. This means that Egypt harbours no hostile intentions towards any other state and will never be party to an aggressive war. More particularly, it means that Egypt will continue to make every reasonable effort to ensure that hostile incidents along the armistice line between Egypt and Israel do not become the occasion of war, and I assure you that, on Egypt's part, every effort will be made to prevent the incidents themselves. Any person under Egyptian jurisdiction found responsible for improper conduct in this respect will, moreover, be suitably punished. The establishment of Israel in Palestine had been beyond a doubt the gravest imaginable challenge to the peaceful preoccupation of the Arab people. Notwithstanding the sense of injustice which will linger among generations of us, Egypt, however, has indicated her acceptance of the UN resolutions concerning the dispositions of Palestine and of the two million Arab refugees displaced by Israel. In doing so Egypt has recognized the ultimate desirability of any understanding between the Arab States and Israel which will bring a permanent peace to the area and which will respect the fundamental rights and aspirations of the Arab people.

It may now be time to clarify further the principles upon which, in my view, such a permanent peace might be achieved. The basic issue is that of territorial adjustment, and I am confident that justice demands that Israel concede such territory as she now occupies as will permit the Arabs of Asia and Africa to be joined together by a continuous and substantial land area under Arab sovereignty and peopled by Arabs. Other rectifications which may be desirable to convert the present demarcation lines into permanent borders can be made, I am sure, on a mutual basis.

Once a just and reasonable solution of the territorial problem has been reached, I am convinced that agreement on the resettlement or repatriation of the Arab refugees can follow readily. I regard it as essential, however, that the refugees be given their freedom to choose repatriation or compensation for the loss of their former homes and property in Palestine. It would seem to me to be wise to grant all refugees the opportunity of electing to receive compensation immediately if they so choose; but as for those electing repatriation, account must be taken of Israel's absorptive capacity, and actual repatriation would have to be phased over an appropriate number of years. Meanwhile, suitable resettlement undertakings could be got underway.

With respect to the primary status of Jerusalem, it is my feeling that the Kingdom of Jordan should have the right of decision, and I would not object if the Kingdom of Jordan elected to retain the present division of Jerusalem. It goes without saying that the exercise of belligerent rights, such as blockade and secondary boycott, would cease upon the effective date of any settlement envisioned above: and in the event that suitable guarantees of a forthcoming settlement were presented, it would appear quite possible that the exercise of these rights could be terminated in advance of an actual announcement of the settlement. As for the matter of future trade relations between the Arab states and Israel I regard this as within the competence of each of the sovereign Arab states to decide in accordance with its own desires and interests. I do not profess to know whether Israel could ever come to a recognition of the propriety of the above suggestions, nor indeed at this moment do I have a conviction that Israel desires to seek peaceful solutions. In writing to you, Mr President, I have wished to inform you of the possibilities for peaceful settlement which I and my government can foresee and which we would earnestly entertain and support with regard to the other Arab states.

Then followed the suggested 'principles for a permanent peace'.

    I. Territorial
      A. The establishment of Arab sovereignty over a satisfactorily

substantial territory connecting Egypt and Jordan and forming a part of one or the other of those two states.

B. The establishment of permanent boundaries by means of alterations of the Armistice Demarcation Lines for such purposes as:

1. Restoring to Arab border villages adjoining farmlands and groves formerly tilled by the inhabitants of those villages.

2. Improvement of communications.

3. Improvement of access to water supplies, and

4. The general rationalization of boundaries.

II. Refugees

A. Arab refugees from Palestine to be provided with a choice between repatriation and compensation for loss of real property.

B. Phasing of the return to assume all rights and obligations of Israeli citizens.

C. Refugees granted repatriation to assume all rights and obligations of Israeli citizens.

D. Refugees electing resettlement and compensation to be moved from the refugee camps and resettled as rapidly as possible.

E. Assistance to be provided by the International Community, probably under UN auspices, for the re-establishment of all refugees.

III. Jerusalem. Formulation of solutions to the problems of territorial division and supervision of the Holy Places which are acceptable to the world community.

IV. State of belligerency and economic restrictions deriving therefrom.

A. The parties to recognize formally the termination of the state of belligerency.

B. Following the termination of this state of belligerency:

1. Lifting of the secondary boycott — that is, discontinuance of all measures taken by the Arab states to prevent trade with Israel by non Arab countries and non Arab firms, and

2. Removal of all restrictions on shipping, other than normal maritime regulations.

V. Unified development of the Jordan Valley. The state affected to agree to the proposals for the unified development of the Jordan Valley developed in discussions with Ambassador Eric Johnston.

APPENDIX 3

Text of proposed letter from Egyptian President Nasser to Eugene Black at the World Bank.

The proposed letter to the World Bank began by rehearsing the discussions which had already taken place between it and the Egyptian government. The American and British governments, it was confirmed, were 'willing to provide on a grant basis part of the foreign exchange requirements for the [High Dam] project. The government of Egypt would like to be assured that the bank will participate in the financing of the project in addition to such grant or aid.' Specifically, the request was for a loan from the bank of $200 million. Paragraphs 5 and 6 of the letter read:

> 5. Having regard to the unusual scale of the project, involving weighty financial burdens and a long period of construction before its full benefits can be realized, and in view of the difficulties which must be overcome in order to accomplish the successful completion of the project, the government of Egypt realizes the necessity of maintaining sound financial and economic policies, including an investment program which will recognize the priority of the High Dam project and the need for adjusting total expenditures to the financial resources which can be mobilized. The government of Egypt further realizes that the execution of the project and the implementation of the foregoing policies will require special planning, organization and administration. Therefore, it agrees that it will maintain those policies and adopt and carry out measures appropriate for the accomplishment of the foregoing objectives.
> 6. In particular the government of Egypt agrees that it will:
> (A) Adopt and apply, in the provision of its own financial contribution to the project and in the incurring of external financial obligations, policies which are prudent in the light of Egypt's circumstances and calculated to maintain Egypt's ability to service

the external debt which it will need to incur for the carrying out of the project;

(B) Plan and carry out the organization, administration and execution of the various phases of the project so as to assure its efficient and economical accomplishment along the lines presently contemplated, including provision for appropriate competition as a basis for the awarding of contracts, not to be departed from except in case of duly established necessity.

This was to some extent a technical matter on which considerable progress had already been made, but insofar as the letter gave the World Bank the right to supervise Egypt's foreign indebtedness, it too was unacceptable.

꙰ ꙰

APPENDIX 4

To His Excellency President Gamal Abdel Nasser from Jawaharlal Nehru, Prime Minister of India.

I am happy to find that the Anglo-French and Israeli troops will at long last be withdrawn by them from Egyptian territory. I feel sure that this would not have been possible had not world public opinion overwhelmingly stood by Egypt. It was a great relief to us to find that, despite their long and close alliance in many matters of international policy, the United States of America also stood firm on the question of withdrawal of the aggressive forces from Egyptian soil. While we can permit ourselves the hope that the worst will soon be over, there will still be need for continuous vigilance for some months to come at least. I am anxious that the revulsion of feelings caused by aggression against Egypt should not be side-tracked by extraneous factors. As it is, developments in Hungary have to an extent come in the way of concerted action against aggressors in Egypt. I feel, therefore, that it is more than ever important to prevent other things from coming in the way of the sympathy of the world expressing itself fully in favour of Egypt.

In this context I venture to draw your attention to the reports which are circulated abroad that considerable pressure direct and indirect is being brought to bear on the large number of British and French nationals and persons of Jewish origin in Egypt. Some of the latter have, I am told, been residents in Egypt for generations. As you may be aware I asked our Chargé in Egypt to mention the matter informally to your Government and I am told that he has already done so and had a discussion with Ali Sabri. I would repeat the assurance which Rajwade has already given to Ali Sabri that it is farthest from our mind to interfere in any matter which is in the full discretion of the Egyptian government. But, Mr President, I feel sure that you will be concerned as much as I am at anything being done which might create an unfortunate impression on world opinion and alienate sympathy from Egypt at a time when most countries in the world are supporting your cause. You have in the recent past showed exemplary patience in the most provocative circumstances. If I may say so, this has impressed the world almost as much as your courage through this critical period. I would request you therefore not take steps which would compel a large number of persons to leave Egypt in penurious circumstances. Considerations of security have of course to be borne in mind. But it would not be in the interest of Egypt herself to allow the impression to grow that an attempt was being made to recoup losses suffered by Egypt as a result of aggression by UK and France and Israel by sequestering the properties of British and French nationals.

This action is certainly justified against those who have abused the hospitality of Egypt by subversive activities. But the large majority of these are innocent victims of the wrongs committed by their governments and I would request you to show them compassion. If you do not wish any British or French national to remain in your country they might, I suggest, be given reasonable time to wind up their affairs and not be forced to leave immediately. Even from the short-term point of view a little patience and tolerance at this stage would help in the discussion of higher issues in Egypt, in the UN and elsewhere. I would not have made this appeal to you had I not felt sure that you would not misunderstand me.

With kind regards — Jawaharlal Nehru.

Index